Riddledom

Other books by David Astle

Puzzled
Puzzles and Words
Cluetopia
Puzzles and Words 2

Riddledom

101 riddles and their stories

DAVID ASTLE

ALLEN&UNWIN
SYDNEY•MELBOURNE•AUCKLAND•LONDON

First published in 2015

Copyright © David Astle 2015

Allen & Unwin
83 Alexander Street
Crows Nest NSW 2065
Australia
Phone: (61 2) 8425 0100
Email: info@allenandunwin.com
Web: www.allenandunwin.com

Cataloguing-in-Publication details are available
from the National Library of Australia
www.trove.nla.gov.au

ISBN 978 1 76011 260 8

Extract from Kit Williams, *Masquerade*, Jonathan Cape, 1979,
reproduced by kind permission of The Viney Agency, London, UK
Text design by Nada Backovic/Bookhouse
Text illustrations from iStock
Set in 12/14.8 pt Adobe Caslon Pro by Bookhouse, Sydney
Printed and bound in Australia by Griffin Press

10 9 8 7 6 5 4 3 2

To Heather May
for her might

CONTENTS

Life & Death

Anti-riddles

Letters & Numbers

Lost & Found

War & Peace

Famous & Forgettable

Body & Soul

Enigma Variations

The 'silly' question is the first intimation
of some totally new development.

A.N. Whitehead

1

What needs to breathe yet doesn't live?

Have you heard the one ... ?

Unlikely, not here, not with the trip we're about to take. In one wild spin we're bound to visit 101 riddles from around the world and across time.

Think Ireland and Siberia, an ivory maze and a Chinese ambulance—anywhere a riddle might be lurking. We'll dig up tricky questions in Pompeii and Quetzaltenango, exploring the stories that lie beneath the punchlines. Shakespeare and a Japanese game show. The steppes of Mongolia and the corridors of Hogwarts—our riddle race is set to start.

Or that's the plan, assuming you're game: flying to Zanzibar and Myanmar, meeting Gulliver and Galileo, bumping into Einstein and a Scottish robot. We'll swing by the Vatican, the Philippines, the Sikh mutiny—all in the name of riddling. Everywhere we turn, every rock we flip, a riddle will be hiding.

We'll eavesdrop on coffee slaves in Brazil and hunt bear in wild Alaska. Truth being, if you think riddles are solely the stuff of schoolyards and Christmas crackers, you're about to have your head refurbished.

Even riddle—the word—is a booby-trap. Once upon a time, goldminers relied on cast-iron riddles to separate grit from eureka. Ditto for winnowers who winnowed with steel-mesh riddles to divide the chaff from the grain. The crux is separation, arising from the German root of *reiter*, or sieve.

Visit any champagne estate and you might tour their riddling cellar. Again the gist is sifting, with traditional vintners rotating new bottles a few degrees each day to separate the yeast from the elixir.

But don't be fooled. None of these rituals apply to the riddles we're booked to meet. Our verb is a different branch, sprouting from *rædels* in Old English, a word variously meaning opinion, or guesswork, or imagination. Take your pick. All three apply inside these covers.

How many birthdays do most people have?

As for drafting a working definition for riddle, that's a separate madness. Questions are close cousins, of course, minus the twist that's central to the riddle. Questions seek knowledge or car keys. They tend to be polite, or nosy. Riddles on the other hand are built to baffle, their kinky shapes concealing a pre-loaded answer.

Or that's my understanding for now. No doubt the riddles around the corner will only shake and stir that idea. Riddles do that anyway, catching you off-guard, making the guesser appear a dunce.

But enough chitchat. Let's head down these stairs. Careful, the stone is slippery and the door's a trick to open. Welcome to the world's own riddling cellar, a room without end. Everywhere you look the vault is stacked with bottles, each blend a riddle to sample.

If you're feeling overwhelmed, you're not alone. As a full-time puzzle-maker I know my share of word games, but this cellar takes things to another level. Riddles can be daunting, to both solvers and collectors. Hence my plan, a token bid to lend our tour some shape. To keep us from drowning I've chosen a finite rack of labels, a premium selection of myth and romance, filth and frolic, life and death, Popsicles and Wonderland.

In a spirit of bravado I've sorted the batch into varietals, from nature to novelty, from war to worship, though folklore is seldom so obedient. You'll notice some labels will overlap with others, while just as many riddles laugh at their pigeonholes. Like this riddle, our first:

What needs to breathe yet doesn't live?

That's how we roll in *Riddledom*, each chapter presenting its own curly question to see if you can snare the answer before the tippling's done.

In essence, that's our challenge now. With one vast room to roam, let's rest our hands on 101 small mysteries—the dry wit of Greece, the sparkle of Finland—and turn each bottle like so many doorknobs, opening to the universe awaiting on the other side. We do this right and every riddle will live and breathe.

Yes, you guessed it. Wine is the answer to Riddle 1, a potion that needs to breathe before it can animate the senses. Take a sip, if you like. The Dutch courage will do you good, a dash of medicine to help prepare for our next 100. Though I should warn you—this opener is a teaser. Upcoming riddles have far greater complexity, more than a few destined to unmoor your mind.

So let's begin. Let's turn and open, sample and solve, illuminate what marvels lie behind each 'dark saying', to quote the *Shorter Oxford*. Rather than expend precious oxygen trying to define riddles, or wonder why their trickery pervades every corner of the planet, I say we go riddling.

⌐⌐ 2 ⌐⌐

When is a boy not a boy?

Milk can turn without moving. Parrots speak in polysyllables. You only need two fingers to make a Venetian blind.

I learnt these facts when riddling as a kid. Every week, every car trip, every stretch of downtime, I discovered how boiled eggs are tough to beat, while icicles are eavesdroppers.

My principal text was canary in colour, a 1959 hardback from New York City published by Platt & Munck. A lifetime later, the book's still with me, a template for the volume in your hands.

Over the years the canary cover softened to margarine, but nothing else has changed. The gags are just as dusty. Quaint line drawings by George L. Carlson, the book's compiler, struggle to aerate the type, the riddles numbered like so many commandments down the page, from 1 to 1001. Yes, that was the title: *1001 Riddles*.

Perhaps the tally rings a bell. It should, since we're about to drown in 101 mind benders, or 99 from this point onward. The echo's no fluke. *Riddledom* is my bid to square an old debt. If not for Messrs Platt & Munck, I swear my brain would never be so devious.

The obvious homage was to modernise the relic, to build a cold list of 1001 substitute riddles. But why take a trodden path? Libraries and bookstores are swamped by wacky collections, each volume jostling to be the next Platt & Munck. The universe, I figured, didn't need another chew-chew train.

Who has a stomach into which you can see?

Whatever tack I took, my job was simplified by the passion the boyhood book had infused. Or, quoting Riddle 2 from that same yellow bible:

When is a boy not a boy?

In theory the riddle invites several answers. When he's a man, say. When he's dreaming or acting, possibly. When he's not feeling himself. Before I tell you the actual solution, a few more words about that riddle addiction.

Growing up I adored the duplicity of English, how a blind carpenter picked up his hammer and saw. How MTGG was a hungry horse, or the tastiest dog was a melon-collie. Sure, the puns are punishing now, but back in the day, late primary school, this here joke-junkie was agog in a stream of homophones and double meanings.

Now and then my parents despaired. Mum feared she'd sneezed too hard while I was in her womb, dislodging some vital helix in my DNA. For his part, Dad could never fathom how a sea captain with a love of carpentry had sired a pun-geek. Worse, a kid who couldn't even spackle without leaving streaks.

I argued back, of course. Those long car trips seemed ready made for philosophical disputes. Riddles, I told them, could be practical. Survival in the desert was guaranteed so long as you could drink your watch's spring and eat the soles on your feet. Pretty soon the car returned to silence, my parents staring at the road while their make-believe scholar resumed his studies.

Looking back, I was, accidentally, kind of right. Riddles can be practical. Like few other diversions, they spur your brain to build outrageous connections. If I had any major beef among the 1001 in Carlson's collection, it would be Riddle 82:

What goes up but never down?
Your age

Bunkum, in my books. You'll never reverse the calendar, or turn back the clock, but you can continue to stretch the imagination, using riddles to keep the mind elastic. Thanks to 1001 crafty questions, I know that jackets and jalopies are both worn out. Or that pages are attached

Fish trap [Fiji]

to both queens and books. I'm here to report that spells, codes and mustangs can each be broken, while Pisces and Libra depend on scales. I'm not saying the links are hilarious, but the pretzel logic reboots the neurons, diverts your focus in fresh directions, attunes the art of lateral thinking. Or, to quote Riddle 781:

What is the difference between an engineer and a school teacher?

Engineers engineer, of course. They build bridges or vacuum cleaners, leaving teachers to bestow the alphabet, explain fractions, tell the class the capital of Peru or how photosynthesis works. Said more wittily:

One minds the train, the other trains the mind.

A cute gimmick for an answer, but never neglect the power of riddling to teach, or the joy of novel language to engineer. The cunning needed to reach a crooked answer requires a special brand of genius in a young mind—or an old mind kept young by riddles.

Somehow I sensed that even as a boy, back when I wasn't a boy, arguing the toss with my parents. Have you solved our riddle yet? It's thorny, though I murmured the answer a few paragraphs earlier, recalling the rapture I felt on the road, the holy book spread across my lap. Check back and you'll see I was agog, versus a boy: the answer you've been seeking.

Years on, of course, that agogness hasn't quit. The slightest sleight-of-language has my system humming. Old or new, riddles have the power to rock the way you think. Stick with me and you'll feel the same rush, as we speed headlong into the mysteries of inner space.

What's the best way to drown a hipster?

Immerse him in the mainstream

Birds & Bees

Not what you're thinking—that comes next.

Instead a start among real birds, the buzz of nature, as we meet some early riddles (a few quite familiar) that seek to make sense of wild things.

⊐ 3 ⊏

Why did the chicken cross the road?

Somewhere in the course of evolution, *Gallus gallus* found the gumption to brave a road. The big question is: why?

The daredevil's first written mention appeared in a literary magazine called *The Knickerbocker* back in 1847. As the name suggests, the monthly emerged out of New York, where knickerbocker identifies a Manhattan elitist, the word echoing the Dutch aristocracy that once called that city home.

The man to dream up the Knickerbocker name was the satirist Washington Irving. His best-known character was Rip Van Winkle, or maybe the headless horseman of Sleepy Hollow.

Irving was born in the week America shook off British rule, back in 1783. He grew up in Manhattan, amid the merchant class, and in his late teens he turned his hand to literature. His first major work was a lampoon in 1809, entitled *A History of New York from the Beginning of the World to the End of the Dutch Dynasty, by Diedrich Knickerbocker*. Note how the so-called author was in italics, too, since Knickerbocker was part of the fiction. An elaborate part, where Irving pretended the Dutch historian was real—and missing.

The ruse was brilliant. Irving, as the real author, placed ads in the New York press seeking information on the spurious author, last seen wandering the city's streets. An early example of viral marketing, the hoax ensured strong sales for the book, plus the lasting popularity of Knickerbocker, the name. Indeed, the New York Knicks is the only basketball team in the world named after a fake Dutch intellectual, while *The Knickerbocker* magazine, launched in 1833, became a nest of fine literary talents, hiring the likes of Irving himself.

Handy details when it comes to appreciating our celebrity chicken. The early 1800s was a time of American pride and literary airs. The Brits were gone, replaced by profiteers. Cities rose in height and

Chicken recipes

Why did the chicken cross the road?
To see his flat mate

Why did the chicken cross the road halfway?
To lay it on the line

Why did the chicken cross the Moebius strip?
To get to the same side

Why did the rubber chicken cross the road?
To stretch its legs

Why did the turkey cross the road?
To prove it wasn't chicken

Why did the dinosaur cross the road?
Because chickens weren't invented yet

population. The west was unlocked, claiming new ground for cotton and wheat, beef and dairy. Rail networks webbed the map, in league with a growing crisscross of roads.

Enter the chicken, standing on one kerb and aspiring to reach the other. Damn. I just blabbed the answer, assuming you've never heard the riddle before. Hardly likely, but still—I need to sidestep spoilers. Lewis Gaylord Clark was underwhelmed with the pay-off anyway. In the March 1847 issue, as part of his long-winded musings, the *Knickerbocker* editor wrote: 'There are "quips and quillets" which seem actual conundrums, but yet are none. Of such is this: "Why does a chicken cross the street?" Are you "out of town?" Do you "give it up?" Well, then: "Because it wants to get on the other side!"'

Sad but true: that's the answer. The reason that the ur-chicken crossed that ur-road was to reach the other side. An anticlimax in light of this elaborate lead-up, yet that's the riddle's essence. Replace 'chicken' with 'boy', say, and the conundrum presents more as a question.

A nail in a horseshoe

Eyewitness reports

Q: Why did the chicken cross the road?

Albert Einstein: The chicken crossed the road or the road crossed it—that depends upon your frame of reference.

Buddha: If you ask this question, you deny your own chicken nature.

Charles Darwin: It was the logical next step after coming down from the trees.

Karl Marx: It was an historical inevitability.

The Sphinx: I ask the questions.

Ernest Hemingway: To die. In the rain.

Of course we all know boys cross roads in order to, well, cross roads. But reinvent the pedestrian and the brain loses balance, at least the brain of 1847, back when the answer was a revelation.

This important riddle element is known as the block. Nothing to do with handyman shows, it is related to the inbuilt obstacle most riddles carry, preventing the guesser from seeing the answer immediately. Usually the block entails wordplay—a splash of double meaning, a homophone, a pun. Or here in the chicken case, a perverse misdirection, having the askee think along comical lines, rather than the practical.

Ho-hum for Lewis Gaylord Clark, but I like how the quip invites a flight of fancy, whereas the answer was down to earth from the outset. The brain needs to readjust genres as much as gears, since the so-called riddle is far more a straightforward inquiry.

Such a tactic borders on being an anti-riddle, you could argue. This is a recipe to warrant its own section of *Riddledom*, where curveball questions play tricks under the guise of riddles, but let's move on to the hen herself.

Whatever the chestnut's designs, the riddle launched the gallant chook into the status of meme, long before Grumpy Cat and Willy Wonka stole the limelight. This one iconic bird has been weaving through traffic for 160 years. What began as a cognitive gotcha has morphed into multiple variations, as our first riddle box vouches.

What did Captain Kirk say when the ship hit meteors?

Despite her vintage, her serial risk-taking, the road-crosser is here to stay. A recent episode in Portland, USA, reminded us of the chicken's permanent roost in our culture. While neither speaker was identified by name, the following dialogue is part of a genuine 911 call from August 2014:

CALLER: Hi, this is actually not a prank call, but there is a chicken trying to cross the road in Linnton, off of Highway 30, across from The Lighthouse.

911 OPERATOR: Is it causing traffic problems?

CALLER: Yes, it's really trying to get into the middle of the road.

OPERATOR (chuckling): Um, ah . . .

CALLER (chuckling): Pretty ironic but . . .

OPERATOR (still laughing): Is it just the one chicken?

Of course it was. That's the rule of the riddle. One road, one chicken, always and forever, riddle without end, amen.

⌐ 4 ⌐

Why is a raven like a writing desk?

Lewis Carroll could make the dead live. You never knew the author was also a miracle worker? Wait, before you edit the Wiki page, take a look at this:

DEAD

LEAD

LEND

LENT

LINT

LINE

LIVE

The writer invented this word ladder as a parlour game, a novelty he'd call a doublet. The puzzle was picked up by *Vanity Fair* magazine in

1879, becoming the sudoku of its day. Some transitions were elaborate, such as the six-stepper of SLEEP to DREAM, while others were MORE or LESS solved in a snap: more-lore-lose-loss-less. (If you're not awake to the SLEEP/DREAM sequence, I've tucked the answer deeper into this chapter.)

Anyhow, by the time the doublets dazzled the public, Carroll was already the creator of two fabulous chronicles, both following the adventures of young Alice. No matter where the child went—down a rabbit hole or through a mirror—she'd meet the strangest creatures, from pipe-smoking caterpillars to argumentative eggs. She bumped into mock turtles and vanishing cats. For an Oxford don lecturing in mathematics, Carroll owned a measureless imagination.

Indeed, the logician was a magician on the page, his fiction a kaleidoscope of his various selves. The dodo that wanders Wonderland, say, is deemed an allusion to the author's actual name, Charles Dodgson, or so claims biographer Jenny Woolf in *The Mystery of Lewis Carroll*. In the same vein, Alice was inspired by the Oxford dean's daughter Alice Liddell.

Alice was almost five when she and Carroll first met. The girl and her three older siblings would share summer days boating on the nearby Thames with Reverend Dodgson. The plan was to pile aboard a rowboat and find the ideal picnic spot. From such free-floating afternoons the madcap stories arose. Timeless stories, filled with serendipity and farce—plus one annoying riddle.

Half-riddle could be a fairer label. Can a riddle be a riddle without an answer? Hardly seems polite to deliver a question without the solace of an answer, but that's the vulgarity committed by the Mad Hatter at his tea party. As host, I suppose, the milliner can do what he likes. And being mad, of course, comes with its own etiquette. All the same, throwing a conundrum at your young guest and then reneging on the solution won't win you too many bouquets on the social pages.

On the surface, the riddle seems so simple:

Why is a raven like a writing desk?

The hatter plucks the question out of thin air. Alice warms to the challenge, convinced that she can find an answer. 'Come we shall have

How do you make holy water?

some fun now,' she says, the we in this case being the other guests at the table—the fidgety March Hare and the comatose Dormouse. The small talk derails her task, however. As often happens in Wonderland, the conversation turns to the muddle of semantics, that pickle that exists between what is said and what is meant: a case of the Oxford logician peeking through the fabric. By the time the tangent concludes, and Alice returns to the riddle, the Mad Hatter is empty-handed. He doesn't know the answer—never did. The little girl is cranky, and she wasn't alone.

Carroll's readers shared her disgruntlement. Using flamingos as croquet mallets was perfectly fine. That sort of lunacy was Wonderland's charm. But serve up a riddle without an answer, and an Anglican deacon was liable to be hanged for heresy.

Umbrage turned into uproar as *Alice's Adventures in Wonderland* grew in popularity. The first print run in 1865 was a meagre 2000. Copies soon vanished, as larger and larger reprint numbers ensued. Translations followed close behind. Yet regardless of the destination, be it the German *Wunderland* or the French *Pays des Merveilles*, readers were sure to be nettled by the incomplete *Rätsel*, or *énigme*.

Carroll himself felt the heat. More and more letters arrived from fans demanding the Mad Hatter close the deal. So bad did the hounding get, the writer added a solution as a preface in later editions: *'Because it can produce a few notes, tho' they are very flat; and it is never put with the wrong end in front!'*

Flat indeed. A lacklustre postscript to the whole raven saga, but the hatter's riddle wasn't so quick to be reconciled.

In 1976, a gentleman named Denis Crutch found a neglected pun among the author's papers, the sort of wordplay you'd expect from the doublet's inventor. Originally, when Carroll penned the answer above, his 'never' was misspelt 'nevar'. Even a sleepy Dormouse could spot the rationale, as opposed to a proofreader who changed the deliberate reversal of 'raven' to the version you've just read, ensuring that Carroll's flat offering fell even flatter.

Pun or no pun, the belated answer still fell short of Wonderland's lofty standards. Readers' unrest only deepened. Bloody ingrates, if you ask me, but the discord's been a healthy one, since that nagging sense

Boil the hell out of it

of incompletion has gone on to spark some splendid alternatives from big names and no-names alike.

So then, why is a raven like a writing desk? American Sam Loyd, father of the chess puzzle and other strategic games, suggested, 'Poe wrote on both.' A deft connection, but I wouldn't fancy the Mad Hatter to be familiar with Edgar Allan's backlist.

A second author, Aldous Huxley, adhered to Wonderland illogic with his proposal: 'Because there is a B in both, and an N in neither.'

A century later, we're still none the wiser, presuming Carroll's 'flat' punchline was never the Hatter's intention. You may have your own theories regarding a writing desk vis-à-vis a raven, but I've only lately found my favourite, a wangle of words that has let me sleep soundly, perchance to sleep-bleep-bleed-breed-bread-dread-dream.

Sound, in fact, underpins the new suggestion. The idea came from Esther Inglis-Arkell, a contributing editor with the science-y website *io9*. In a piece she wrote back in 2012 about this infamous riddle Inglis-Arkell took the homophone route. A raven is like a writing desk, she believed, as neither is approached without 'caws'.

'Off with her head!' to quote Wonderland's Red Queen—or maybe I'm being too harsh. The pun is better than most, and a long chalk better than Carroll's own bid. Then again, the *io9* article inspired the best solution of them all, with a contributor known simply as MisterGone trumping the field in a single post. Better still, the mystery correspondent also involved an Oxonian peer of Lewis Carroll, namely Reverend Spooner, who's scheduled to reign in Riddle 50. To quote the chatroom's immortal MisterGone:

> *Why is a raven like a writing desk?*
> *One is a pest for wrens, the other is a rest for pens.*

What's red and smells like blue paint?

⊐5⊏

Riddle me, riddle me, rot-tot-tote!

On the first day the squirrels arrived with three dead mice. They laid them before Old Brown, the owl who lived on Owl Island, and the bird was pleased. He let the squirrels forage the copse for chestnuts, though one squirrel had other plans. While all his friends searched the island, Squirrel Nutkin danced and pranced around Old Brown; he hurried and scurried in a red-fur blur, all the while singing:

> *Riddle me, riddle me, rot-tot-tote!*
> *A little wee man, in a red red coat!*
> *A staff in his hand, and a stone in his throat;*
> *If you'll tell me this riddle, I'll give you a groat.*

Old Brown didn't give a hoot. He closed his eyes in the vain hope that Nutkin might tire of his routine and skitter off. Not a chance. The squirrel bounced and bobbed. He twitched and chittered. If Ritalin had been available in 1903, this animal was a prime candidate.

Even on the second day, when the squirrels crossed the lake on sticks, Nutkin was off the wall. This time the squirrels arrived with a dead mole as peace offering, yet Nutkin offered Old Brown no peace whatsoever. He danced and pranced. He whirled and twirled. He ruffled Old Brown's feathers with a nettle branch, and once again chanted a riddle the bird did his best to ignore.

You can see the fairytale shape of Beatrix Potter's story, which the author described as 'a tale about a tail'. As winter loomed, the squirrels hit the island six days straight, each time bearing a gift, and each time the owl's serenity was trashed by the hyperactive Nutkin.

Being wise, Old Brown did his best to overlook the pest. In similar fashion, Beatrix Potter had struggled to ignore the strange woman who'd shared her train ride seven years before the author devised the Nutkin story. This strange revelation has emerged only recently. As well as writing a library-load of children's tales, from Peter Rabbit to

Red paint

Jemima Puddle-Duck, Potter was also a prolific journal writer from the age of fourteen onwards. To keep things private, she developed a code, where one letter doubled for another. For all her trouble, a rabid Potter fan cracked the secret language in 1958, fifteen years after the author's death.

If historians were hoping for scandal and scuttlebutt, they were crestfallen. What Leslie Linder uncovered was a young Victorian woman who aired occasional bitterness, as well as making notes on family life, Bible quotes, art show impressions and her regular train trips to visit relatives. On one such trip, in 1894, the 28-year-old Potter was affronted by a passenger who refused to sit still: '[The woman] appeared incapable of holding her tongue or her limbs, which I rather misliked when there was a tunnel.'

Ring a bell? Add a bushy tail, toss in a riddle, and the woman seems the prototype for Squirrel Nutkin. The theory was proposed by Liverpool University's Dr Gareth Williams, writing for *The British Medical Journal* in 1995. Beyond the Nutkin link, the article suggested that the woman on Miss Potter's train suffered from Tourette's syndrome.

'Nutkin does seem psychologically challenged,' said Williams. The doctor did some digging, finding the train incident and extrapolating from there. Old Brown would be the first to tell you about the squirrel's antisocial ways, plus the emotional disconnection, the frenzied mannerisms. While the squirrel never cusses, unlike most Tourette cases, his rampant word invention accords with the clinical literature. On Day Five, when the squirrels lobbed with wild honey, Nutkin pestered Old Brown with 'Hum-a-bum! buzz! buzz!', in keeping with the 'rot-tot-tote' of his initial teaser. Perhaps the addition of riddles, one ditty per day, was Potter's fairytale way of increasing our sense of the owl's sufferance, the same as she'd felt when discomfited on a train.

By the way, have you identified the riddle's wee man in a red, red coat? Let's just say that Helen Potter, better known as Beatrix, would blush like a cherry if she ever knew we'd cracked her private diary. Worse, she'd chafe to hear that we've merrily drawn parallels between neuropsychiatric disorders and a most impertinent squirrel.

What do you call a robot with a nasty bug?

⌐6⌐

Dvi lentutės, dvi geldutės, ylos kotas, katile dugnas . . .

Two little planks, two little shells . . .

Lithuania is one big veggie patch: a land smoothed by ancient glaciers leaving loamy soil in their wake, heaven made for farming. National cuisine reflects as much, in tandem with homegrown riddles. Even today, the menus of Vilnius list your staple pork and chicken, the meat either buried in beets and radishes or stewed with potato. Cabbage is popular, too, as encoded in the nation's riddle-bio: *From birth to death it stays on its foot.*

Other veggies get similar treatment beside the Baltic:

The leaves are round, the breasts are blue. (Turnip)
A boat is full of white, small spades. (Cucumber)
Many brothers—one cradle swinging. (Peas)

Fine when the sun is shining, good rain is falling, and the harvest is ample. But some seasons can be fallow, compelling the household to forage beyond the fields. Again the riddles betray the story:

One with nine hearts. (Wild apple)
Two little planks, two little shells, the handle of an awl, the bottom in a cauldron.

The only thing missing from our principal riddle is an Allen key to assemble the inventory. Of course, where riddles are concerned, that unifying element is the answer, the absent piece that, once added, clicks the hodgepodge into shape. In this case, the answer is *Gilė*.

Sorry. You may not speak Lithuanian. And even if you do, the allusion may remain too tough to solve. Botanists have a better chance of gathering the answer, just as hungry Lithuanians once gathered the real *gilė* in the forests, a food gobbled by deer and mice alike. The windfall was a handy

Lithuania mania (late 1800s)

*A slender woman with a wide head has only one tooth yet she gnaws
    the earth.*
Rake .

On the neck is a beam, on the hands, small bells.
Water carrier bearing two buckets

*Here comes a nobleman on two peg legs, with a meat beard and bone
    mouth.*
A rooster

*The road is without trash, the horses without nostrils, the whip without
    a knot.*
A boat and oars in a river

supplement through leaner times, the basis of poor man's coffee, as well
as a nutty mash to help a family eke through winter.

Can you guess the food? Squirrels love them, by the way. Broken
down, the morsel comprises two planks and two shells, plus a haft and
a bowl. In a nutshell, the riddle is all metaphor. The moment you slice a
gilė in half, you will expose the imagery: the pinkish pith that mimics
fresh-cut planks, the wooden husk, the handle-cum-stem connecting
to the lower hollow, or cupula as the botanists prefer.

Early surgeons resorted to equivalent imagery when slicing open
the human brain, applying creative associations to the segments they
exposed. The 'cortex', which protects the grey matter, is Greek for bark.
Probe deeper into the medulla (or pith), and you'll reach the amygdala,
the neural bundle vital to memory and emotions. In English, 'amygdala'
translates as almond, a reference to its nubbly shape, and a tasty curio to
bury in the memory for the next trivia night. Our brain, you could say,
was a prequel to the Baltic moment an acorn was split. The surgeons, like
the riddlesmith, applied their poetic eye to the mystery of nature's interior.

The fly can't settle on the lion's blood.

⅃7⌐ 7

I know the *imazi ihobe*

I know the female dove

In Xhosa, one of the languages of Africa's Bantu people, the word for knot is also the word for riddle. That's why 'an old crone standing all alone on a vast plain' is not literally an old crone standing all alone on a vast plain, but rather an *iqhina* to untie.

The answer (or *impendulo*) is the unravelling, removing the snarl from the description. We see the same idea sustained in the French word *dénouement*, which means unknotting, where Mrs Marple untangles the murder's timeline and places Reverend Green in the kitchen with a candlestick. And in the case of the old Bantu crone, our *iqhina* example, a knot is also a clue.

Can you guess the answer? Consider your body for a moment. Readers with an outie may have more success, since the answer is the navel—the umbilical knot occupying the plain of your belly. Poetic licence, granted, but that's your typical Xhosa riddle: a metaphor that spurns a question, a knot demanding denouement.

Veering from this standard formula is the bird riddle, a variation unique to Xhosa. The recipe was first reported by Dr A.C. Jordan in the early 1970s, though the bird riddle's 'battle' style had likely been raging for years.

Again, as with the classical knot, the *intaka iqhina* hinges on elusive imagery bundled up into a terse statement. This time round, though, the answer is served up first, daring the listener to prefigure the poetry. Here's a customary contest between Cape and Town:

> *Cape: Do you know the birds?*
> *Town: I do know the birds.*
> *Cape (unimpressed): What bird do you know?*
> *Town: I know the female dove.*
> *Cape: What about her?*
> *Town: That she is a lazy woman.*

Fire [Swahili]

Cape: Why so?
Town: Because instead of building a nest, she collects a few sticks and
lays her eggs on them.

The female dove—or *imazi ihobe*—can also be a jealous wife, as she never allows her husband to go out alone. Both analogies depend on a keen eye for nature. That is the subtle bonus of the bird riddle, the formula a spur for Bantu children to notice the behaviour of the birds around them. Owls are sorcerers, for they only hunt at night; butcherbirds are the nemeses of sorcerers, since they impale their victims on thorns; the wagtail is a shepherd for always attending cattle.

Curiously, the format doesn't deviate from birds—sidestepping mammals, insects, trees. The topic is as fixed as the contest element, where the challenger (Cape in our case) must always act unimpressed, holding the proposer's supposed knowledge in contempt. For a few beats anyhow, just until the field notes are explained in the final line. This is the moment of tension, when the knot vanishes before your eyes, the birdwatcher untying his analogy to undo the challenger's disdain. Question being, will he soar like an African fish eagle, or become *Nettapus auritus*—the pygmy goose of the sub-Sahara?

⌐8⌐

A man that was not a man
hit a bird that was not a bird ...

Time to crank the time machine back to old Greece. Though before we hit Go, a quick reminder about the block I've just mentioned, that logic trap that makes a riddle so treacherous to answer.

In many ways the Greeks invented the feature, dreaming up the word aporia, an impasse that obstructs you from finding an obvious outcome. That may sound frustrating, but there's a pleasure implied in aporia (literally the absence of a passage, or portal), since the seeker must truly think to reach enlightenment. And if that sounds

What do you call an old snowman?

lofty in tone, then let's meet a man who elevated the mind to giddy heights.

A noble by birth, Plato was a riddling master who adored aporia, the man toying with blocks long before Lego left the assembly line. His stamping ground was Athens, some 2400 years ago. A passion for learning saw him study under Socrates, where he soon developed his own reputation for radical thinking. Plato's major claim to fame was turning the visible world on its head, devising a philosophy he labelled the theory of forms.

Let's say you're currently reading a book. Or are you? Nurse the object in your hands and consider its realness. (For those who opted for the e-version, dandle your Kindle and muse along similar lines.) Pragmatists will doubtless be convinced. Of course this is a book! Just as that's a table, this is a chair, and yonder is a flyscreen—but Plato had his doubts.

His theory put convention under fire—every stick of furniture in the household, every statue in the temple. A tree, say, was not a real tree but a reflection of the truly real. Yes, you can feel its bark, climb its branches, or pulp the whole thing into a book if you wish, but ultimately a tree is an idea embodied by its material representation.

Head-spinning now, as it was then. Which is why I'm keen to crown Plato as a great among the riddling pantheon. In his universe, the chicken is the quintessential embodiment of chicken-ness, yet in the same breath isn't a true chicken. Rather the bird is an envoy of the eternal form, a reminder of the fundamental. Particulars might come and go, but form is inviolate.

Indeed, Plato's theory overlaps with riddles in a curious way. Both view the world through a prism. Both challenge orthodoxy. But where Plato's idea enshrines the singular—claiming every apple is one apple— the riddle delights in multiple choice.

A cat in the Platonic universe is Everycat. A cat in riddledom may allude to a Persian, a panther, a whip or a snowmobile. Maybe it's a drawing of a cat. A toy cat. A cat logo. Perhaps it's a brain scan, or a twin-hulled sailboat. Or then again the animal may symbolise a creeping mist, a lapping breeze, a sex kitten, anything behaving in feline fashion. Regardless of which way the wind blows, the umpteen options still own the one label.

Water

Working in cahoots, the theory of forms and the history of riddles help unstitch the world we think we know. Both brands of thinking poke fun at presumptions, what your eye sees versus what your brain must redefine. This mental tussle is captured in Plato's own riddle, a four-part poser that aims to sever the cords with reality:

A man that was not a man hit a bird that was not a bird, perched on a branch that was not a branch, with a stone that was not a stone.

To give you time to solve the paradox, a word about the riddle's source. Or maybe that should be sauce, as recipes are involved.

Despite kicking the bucket in 348BC, give or take, Plato survives through his masterpiece, *The Republic*. The book—at least it seems a book—is a dialogue of some 125,000 words. The principal speaker is Socrates, the same intellect to nurture the younger Plato. Tape recorders weren't part of Athenian life back then, so we can be grateful for *The Republic*, as the interchange between mentor and students is the next best thing to eavesdropping on the famous academy.

At one point, amid talk of justice and politics, the argument drifts into semantics. The key inquiry comes from Glaucon, Plato's older brother, who ponders, 'And can any one of those many things which are called by particular names be said to be this rather than not to be this?'

Socrates replies, 'They are like the punning riddles which are asked at feasts or the children's puzzle about the eunuch aiming at the bat, with what he hit him, as they say in the puzzle, and upon what the bat was sitting. The individual objects of which I am speaking are also a riddle, and have a double sense: nor can you fix them in your mind, either as being or not-being, or both, or neither.'

Cagier readers will now realise they've just been told half the riddle's answer. Socrates is the culprit, blurting the details with no regard for spoilers. The whole business revives the planks and cauldron of a Lithuanian acorn, where figurative language parades as the actual, and thus spurs the listener to bark up the wrong tree. Returning to the opening riddle:

A man that was not a man hit a bird that was not a bird, perched on a branch that was not a branch, with a stone that was not a stone.

Who's the loneliest opera star?

Asked another way: what man isn't a man? What bird isn't a bird? And so on. Fittingly, the solution is equally elaborate. According to Plato, the man in question was a eunuch with failing sight. What he took to be a bird on a branch was actually a bat on a reed. Though I'm still not sure why he felt the urge to throw a chunk of pumice (not a real stone) at the creature.

Before you start whining about such a contrived story, let me pull another excerpt from *The Republic*:

> . . . *is not this rather like a dog who cannot get at his assailant, quarrelling with the stones which strike him instead?*

In short, don't blame me. Or Plato in particular. This was a gag du jour, a brainteaser doing the rounds of social media back then. The philosopher adopted the enigma, as it went to encourage suspicion towards what we see and understand. Better than that, the riddle highlights the golden rules of solving: Never fall for face value. Sift the so-called facts with a critical eye.

To solve a riddle means solving the question wrapped inside the question you've been given—finding the portal beyond the aporia. Master that art, grasshopper, and you'll unravel any riddle, for Plato swears that all riddles are ultimately the one riddle.

⌐ 9 ⌐

M'aan cwii tsan'iieen jeen chian'iie

There is that person who is like a crybaby

Xochistlahuaca is not on the gringo map. Nor is Tlacoachistlahuaca. While I did ride a bus over the Yacuyagua mountains, where both villages lie, that was in transit, half-asleep in the half-light. All I retain from the bus trip was an image of the rank of crucifixes standing prim along a clifftop, a tribute to other buses less fortunate.

Enrico Crusoe

Sonic riddles

From Japan:
Sasa-no-ha-ni imo-no-ha
(A sound effect as riddle, describing the sough of bamboo leaves)

From Ghana:
Kerbu kerbu njolla
(The clunk of goat hooves on rocks)

From Mozambique:
Shigiligigi shigi
(The sound of morning rain on palm fronds)

From North America:
My mother went over to your mother's house to borrow
A wim-babble, wam-bobble, a hind-body-fore-body,
Whirl-a-kin-nibble.
(A loom)

From Australia:
How do you make a cat go woof?
Soak it in petrol and throw a match.

Hang on, that's not true. If I close my eyes, which I often did along that road, I can retrieve the vivid Indian girls who filled the aisle during one fuel stop. '*Manzanas! Manzanas!*' Their apples were small but sweet, like crisp nectarines.

Dredging deeper, I see the Braille of coffee beans drying on roadside roofs. The whitewash messages on boulders. The piebald dogs keeping vigil on doorsteps. The spectres of drying laundry. We were still an hour from Oaxaca, zigzagging through mist, the scream of gears a constant din, the squeal of brakes, the squeezebox music pulsing on the driver's cassette.

Noises, in fact, are my lasting souvenirs of Mexico. Beer labels and photos can only salvage so much of that 1993 escape, compared with

And who's the fakest opera star?

the gargle of roosters, the walloping of wet clothes, burro whines and fountain dribble. In Xico, near Xalapa, a rushing creek sighed through a shoal of pebbles. VWs growled around San Cristobal, blaring propaganda through a rooftop tannoy. And thanks to Charles T. Scott, an American anthropologist who spent some time living in the Yacuyaguas back in the sixties, I can now hear the Amuzgo.

These were the apple girls, the indigenous faces I glimpsed in the fog. The Amuzgo belong to the broader Mixtec band of people, and it's only now, via the riddles that Scott shared in *The Journal of American Folklore*, that I hear their voices, and their homes:

M'aan cwii tsan'iieen jeen chian'iie.
There is that person who is like a crybaby.

Who is this grump? you ask. As a clue, none of the homes I saw on that Yacuyagua road had state-of-the-art furnishings. As we wove I never saw the handiwork of a master builder. Instead the way was bordered by impromptu shacks, cardboard glazing, hessian curtains, plus many a sagging bamboo door—the riddle's answer. Minus a solid frame, and with only straps for hinges, the bamboo drags against the door jamb every time it's swung. Shut your eyes and you hear the crybaby's groan, for riddles wield that power too, every offering a coded means of passing through a doorway into elsewhere. Old Greeks talked about aporia—the blocked path—yet here on the Yacuyagua road, that bamboo obstacle has just moaned open for you. One eloquent sound allows the outsider to cross the threshold into elsewhere.

⌐⌐ 10 ⌐⌐

An old woman is made to break wind by an angry old man

Pause for a moment and consider living on the edge of the East Siberian Sea. We're talking Arctic Circle, where winter temperatures plunge below zero—and stay plunged. Permafrost turns the tundra into concrete, the Anadyr River glassing up with ice. Edible plants are buried under snow, meaning your diet depends on the catchability of fish or reindeer. Yet somehow the Chukchi people of remote northwest Russia consider riddles to be the hard things in their lives.

That's the phrase they use: *Qolo'-wêthau'tê*, or hard words. Many anthropologists, including the ground-breaking American Frank Speck, consider riddles to be more a Russian import, in contrast to Chukchi's richer veins of proverbs ('being words') and tongue-twisters ('hurry-tongue-competition words').

Museum dioramas might label these hunter-gatherers as Paleo-Siberians. Another way of saying the race is big on tradition. Their early dealings with Russia in the 1600s were fractious at best, as the Chukchi prefer their own space. Sleeping in deerskin tents and subsisting off walrus fat may not be everyone's cup of tea, but the Chukchi aren't the kind to wait for better offers. Until last century, with the onset of more comforts, their only sense of restlessness lay in their nomadic lifestyle, chasing the seasons year after year.

Their so-called hard words bear this out. Even if Russia bestowed the genre, the Chukchi have made the wordplay their own. Each riddle captures the spirit of life around them. The alder tree, say, 'enters from the outside with clothes' and is later debarked and trimmed to be 'undressed in the outer tent'. A kayak 'cuts but draws no blood'.

The truly ancient is embalmed in the borrowed form, too. 'A grass-bound shoulderblade' alludes to the oracular powers invested in burning bones over the fire. Deer or seal, the scapula is wrapped in grass and roasted until it carbonises, the cracks a cipher to the future. Different patterns spell different destinies. Should cracks emerge on the bone's rise, then mountains are implied in the clan's impending move. By contrast, cracks under the scapula murmur evil, or the proximity of wolves. Scapulimancy, as the custom is known, will also recommend directions for the next day's campsite or hunt.

Turning to more recent customs—the trappings of a new world—even these are given the Chukchi overlay:

I have four holes and only one road.
A wooden house

Here comes Kaka, walking with an open leg.

> *Its eye is poked by women; it gets angry, bites its lip, and ascends*
> *skyward.*
> *The lamp*

As for the riddle in our title, just imagine an Arctic evening by the Bering or Okhotsk Sea. There you are, swaddled in fur, lying in your *yaranga*, that mobile home of alder frame and deerskin, deep in the taiga forest, the gales howling through the pines, when you hear:

> *An old woman is made to break wind by an angry old man.*

That's how the noise might strike a newbie. But generations of hunters, and centuries of evenings, have taught the Chukchi a thing or two. Forget the farting pensioner, the ruckus belongs to polar bears doing the wild thing in the Chukotka wilderness.

⊐ 11 ⊏

Дүлий хонь өглөө хамтдаа хийж, орой нь тусгаарлагдсан байна

Dumb sheep are put together in the morning
and separated in the evening

Take your pick, English or the original Mongolian, the statement still sounds like twaddle.

You mean to say that some sheep are smart? Or wait, isn't the day/night distribution in arsey-versey order? If I was running a sheep station outside Ulan Bator, then I'd muster the flock come evening to guard against the wolf, and let the animals wander the steppe during the day. Or maybe I'm the dumb one, though Mongolia does have wolves—I know that much. The wolf riddle tells me:

> *It runs trotting along, with dun-coloured boots and two ears perked up.*

Foxes, too:

Scissors [Philippines]

Flattening itself out with a garment as yellow as a dry leaf.

Animals in general dominate this pocket of riddles. Sheep are the clear winner, with page after page of Archer Taylor's seminal collection of Mongolian riddles (1954) in an ovine vein. The typical ploy, keeping things terse and declarative in the Mongolian way, is to use sheep to symbolise objects:

A sheep that has 100 coats in severe winter.
Onion

A grey sheep with a hole in its navel.
A lock

A stable full of sheep, among the sheep a golden ram.
Stars and sun

Speaking of symbols, the modest flock above does a fair job of representing the bulk of Taylor's collection. The Mongols love metaphor almost as much as brevity, with so many of their riddles a single line, free of question mark, rich in figurative language, an animal never too far away:

A bluish horse with perspiring sides.
Whetstone

A swamp frog with nine sinews.
Saddle

A big-bellied snake on top of the yurt.
Rope

Four geese on an anvil.
Udder

Five flies on a shelf, therefore, are not five flies on a shelf but a row of buttons on a pillowcase. A lame crow licking a burial mound has nothing to do with a crippled black bird defiling a grave but is a pair of scissors cutting hair. When reading Mongolian riddles, your imagination needs to leap almost as high as a screaming rabbit getting its ears twisted, which is a balalaika.

What's lengthened by being cut at both ends?

So then, a dozen metaphors into the genre, the template established by a who's who of Central Asian zoology, can you identify those dumb sheep mentioned in our opening riddle? The answer has just been dropped in passing. Read the last paragraph again and you might channel your inner Mongol. Not scissors, which the corpus also calls a gaping mouth with no throat for swallowing. Not a pillowcase, which locals encode as the torn belly of the grey ram. But the buttons on your shirt, or the cotton caftan (*deel*) that locals favour, or possibly the silken jacket (*khantaaz*) that appears on festival days.

Before plastic arrived, Mongolian buttons were made of bone— either cattle or sheep. Wood was around, of course, but nomads knew better than to waste good fuel on haberdashery. Thus the button riddle works on the actual and metaphorical levels. As bone, the buttons are sheep, and the dumbest sheep is a lifeless one. Converted to buttons, the animal has new life, gathered into service by day and set loose at nightfall. In true Mongolian mode, the action also underpins the national pysche, where the imagined interlocks with the material.

⊏⌐ 12 ⌐⊐

Eu sou mineiro, não bule comigo não . . .

I'm a mean miner, don't mess with me . . .

From the 1500s, slave traders from Brazil ventured as far as Gabon in western Africa. They called on Namibia. They travelled up the Kwanza River to raid the Mbundu of northwest Angola. They took their pick of human capital among the Ovimbundu in the Benguela highlands, the Kongo people in the Zaire basin, the Bantu of Ndongo. They kidnapped men and women—the better to breed—and shipped their booty home to South America, back to the red loam east of São Paulo where they told the captives to dig.

And plant. And reap. And tear down forest. And lug the crop to market. By the late 1700s, coffee was the West's new drug and Brazil

A ditch

was there to cater for the addiction. Plantations spread from Pará in the north to the fertile hinterlands of Rio, the region known as Vassouras.

For the slaves, escape was next to impossible. Not with vigilant owners, plus the extra predicament of young families to raise. So it was that work became a type of cure, alleviated by the songs the slaves created to maintain a physical rhythm, as well as nourish memories of Africa. The children learnt to sing along as soon as they could talk. The custom was a secret to survival. In the fields the singing kept the hoes moving in unison. And later, in the *senzala*, the slave quarters attached to the farm, different songs unchained the workers' spirits.

Night songs were known as *pontos*, where *ponto* is a knotted stitch in Portuguese. (The same metaphor also evokes Africa, as you may recall, where the Bantu people know the riddle as *iqhina*, or knot.) Separate from the work tunes, the *pontos* had different beats and purposes. The *ponto de porfia*, say, was the song of strife. The *ponto de demanda* was the challenge song, a terse stanza thrown to the listener in want of a response. Not a singsong echo this time, as may happen in the field to keep the knife swinging, but a clever answer to match the master-singer's demand.

Não senta não, não senta não,
No toco de embaúba tu não senta não.

Don't sit down, don't sit down,
Don't sit on the stump of the embaúba.

If this leaves you bamboozled, then you join the ranks of the plantation owners, those who ignored the nocturnal drumbeats on the proviso of steady profits. On Sundays, if the season was right, a boss might grant his labourers an empty patio (the clay tier where the coffee beans dried) to host a *caxambu* ceremony.

Warm brandy would flow, a heady homemade liquor called *cachaça*. The drumming was constant, heart-like, mesmeric. Large *tamburs* drove the tempo. The smaller drums—the *cuíca* and *guzunga*—hung off shoulders and embellished the musical trance, working in tandem with the basket rattles, the *guaiás* filled with stones. The *ponto* dance was samba-like, slow and anticlockwise, a semaphore of elbows and

Say me and I'm broken.

hips punctuated by navel-on-navel collisions. The master-singer was the *jongeiro*, he who threw his riddles to the wheel that moved around him.

Eu sou mineiro, não bule comigo não,
Eu sou mineiro, não bule comigo não.

I'm a mean miner, don't mess with me,
I'm a mean miner, don't mess with me.

A logical verse if the *jongeiro* was a miner, but planting coffee is a different drudgery. What was the meaning behind the lyrics? Where would you start to untie the knotted stitch?

The secret lay in digging—or *escavação* in Portuguese. A central theme of any *ponto* was the notion of cutting a line, just as the daytime mattock dug a furrow in the field. Slicing the earth to make a road required the same sure strokes as the *jongeiro* needed to carve out his *carreador*, or the song's main trail. The armadillo, by the same token, was a totem revered among the slaves. Old *tatu*, as the creature was dubbed, was the grand excavator, and its blood was deemed capable of curing deafness and reviving the power of smell. Another important trait was the armadillo's knack of moving as fast in reverse as forward, this sense of returning to its burrow another powerful metaphor for the displaced dancers. So it was the wise *caxambu* would answer the so-called miner:

Oi mineiro, mineiro, mineiro,
Acompanha a minha linha.
Oi mineiro, mineiro, mineiro,
Acompanha a minha linha.

O miner, miner, miner,
Follow my line.
O miner, miner, miner,
Follow my line.

Thus the challenge was met, the triumphant solver becoming the new *jongeiro*. He, too, would step forward to hold the floor. He'd phrase a fresh riddle to the drumbeat, another *ponto de demanda* for his people to untie. Regardless of the subject, his language would be terse and swift, blending Portuguese and stray bits of Bantu. This mixture was crucial. In some field studies, the *jongeiro* is dubbed the *cumba*, a link to the Bantu word for braggart, since pride was a key ingredient of the ceremony, the antonym of serfdom.

But the same emotion was also asking for trouble. No coffee boss would sanction defiance. Hence the riddle-talk evolved, the covert metaphors and language salad—all the better to camouflage meaning from guesser and owner alike. Where the adopted African totem was the armadillo, the plantation masters were furtively compared to the agouti, the vermin relying on the diggings of other animals for its lair.

Still with the slurs, the *embaúba* is the punkiest tree in Brazil, soft as cheese and useless for building. Shrewd readers will recognise the species, the word appearing in our maiden *ponto*, the type of stump you should never sit on. The gist of the verse is power, not timber.

If the dancers can't match the *jongeiro's* demand, they are free to yell out *machado* (axe), the cue for the singer to give a fresh riddle—for the *ponto* is too heavy, as they say. However, should one dancer see the stanza's deeper meaning, then he might grab his moment and reply:

> Com tanto pau no mato,
> Embaúba é coronel.

> *With so many trees in the forest,*
> *The* embaúba *is the boss.*

And on it goes, like the wheeling *jongo* dance that still survives in parts of Vassouras, some 150 years after slavery has been abolished. A drug as strong as coffee, the *ponto de demanda* has remained in demand, the element of pride as vital as ever to the African diaspora. While the yoke has lifted, the pull remains strong.

What do you call an Italian with his hands in his pockets?

Mute

Lust & Love

Humans are hard-wired to find food, shelter—and a mate.
This section is the mating side of the equation.

From songs to opera, from erotica to graffiti, riddle-making seems hard-wired too.

13

I gave my love a cherry
that had no stone

'John Belushi was like Babe Ruth,' claimed his acting accomplice, Bill Murray. 'He could eat 50 hotdogs and he could hit 60 home runs.' And he could also steal a movie with one mad act of violence involving a folk singer.

The movie was *Animal House*, shot in 1978, a college comedy emerging from the National Lampoon stable. Belushi played a rabble-rouser named John Blutarsky, alias Bluto. In the critical scene he's dressed in nothing but a bedsheet, his token toga for the frat party. In contrast, the folk singer—Charming Guy On Stairs, or Stephen Bishop—is clad in bohemian skivvy with slimline jeans. His guitar is angled across his knee, troubadour style, the better to serenade the vestal virgins perched nearby:

> *I gave my love a cherry that had no stone*
> *I gave my love a chicken that had no bone*
> *I gave my love a story that had no end*
> *I gave . . .*

That's as far as Charming Guy got before Bluto seized the guitar and smashed it against the wall. Not once, but a brutal whack for every riddle the singer never had the chance to answer.

'Sorry,' shrugged the vandal as he handed back a fretboard, no strings attached.

The virgins looked appalled. If the violence didn't rock their evening, then it was the lullaby's breach of contract. Some things are traditional, just like 'The Riddle Song', and traditions need respecting. Didn't Bluto know that the song had emerged in the 1400s as a standard of English balladry, more recently covered by the likes of Joan Baez, Carly

Simon, Burl Ives, Pete Seeger and a funky makeover by The Meters? You know, maybe he did. There's only so much romantic folklore a toga party can stomach, and Charming Guy, or more specifically his Yamaha six-string, paid the consequences.

To play the song in full, the first verse itemises four contrary presents for the singer's sweetheart. (The unsung gift in the interrupted verse is 'a baby with no crying'.)

By now the listener is wondering how all these items are possible—cherries without stones, boneless chickens, etc. The second verse anticipates the confusion. Riddle songs are designed that way: the tease, then the payoff. At the very least, if the melody doesn't beguile your audience, there's always the promise of clarity.

The cherry, it's been argued, is an allusion to the hymen being broken, the sexual shift into womanhood. Perhaps this explains the virgins' interest, though the lyrics play coy, opting for the botanical interpretation. Indeed all four riddles, including the potential innuendo of giving a maiden a snivel-free baby, are furnished with tasteful solutions:

> *A cherry when it's blooming, it has no stone*
> *A chicken when it's pipping, it has no bone*
> *The story of how I love you, it has no end*
> *A baby when it's sleeping, it has no crying.*

Variations abound. In some versions the endless story is replaced by an endless ring, a love token to bind the singer and his squeeze. (As for pipping, that's a troubadour's way of saying the chicken's inside the egg.) In other covers, the riddles are shuffled, the eternal romance relegated to the song's finale in order to boost the mush factor. Come to think of it, maybe that's what Bluto dreaded on the stairs, knowing where the melody was leading and therefore taking the romance into his own hands.

Poke her face

⌐ 14 ⌐

Ciò che il ghiaccio può fare fuoco?

What ice can make fire?

Three riddles, one chance. Give one wrong answer and the royal axeman will tend to your neck in the square. That grisly task begins the opera. We see a nameless Persian prince being led to the chopping block, watched by a throng of understudies. Above them, the ramparts are decked with skulls: the head-count of hapless suitors who deemed themselves equal to the riddles. The prize, should any young man survive the enigmas, is the lily-white hand of Turandot, princess of the Forbidden City.

Death and romance, in fact, are part and parcel of the story, both onstage and on the drawing board. The work was the last by Giacomo Puccini, the fatal Chinese tale proving his undoing, the composer putting down his pen in 1924 with most of Act 3 still to compose.

Handily, Puccini's desk had a pile of sketches and story notes, giving fellow composer Franco Alfano the bones on which to flesh out the remainder. Failing that, there was also the Persian legend that fuelled the libretto, one of several tales where riddles often stood between love and destruction. Folklore calls them neck riddles. *Oedipus Rex* is the original example, and *Turandot* one of the more resplendent.

The opera begins with a bloody whack, the prince dispatched before laggard patrons can find a seat. The onstage crowd bays approval. One observer is a tenor called Calàf. He sees Turandot from a distance and falls into a stupor. He must win her heart. Timur, his father, begs him otherwise, as does a slave girl called Liù. By this stage I should issue a spoiler alert, though just like Alfano, you can probably guess the climax. Calàf won't be told, of course. He seeks out the princess and agrees to put his neck on the line. Turandot accepts his folly. She calls for three sages, each one bearing a scroll—the riddles of fate. The scene is attended by the emperor himself, plus the servants Pang, Ping and Pong, not to mention a mandarin, the terrified Liù and a ghostly chorus of suitors past.

What's the laziest bird in the world?

What is born each night and dies at dawn?

The first riddle is sung. Calàf wastes no time. He believes the answer is Hope. The sages unfurl the initial scroll and declare the man correct. Turandot is impressed, spurring her to voice the second enigma:

What flickers red and warm like a flame, yet is not fire?

Turandot's father, the emperor, implores the young man to reconsider his endeavour. Your life is at stake, wail the phantoms. Your love is at stake, croons Liù. But Calàf is defiant. He still can't tear his eyes off the bodacious Turandot. Pushing his luck, he replies this time with Blood, an easy guess for a man whose veins blaze with the stuff.

Two out of two. The court is aghast. The crowd inhales, angering Turandot, who orders her guards to lash the wretches. If death isn't deterrent enough, then surely this brutality should dissuade Calàf from thoughts of conjugal bliss, but no dice. He awaits the final riddle:

Ciò che il ghiaccio può fare fuoco?

Relax, Turandot is cruel but she's not vindictive. That last-minute switch to Italian was mine, not hers, a reminder of Puccini's libretto and how the work delighted La Scala's audience at the 1926 premiere, two years after the creator's death. However, first-night patrons were short-changed. In a gracious touch, Arturo Toscanini, the conductor, rested his baton midway through the final act. He explained to the audience that this was the point Puccini himself had reached, and thus the premiere ended prematurely. The crowd applauded and left the auditorium in suspense, obliged to buy more tickets to see if the couple made the altar. Frazzling, I know, but at least the first-nighters got to hear Riddle 3 being sung and solved:

What ice can make fire?

Turandot, as Calàf sang—his third answer. Once more, he was right, his neck intact. By fluke or fate, Calàf had met the challenge, sensing that the princess's icy veneer was merely a screen for burning desire. Be that as it may, Turandot had cold feet. She refused to honour the deal, resenting the notion of being somebody's booty, so to speak, no better than a slave getting offloaded to a stranger. In short, the princess was a total princess about it, shocking neither the Forbidden City nor La Scala.

True to his heroic nature, Calàf offered his neck in recompense, despite solving all three riddles—on one proviso. Until now, the libretto, and the court, had only identified the suitor as the Unknown Prince. Calàf was happy to cop the axe by sunrise, assuming his beloved could find out his actual name before the cock crew. Should the princess miss the deadline, then the executioner's hood would lose out to the bridal veil, and all would be peachy in *il mundo di Puccini*.

Go on—dare to map the finale? You've got three guesses.

◰ 15 ◳

Hyse cwom gangan pær
he hie wise stondan . . .

Corrr—if that sentence doesn't quicken your pulse then you'll need to collect on your life insurance. Oops, sorry, the line is Old English. Let's upgrade it:

> *A young man made for the corner where he knew she was standing . . .*

Feel the electricity now? The animal kind, as lightbulbs weren't around in AD980, roughly the vintage of the *Codex Exoniensis*. The Latin title is the work's formal name, as registered in 1072. The book was bequeathed to Exeter Cathedral by the city's first bishop, a man named Leofric. In his will, the cleric identified the book as '.*i. mycel englisc boc be gehwilcum pingum on leoðwisan geworht*', which was Leofric's way of saying 'One large book in English verse about various subjects'.

While that description's fair, you could also say that *The Collected Works of Shakespeare* is a fat book of plays dealing with several matters. Simple fact being Leofric fails to tell the full story. True, his large book is full of verse, but each segment is a trove, from early Christian

I'm tall when young, short when old.

poems to the elegiac kind about our brief term on earth. Inside this single volume are the Lord's Prayer and pagan Germanic tales. Peter Thomas, the cathedral's librarian, wasn't exaggerating when he recently told the local press, 'Given that it's the oldest English literary book in the world, you could regard it as the foundation of all English literature. As far as I'm concerned it's priceless.'

Perhaps Leofric had a flair for understatement, or the codex's value has only been realised in the intervening millennium. Either way, the same chap also neglected to say the book holds an abundance of riddles. Ninety-six in total, though some have frayed to single lines, while others are AWOL, causing the sequence to skip. Before you ask how such imperfections are possible, bear in mind that *The Exeter Book* (its lay name) has suffered fire and water damage over the journey. Before bibliophilia became a fetish, the volume was also used as a cutting board for cheese, as well as a beer mat.

As for naming the riddlesmith(s), that's a lottery. George Krapp and Elliot Dobbie, seminal editors of the work, date the verses to the early 700s, the transition phase between Latin and Anglo-Saxon. A shadowy figure called Cynewulf, one of few period poets we know by name, has been implicated, though he's more likely to be one of many.

Turning to the actual riddles, the 96 cover the gamut of mediaeval life, from the bellows to a battering ram, many samples ending with the taunt: *Saga hwæt ic hatta* (Say what I am called).

Bagpipes get a mention—the sword and the sun, the flail and the badger. At least, badger is the prevalent guess for Riddle 15, as splinter groups favour the porcupine, the fox and/or the hedgehog, depending on which hairy-cheeked hole-dweller tickles your fancy. For that's the rub with *Codex Exoniensis*: the book boasts 96 riddles and not one answer.

Thankfully, several solve themselves. The bookworm is a case in point, Riddle 47: *The stealing guest was not a whit the wiser for the words he guzzled . . .*

Compare this to the iffiness of Riddle 10: *I burst to life when from the lap of brine and branch I came in black robe . . .* Sleuths are split into five camps, peddling theories as diverse as a bubble, an anchor, a waterlily or the trough between waves. The fifth and strongest lobby pushes the

A candle

barnacle goose, a bird once thought to hatch from barnacles and feed on driftwood sap, as captured in this telling line: *I matured in the sea, above the milling waves, my body locked to a stray floating spar.*

Anglo-Saxon biology might have been off-kilter but their hints could be pretty faithful, unless we consider the riddle cluster that carried deliberate alternatives. This set is known as the obscene group, or the innuendo riddles, written proof that bishops like Leofric might have been pious but were not always prudish.

Take the battering ram I mentioned earlier. As phallic symbols go, the weapon gets off lightly. Not so the fire poker, the gimlet or the key: *A strange thing hangs by a man's thigh, hidden by a garment . . .*

Women get their moment via onions, ovens and a helmet: *Then he poked his head inside me, pushed it up until it fitted tightly . . .*

But the riddle to make the sweetest music, with nary a lute in earshot, must be the po-faced porn of Riddle 54:

A young man made for the corner where he knew
She was standing; this strapping youth
Had come some way—with his own hands
He whipped up her dress, and under her girdle
He thrust something stiff as she stood there,
Worked his will; they both shook.
This fellow quickened: one moment he was
Forceful, a first-rate servant, so strenuous
That the next he was knocked up, quite
Blown by his exertion. Beneath the girdle
A thing began to grow that upstanding men
Love heartily and buy with money.

Forget Mills & Boon. This is hot & steamy from a time when mills made flour and boon meant a blessing. Nameless poets from the Middle Ages could make the blood churn as surely as the modern bodice-ripper. Who needs *50 Shades of Grey* when the *Codex Exoniensis* can summon the raunch with one hand tied behind its back?

Heaven knows how Bishop Leofric interpreted the quickening fellow. Have you guessed the answer? The last paragraph carries a clue. Nothing to do with flour, but bread is getting warmer. The innocent

How many months have 28 days?

solution is a butter churn, or the act of churning, where the strapping farmhand removes the lid to work the plunger. The upshot—or growing thing—is the frothy concoction called buttermilk, the energy-rich elixir men enjoy and buy with money. All that's missing is a tablespoon of sea salt, plus two creamy cups of double entendre.

⌐ 16 ⌐

Out of the eater, something to eat.
Out of the strong, something sweet.

SCENE: A wedding feast in sandal times. Samson sits at the table's head with his bride, a young woman from Timnah whom the Bible fails to name. Still, we can confirm the woman is a Philistine, which sounds like a snub, but Timnah belongs to that part of the Levant. Same applies to the 30 groomsmen surrounding the couple, Philistines one and all. Only Samson, the Israelite, is the exception.

SAMSON: Gentlemen, if I may, I'd like to propose a riddle.

PHILISTINE 1: Don't you mean toast?

SAMSON: Out of the eater, something to eat. Out of the strong, something sweet.

PHIL 2 (raising glass): Good health!

PHIL 1: Out of the eater, what?

SAMSON: That's for you to decide. You have seven days.

PHIL 1: Or what?

SAMSON: Let's talk robes. The good gear. Solve my riddle in a week and I'll deck you all in finery.

PHIL 3: Hear, hear! (raising glass) To Samson and his Timnah woman!

SAMSON: Fall short, however, and I will expect the same in return—30 robes of the finest quality.

BRIDE (whispering): Do you think that's wise, honey?

SAMSON: Shhh.

Shhh, because honey was a hint. By chance, that was the riddle's sweet bit, not that Anon of Timnah knew that. Nobody did, bar Samson. Cracking the riddle relied on knowing about a certain incident in the Sorek Valley, a small matter involving Samson and a lion. The lion was the riddle's strong ingredient, but 30 men had no idea, since no witnesses meant no solvers. Samson sat back, thinking how his cleverness would wangle a wardrobe. Strong and clever—no wonder he was a catch.

As for the riddle's catch, you needed to know how a lion had sprung from a Timnah vineyard a few days prior to the wedding. Samson tore the beast apart. That's the verb the Bible uses, or toreth in the older editions. The spirit of the Lord entered the young man's biceps, allowing him to rip the lion to shreds.

Did he tell his parents? Judges 14:6 says no.

Did he tell the hottie from Timnah? Perhaps. But she hadn't heard about the bizarre aftermath, when Samson passed the lion's carcass a few days later. He noticed that the air was busy with bees. Against all reason, a swarm had built a hive inside the animal, the sweet within the strong.

Samson grabbed some honey, a scoop for the walk, and a scoop for his sorrowful parents. As Israelites, Manoah and his nameless wife were lamenting the fact that their macho son was marrying a Philistine goy (not to mention the banquet bill). Even if Samson told them the honey came from a lion's guts, they were in no shape to listen. Consequently the wedding riddle was a locked vault. A shutout. The groom's garments were safe, or so he figured.

But the groom wasn't in the loop about his bride's treachery, where clearly blood ran thicker than matrimonial wine. The bride crooned and cajoled her lover. She ran her fingers through his miraculous hair and pleaded for an eensy-weensy clue.

Being made of flesh, Samson relented. He told her about the lion episode. The bees, too. What the hell, he gave her the whole answer, only for the drama to hit its flashpoint somewhere near the tiramisu. Okay, so the menu's conjecture, but the riddle's answer is quoted directly:

PHILISTINE 1: What is sweeter than honey? What is stronger than a lion?
SAMSON: If you had not ploughed with my heifer, you would not have solved my riddle.

Higher than a horse, lower than a pig.

Them's fighting words, and not a little lewd. Bottom line being, Samson had to conjure 30 garments out of thin air. Curiously, some Bible scholars assert this outcome to be the riddle's key role, the bride's betrayal the impetus for Israel to take up cudgels against the Baal-worshipping Philistines. The riddle was a trust test and Samson's wife had failed. But rather than confront her with words, he did what biblical hombres knew best. He went smiting.

Craftily, it must be added. Brains and brawn—Samson *was* a catch. He roamed the land and snared 300 foxes, tying them tail-to-tail in pairs. Next he travelled the Philistine grain fields to let the animals loose. The locals were afraid that their land had been cursed by surrealism, a plague of two-headed foxes! Worse, Samson had bound a torch to each coupling. As the foxes ran, their attached flames lit the grain. Thus the Riddle War had begun, ignited by a manic brushfire the Philistines were powerless to quell. Wheat went. Haystacks burned. Olive groves turned to char.

When Samson was named as the culprit, the farmers marched to Timnah and killed the nameless woman's parents. (Vengeance had its own weird logic in the Bible.) Before you could say shibboleth, the Riddle War had escalated. Soon the hotspot shifted from Timnah to Etam, a flyspeck south of Bethlehem, where Samson brandished a donkey's jawbone at his enemies, slaying a thousand Philistines to recoup his wardrobe debt and then some. Meanwhile, God was pleased with what He saw, opening the earth where the jawbone fell, and issuing fresh water from the earth, a spring that bubbles to this day.

Furthermore, after Samson had rinsed off the blood, quenched his thirst and fleeced the corpses, he would venture to Gaza where his new love interest awaited. Delilah was the quintessential bombshell, a far greater turncoat than his Philistine ex. With Delilah's looks, and Samson's abs, the two were the Brangelina of their day. Magnetic. Irresistible. Sheer physical chemistry with no whisper of riddles (or inconvenient wives from Timnah) on record. Mind you, since Samson accredited his primal allure to his deltoids, he failed to see that his lover was more interested in his throat, and how to slit it. Or, put riddle-wise:

> *Out of the strong, something vulnerable. Out of the hot, something coldblooded.*

A saddle [Estonia]

⌐ 17 ⌐

Waq law pampapi huq machucha runtunta champayanankama suqurn

In that flat place an old man sucked on his egg until fibres came out

High in the Andes, a young man needs six things to seduce a young woman:

1. a ukulele-sized guitar called a *chinlili* . . .
2. . . . and songs to play on it
3. a good throwing arm for tossing pebbles at your wooee's feet
4. a lantern for nocturnal meetings
5. cold beers—or better still a lackey to go fetch them
6. a repertoire of riddles.

Good looks help, too, plus a jaunty llama cap. But in places such as Ayacucho, the Quechuan capital of Peru, you won't make second base until you know your share of ambiguous questions.

This assertion was made by Billie Jean Isbell and Fredy Amilcar Roncalla Fernandez back in 1977. Their essay on Quechuan riddle games, appearing in the *Journal of Latin American Lore*, identified word-play as Romeo's calling card, a quick mind being more aphrodisiacal than oysters in the Andean air.

Serenades may win the day in Verona, but in the boondocks of Huanacayo and Quillabamba an aspiring swain needs to get his riddle on. For centuries the banter and pebble-lobbing took place in the pastures edging a town, the quiet grazing lands where a young shepherd might stray upon a nubile shepherdess. Over time, as life became more centralised for the average Peruvian, these pasture games evolved into *Vida Michiy*, which means 'to pasture life'—importing the old-time flirtations into the outskirts of the modern town.

The rules are rubbery, so to speak, though some things have remained unchanged through the flux. The first is the element of ambiguity. Unlike

What path has crazy paving?

standard Quechuan, a language laced with markers to denote the speaker's topic and personal link to the subject, the riddle mode is all but naked in its wording. Which leads us to the second constant: sex.

Among the 109 riddles that Isbell and Fernandez gathered in the Andes, most worked blue. A riddle either presented an innocent question with a filthy answer, or vice versa. For example:

Waq law pampapi huq machucha runtunta champayanankama
    suqurn.
In that flat place an old man sucked on his egg until fibres came out.

Did it make you blush? That's the plan. The *Vida Michiy* thrives on boundary-pushing. *Huevos* in Spanish means eggs, or bollocks, and the same innuendo holds good in Quechuan. Likewise, fibres can be translated as hairs, concocting the image of some old codger in a paddock committing an act of gross indecency, not to say agility.

Until the answer arrives. The egg in question is a mango stone, the fibres being the flesh attached to the pith. With one word the tension is defused, and the riddle game rolls on—with one speed bump.

If the guesser errs, taking the wrong tack, then the punishment is dire. Death awaits in a virtual way, thanks to the phase known as *qaqata wichiykusaq*, or 'I'm going to fall into the abyss'.

Once more, subtext abounds. If an egg is a bollock, then an abyss is a vagina—the ambiguity powering the game like voltage. To make the wayward stab, the sucker has to fall down a ravine in his imagination, reporting on the episode via a series of questions. Here's a snippet gathered by Isbell and Fernandez from a fourteen-year-old boy, reliving his trauma:

SUCKER: *Qaqata wichiykusaq!* (I'm going to fall into the abyss!)
ASKER: *Arí. Wichiykuy ya!* (Yes. Fall now!)
SUCKER: *Ya . . . Bundún! Yàsta.* (Ya . . . Boom! It's done.)
ASKER: *Ya. May qataqaq wichiykunki?* (Ya. Which abyss did you fall into?)
SUCKER: *Wayunku qaqata.* (Wayunku Abyss.)
ASKER: *Mas o menos hayka metrutataq wichiykuwaq kara?* (More or less,
    how many metres did you fall?)
SUCKER: *Yaqachiki kilumetruta.* (It must have been more than a kilometre.)

A psychopath

Quechuan questions

Ojetiyta pukuy—akayta mikuy. *(Blow on my arse—eat my shit.)*
Manka *(Cooking pot)*

Negra vieja piñakun. Yana macho kallpaykuspa upallachin.
   *(The old black woman is making herself angry. An old black man
   running causes calm.)*
Olla y cucharón *(Cooking pot and ladle)*

Splat. The virtual fall leads to virtual death, ticking every Freudian box
on the list—sex, death, blood, shame. Not that the matter ends there.
To deepen the filth, the sucker needs to further his embarrassment,
telling others how his guts exploded, the mess a feast for vultures
and dogs. What next? The same scavengers travel the mountains and
eventually shit his entrails on the high plains. What next? Next the
aqchi bird, the Andean magpie, steps in the crap, and soils its own
nest, where an egg is lying—a real egg. What next? Next the village
priest comes to cook this egg, mixed with the sucker's own guts and
vulture shit, adding a pinch of salt to improve the taste. What then?
Then the father prays . . .

The sequence embodies The Fall in its own Andean way: the
undercurrent of sex and disgrace ending with a celibate beseeching a
god who may or may not exist. On the language front, examining the
banter, you'll notice how English (*kilumetruta*) has entered the fray,
along with *mas o menos* (the Spanish phrase for 'more or less'). Both
corruptions signal a slow diluting of the Quechuan tongue, perhaps to
the point where *Vida Michiy* is less the courtship of choice in Ayacucho.
Though as long as eggs and abysses mean more than eggs and abysses,
then the *chinlili* is sure to be fingered in Peru.

Why did the blind chicken cross the road?

◄⌐ 18 ⌐►

Why are ladies like arrows?

I must have spent months, back in 2012, trying to answer a single question: is English the only language to have cryptic crosswords? The short answer is no. Writing *Cluetopia*, my time-travelling tour of crosswords, I'd found half a dozen cultures with their own cryptic genre, from the visual puns of Sweden to France's fractured poetry. None of it was simple to untangle. Most hinged on idiom. If a pun was funny in the original tongue, then you can guarantee the same gag would asphyxiate in transit.

Drawing a blank with a particular Dutch puzzle, I enlisted help from people with names like Henk and Bruno. The exercise verged on futile. To give you a taste, imagine translating this riddle into a second language:

Why are ladies like arrows?
Because they can't go off without a beau, and are always in a quiver
  till they get one

The solution is a translator's nightmare. First, there's the duplicity of going off, then the homophone of beau/bow, and finally the quaint double meaning of quiver, with the added complication of the breached adjective, a/quiver. Forget about it. Move on. That's far too difficult. The English-speaking brain does enough heavy lifting without the wisecrack needing footnotes for alternative speakers.

Or so you'd reckon. Translators are brave by nature, but there are some pieces of wordplay that defy exporting. Cryptic clues and convoluted riddles are two that spring to mind. Every sign is telling you, GO BACK, WRONG WAY. Still, with the aid of Henk and Bruno, I fought the good fight with *Cluetopia*, just as I've needed bravado (and wise counsel) to get this far into *Riddledom*. Until now. Until this chapter, where I get to sit back to savour that schadenfreude in the shape of a book called *English Riddles: With explanations and notes in Dutch.*

To visit the Birdseye factory

My eyes lit up on seeing the title. In 2012, after so many weeks of crunching clues with polyglots, deciphering emails and splitting nuances, I knew my latest wordplay safari had finally returned the favour.

Fools to a man, Benj S. Berrington and John S. Berrington—the editors hired by the Dutch publisher—had tried to transfer a raft of riddles that didn't care for relocation. Just like the arrow example, none of the riddles was especially droll. All that changes when you accompany each punchline with a clumsy justification from La Hague. Suddenly those same 202 riddles become a scream.

Returning to the arrow pun, let's rerun the Q&A, this time with the Berringtons adding their tuppence:

Why are ladies like arrows?
Because they can't go off without a beau, and are always in a quiver till they get one.
(Arrow, *pijl*; to go off, here *weggeschoten worden*, also *trouwen*; beau, *minnaar*; bow, *boog*; quiver, *koker, trilling*; to get, *krijgen*.)

Laughs in translation

Why is an author the queerest animal in the world?
Because his tale grows out of his head
(Tale, *verhaal*; tail—same pronunciation—*start*; queer, *vreemd*)

When is wine like a pig's tooth?
When it's in a hog's head
(Hog, *varken*; hogshead, *okshoofd*)

Why is an adjective like a drunken man?
Because it can never stand alone
(Adjective, *bijvoegelijk naamwoord*)

If a woman were to change her sex, what religion would she be?
She would be a he, then
(Sex, *geslacht*; heathen, *heiden*)

Why did the lunar restaurant flop?

Now *that's* funny. To consider a pair of Dutchmen at the turn of last century trying to separate their *minnaars* from their *boogs* still gives me a stomach cramp. I'm guessing the book was aimed at language students, equipping competent English speakers with vernacular insights. Though after 202 brain-benders like that little stinker, I can only guess that students left their Amsterdam classroom all a-*trilling*, and not in a good way.

⌐ 19 ⌐

Mulier ferebat filium simile sui . . .

A woman has borne a son of her own . . .

Pompeii sits high on my bucket list. I see the city as my eventual reward for suffering through all those grammar mantras at school, over and over, *amas* and *amat*, locative and vocative, Horace and Virgil ad nauseam. If I can't flex my classical muscle with the man in the street, then maybe I should make for the Pompeii streets, one day, if only to decode the ample graffiti. The crude and the flippant, the arch and the bland, or even the poignant, like this confession:

> *Odi et amo.*
> *Quare id faciam fortasse requiris?*
> *Nescio, sed fieri snetio et excrucior.*

Translated, the pain rises to the surface:

> I hate and I love.
> Perhaps you ask me why I do this?
> I don't know. But I understand that it's happening and I'm in pain.

You can feel the anguish from 2000 years away. The lines are scratched on a column edging the forum, one of 13,000 inscriptions across Pompeii. No small effort for a town that had some 10,000 residents, more than a scribble *per capita*. No doubt more will be found once the

No atmosphere

remnant lava is gouged from the laneways. When Vesuvius erupted in AD79, the disaster preserved a library of popular culture, scratched and painted across the walls, from the grain market to Apollo's temple.

Early in the 1900s, when the major digs took place, archaeologists were deafened by the voices yelling from the masonry. The oldest message they found, dating back to 78BC, was among the more banal: *Gaius Pumidius Diphilus was here.* Other inscriptions answered to epigrams (*Disparagement makes a small wrong into a great one*) and brothel ads, curses and warnings. There were child-like sketches and vows of love. There was the comic (*Guest, do not urinate against this tomb, the bones beg you . . .*) and the ironic (*Nothing is able to endure forever*).

There was a quatrain, too, chiselled into the basilica, the long arcade abutting the main forum. One more poetic fragment to the naked eye, the quatrain was soon revealed to be a *zetema* (or riddle), the rarity even headed by that word to establish the challenge:

ZETEMA
Mulier ferebat filium simile sui
Nec meus est nec mi similat sed
Vellem esset meus
Et ego voleba[m] ut meus esset.

In English the riddle reads:

A woman has borne a son of her own;
He isn't mine nor does he resemble me,
But I wish he was mine,
And I was wanting him to be mine.

Before we go exhuming, a quick note about that bracketed *m* you just met. Amazing how one letter can murmur so much about the Latin of the day, as well as the riddlesmith's own dilemma, scratching the stanza in the plaster. In the original *zetema*, there is no *m*, hence the brackets. The letter has been added by Rebecca R. Benefiel, the American translator, a logical guess to fill a lacuna. Without getting mired in deep-geek detail, the missing *m* is likely a symptom of Latin's glacial shift into modern Italian. Being pure, the word would be *volebam*

What must you add to nine to make six?

(I wanted). Being modern, the mystery scribe omitted the *m*, implying the nasalised corruption spoken in those buried streets.

Fine, but what about the answer? The *ego* responsible for the verse failed to leave a solution. Nor did any passerby inscribe a theory. Instead the guesswork was left to the shovel crew—and us.

Since the quatrain's unearthing, several tangents have been tested. The bluer stabs match the tenor of adjacent graffiti, suggesting that the writer wished to own the boy sexually, rather than parentally. While this is possible, a more persuasive argument came from Karl Schenkl, an Austrian polylinguist who developed a shine for *pecunia*, or money, as the possible answer.

Unorthodox, I admit, but not when you consider the son as *fructus* (fruit), a metaphor for *merces*, or the interest that investments generate. Rather than lust, the riddle reflects class envy within the scribbler: where money begets money, the workaday labourer is never able to own the action. Then again, I'm feeling less sold by *pecunia* the more I'm trying to sell the conjecture. Maybe the riddle is still up for grabs, 2000 years on. If we can't pinpoint the author, perhaps a bright spark will still unmask the poem's mysterious woman and her desirable son. Maybe some feckless tourist will dig up his schoolboy Latin and come to the rescue, some ancient fool in 2040 with a long history of wordplay. Or maybe the *zetema* affirms how far away Pompeii can seem, despite its chorus of immediate voices.

⌐⌐ 20 ⌐⌐

Kyamiso-ru to kakete enpitsu to toku. Sono kokoro wa?

What do a camisole and a pencil have in common?

That's our leading question, the riddle borrowed from a Japanese game show involving colour-coded kimonos and four-kilo cushions.

Shōten has ruled Japan's airwaves since 1966, the country's second-longest-running TV program, behind the costume soapie *Zenigata Heiji*.

Tonally the shows could not be further apart. Where *Zenigata* dwells on protocol and chivalry, *Shōten* excels in smut and mortification.

Every week, six *rakugo* experts converge on the studio wearing lurid kimonos. *Rakugo* is a storytelling mode unique to Japan, a droll narrative where one performer plays every part. Picture a stand-up saga, except that the comedian is sitting cross-legged on a straw mat, a fan and rag his lone props. The custom stems from the feudal period some 1000 years ago, born of Buddhist monks seeking to enliven their sermons.

In fact, the veteran host of *Shōten* is the chairman of the Rakugo Association. Every Sunday night, Katsura Utamaru will fire a set of mental challenges at his contestants, then assess the wit of each response. A typical question is a *nazokake*, or comparison riddle, such as our camisole/pencil poser.

Have you given the matter any thought? The key to a *nazokake* is improv. Often the intended answer has a telltale sheen, presuming there is a set solution, but that doesn't disqualify comical suggestions. How does a pencil relate to a camisole? Let's think about it. Both lead to a point, you could argue. Both are graphic, and highlight outlines. I don't know—I'm freefalling here. With any luck, the studio audience will like what they hear, obliging Utamaru to award me a cushion.

For that's the modus operandi. A contestant gives a smart reply, he gains a cushion. The better the player, the higher the stack he perches on. Sounds aspirational, right? But *Shōten* can be cruel. Imagine that I answered that a pencil and camisole both implied a rubber, and the gag met with silence, or a storm of boos. Utamaru would have no choice but to pluck a *zabuton* from beneath my buttocks. Only the finest *rakugo* artist can boast the magical stack of ten cushions, the ultimate *Shōten* prize.

That's the good news. The bad is where the weird arrives. Japanese game shows have a reputation for the outrageous, and in this regard, *Shōten* doesn't disappoint. Come the *oogiri*, or endgame, the cushions are often ditched for acts of humiliation. To research this chapter I spent a few hours watching GIFs of crazy Japanese moments. And by spent, I mean squandered. I saw the stuff of nightmares in high resolution. Such as a woman scurrying from a Komodo dragon with a pork chop dangling behind her. Or another woman standing in a giant

Black chicken, open stomach.

spindle, her body being swathed in mummy bandages as she's happily addressing the camera—until she can't address anymore. I saw a man trying to eat spaghetti in a tumble dryer, while another bloke attempted to munch on a shoe. You get the drift. Tokyo has a soft spot for the troppo, and *Shōten* is part of the pathology.

To single out a winner, the top riddlers enter a showdown of shame. This time, instead of cushions as trophies, there are indignities as penalties. You get the answer right, you please Utamaru, you make the audience laugh—you're safe. You might even win. Then again, if you blow your chance, well . . . what's the worst that could happen?

Before we answer that question, let's solve our riddle. What do a camisole and a pencil have in common? The intended answer is rather elegant:

Chotto usui no ga ecchi

In Japan, when foreign words (such as television or ice-cream) cross the sea, they are converted into calques, loan words modified to fit the native grammar. For example, those last two newbies are better known as *terebijon* and *aisukurimu* in Yokohama—easier for locals to say, and grammarians to parse. Spelling is easier, too, once the words are modified to match existing patterns. This only leaves the vexatious English alphabet to manage now and then, including the irksome H—pronounced *ecchi* in Japanese, the last word in your *nazokake* answer.

Translated, the punchline reads: *Ones that are lighter are H.*

But how does that relate to a camisole? It doesn't on the surface. You need to plumb the next level down, where the homophone of *ecchi* means sexy. This subversion then sees *chotto* (lighter) shift to mean thinner, a nuance also reflected in English. A thinner blanket of snow, for instance, is also a lighter cover. Hence the subtext is where the sizzle lies:

Ones that are thinner are sexy

Nail that pun and you could own the episode. Flub your chance, however, and you might have a dwarf's backside wheeled inches from your face or a bamboo paddle applied to your hindquarters—just a few of the *Shōten* perils on offer. Tragically, the punishments will repeat if you make one more slip, and I'm not talking camisoles.

Stove [Turkey]

⌐ 21 ⌐

Eine getötet keiner, aber immer noch getötet zwölf

One killed none, but still killed twelve

Ironically, the longest word hiding in FAIRYTALE is REALITY. Though if that seems perverse, how about two German brothers called Grimm who made their living by writing 'Happily ever after'?

The Grimms knew the rules well. As much historians as writers, the brothers combed the breadth of German folklore to adopt and adapt the stalwart franchises we know today: Cinderella, Snow White, Hansel and Gretel.

The pair were born in Hanau, close to Frankfurt, in the late 1700s. In a few short years they experienced both privilege and poverty, owing to their jurist father dying when Jacob and Wilhelm were still wearing shorts.

Later, both studying law at university, the Grimms took an interest in fairytales, possibly inspired by their own riches-to-rags existence. The young men began to identify the tales' common ingredients, from woods to witches, and from damsels (*Jungfrauen*) to riddles (*Rätsel*).

Both elements get star billing in *Rumpelstiltskin*, the best-known riddle tale from the Grimm output. You know the drill: boastful father says his daughter can spin straw into gold; king wants evidence, locking the girl in a tower; overnight the girl relies on a freakish imp to make the magic happen; king wants more; girl promises her firstborn to Mr Imp to turn the latest haystack into bullion, etc.

Being fair-skinned and gracious, not to say an apparent cash cow, the miller's daughter becomes the queen, the royals flourishing until their baby arrives. Lo and behold, the imp returns. Wants his baby, as the girl had promised. But the queen baulks. She offers the imp any riches the realm can dispense, only for the creditor to say, 'If you can guess my name, then you can keep your child.'

As part of folklore gospel, the queen has three days to guess the answer. It's a question more than a riddle, a quest to find one elusive

What did the Jewish Superman say?

answer, with time running out. Thanks to a courtier who overhears the imp singing his own name, the queen manages to keep her baby. She names the imp, so consigning Rumpelstiltskin to exile, or death, depending on which edition you own. In both versions, 'happily' crops up.

Quiz a league of bedtime readers, and *Rumpelstiltskin* will be the obvious riddle/maiden story that most can name, with name the pivotal word. Yet the stronger candidate in the Grimm canon goes by the name of *Das Rätsel (The Riddle)*. Here the question is a bona fide riddle, confronting a princess this time, who once again has 72 hours to dredge up the answer.

To put you in the princess's shoes, Cinderella style, I'll ask you the riddle without giving you the backstory:

One killed none, but still killed twelve.

The Grimms composed their riddle tale in 1812. As you'd expect, the princess has no chance to make sense of the equation. With no inkling of the raven jabbing at the dead horse, she's left to clutch at straws.

What raven? you ask. Which horse? Where *Rumpelstiltskin* illustrates the power of names, just like the *Turandot* saga, *The Riddle* underlines the advantage of privileged knowledge. Time and again you see this device played out in folklore, where a question can only be solved if you share the asker's experience. Look no further than Samson's riddle at his wedding feast. Or even the enigma that is your computer password, based on a name or a touchstone only you know. Riddles are designed to flaunt this advantage, to emphasise the disparity between knower and ignoramus. The ploy makes sense, I suppose, especially if your life is at stake. Let's do a road test. If I'm allowed to electrocute you, but only if I correctly answer one question you ask, then you wouldn't quiz me on the capital of Burundi, or Kentucky Derby winners. If I'm feeling vengeful, I'll turn to Google. Instead you'd opt for the esoteric, plumping for your goldfish's name from kindergarten, or the number of olives you once ate in Valencia.

Getting back to *Das Rätsel*, the synopsis is Fairytale 101. We begin with a witch who tries to poison a visiting prince; the prince's horse drinks the poison instead and dies; a raven flies down and pecks at the body; the prince's servant unwisely kills the raven for supper; the bird is cooked that night in a tavern; but wait, the dozen guests who eat the bird all happen to be murderers. (Damn these tales seem small-g grim in summary.) And thus the prince and his servant are safe to wend their way on to the next plight, meeting a princess who boasts a gift for riddling. To win her hand, suitors have to pose a riddle. Should she guess the answer, the suitor is beheaded. If stumped, she'd tie the knot.

Before we get to 'happily', a word about dirty pool. That's what the princess tries, sending her maids to the prince overnight, aiming to weasel the answer from the young man's dreams. Call me sceptical, but I deem that a euphemism for sleeping with the guy, trying to elicit the answer via seduction. Twice they fail, only for the princess herself to sit on the man's bed, much as parents perch beside their children, reading these timeless stories. While she does crack *Das Rätsel*, she also falls in love in the process. Cue 'happily'.

⌐⌐ 22 ⌐⌐

Seven exit and nine enter, two pour and one drinks

The Queen of Sheba spelt trouble. The woman was gorgeous in the drop-dead category, with lustrous black skin and a killer dress sense. Wealthy, too, arriving in Jerusalem with a caravan of spices, gemstones and gold, her explicit wish to test King Solomon.

The man's wisdom was legendary, such talk reaching the queen's own realm in southern Arabia, where modern Yemen lies. Sheba was in town to see this sagacity first-hand, armed with her looks, her treasures and her riddles.

Solomon, for his part, was on high alert. Sheba attracted her share of hearsay, too, not only for her glamour and her riches, but her hairy legs as well. As a man with 700 wives, and a few platoons of concubines, Solomon was hardly picky. Doubtless his harem contained the odd

Born white, live green, die red, bury black.

frump—a hawkish nose here, a crow's foot there—but hairy legs were a different proposition, at least in 950BC.

No mere hang-up, Solomon's concern related to the demons who pranced through Arabic literature. Known as djinni, evil spirits capable of enslaving men with magic, the breed was confirmed by goat-like legs, a sure sign of devilry. If the test was as simple as upskirting the queen, then Solomon was willing to put his prodigious mind to the task.

That's why, according to the Midrash, the Jewish commentary attached to the Bible, the king awaited his guest in a glass pavilion. A trick with mirrors? Not quite. Think classier, for the Queen of Sheba entered the chamber in her ankle-length finery, surveying the space between door and throne, and mistook the translucence for water. Solomon's illusion worked a treat. The visitor bunched her hem to wade across the space, revealing two hairy legs. Shapely, it was true, but hairy into the bargain. Thus the king knew he sat in the presence of danger. He'd need every shred of his wisdom to survive.

Versions of the meeting vary. Rival translations can also adjust the details. In most Bibles, quoting 1 Kings 10:5, the Queen of Sheba was overwhelmed by what she saw—'the palace Solomon had built, the food on his table, the seating of his officials, the attending servants in their robes, his cupbearers . . .' In other accounts, she gazed at the grandeur until 'there was no more spirit in her'. A minor discrepancy on the page, perhaps, but quite a crucial detail, given Sheba's witchery. Nonetheless, whether or not Solomon's splendour exorcised the queen, she still had her diabolic riddles.

Read the Bible version and you'll learn about the bags of jewels, the spices, the precious almug wood—the many gifts Sheba bestowed on Solomon. Then again, head for the Midrash and those presents morph into prizes, as though the king had to prove his own talents before earning the largesse. Whichever the scenario, the queen would ask four enigmas, the first of these the most riddle-like in form:

Seven exit and nine enter, two pour and one drinks.

Imagine the tension, if you can. Three millennia is a big gap to span, but give yourself over to the moment. There they stand, two powerful figures on the brink of capitulation, the silence as fragile as the glass around them. If Solomon blunders, the demon-queen might claim his hand, his kingdom, or his head. The stakes are cranked to eleven. Turning the tables, if Solomon unravels the string of numbers, Sheba may fall, her charms and chicanery coming to naught.

Nowadays we have game shows or reality series to serve as tropes. We know we need to woo the judges, beat the buzzer or sing our little hearts out to survive another day. Three thousand years ago, that do-or-die genre fell to folklore, including riddle tales, where marriage might be the jackpot, or death the single penalty. Yet somehow the story of Solomon and Sheba goes one better, throwing man and woman into erotic conflict, human versus djinn, empire versus empire, the balance of power teetering between wisdom and allure. Blind Freddie could see why Halle Berry and Gina Lollobrigida grabbed the Sheba role, and a long list of Hollywood sirens before them. Indeed, womanhood was the answer to the queen's mathematics.

Solomon chose his words with care: 'Surely seven days of menstruation exit; nine months of pregnancy enter; two breasts pour and one baby drinks.'

His answer amazed the queen. Solomon deserved his legend, it seemed. The algorithm was on the money. Yet even with the riddle solved, the danger didn't leave the air.

Dina Stein, professor of Hebrew literature at the University of Haifa, argues that the riddle embodied a double risk for Solomon. First came the challenge of cracking the logic, then the threat of igniting desire. As Stein writes, 'The queen of Sheba speaks to Solomon in a metaphoric language loaded with sexual connotations (enter/exit, pour/drink).'

But the king was awake to the plan. He cooled the queen's raunch with his tepid reply, switching the erotic for the domestic, replacing the potential lover of Sheba's riddle with the mother implicit in his answer. Human 1—Demoness 0.

Unfazed, the woman tried her second ruse, a riddle involving a messy family tree that Solomon sliced apart with logic. He showed equal savvy when it came to the final two riddles, the man seemingly a stranger to failure. Sheba had no answer, so to speak, since Solomon appeared to own them all. No sooner was one challenge posed than the king would swerve, and solve, and avidly await the next. In the

Why are the Irish so wealthy?

end, the last enigma nailed, the temptress was left with no choice but to lick her many wounds. By the time she shambled from the pavilion her spirit was most certainly spent.

Outside, that lavish caravan of gold and spices no longer loomed as dowry but as the mother of all scores for the wise king of Israel. The loot was delivered, Solomon praised, and little Miss Hairylegs made good her retreat.

Their capital is always Dublin

Life & Death

Did I mention hard-wiring before? Survival is also high on the list.

Evolution is not just down to the fittest, but the sharpest-witted, too. Prepare to risk your life as we confront more 'neck riddles' (plus other gruesome business).

⌐ 23 ⌐

A fire broke out in a prison

Every week I write a language column for *The Sydney Morning Herald*. Topics can range from the shallow end (the rise of -ish, menu dialect) to the deeper stuff (sexist idiom, Orwell's legacy).

Readers are quick to respond, turning 'Wordplay' into an extended conversation. When the inbox is inundated, one column will beget the next. Though occasionally an email will throw me for a loop, posing a language query too difficult to answer solo. The question might relate to jargon, or Arabic, or deep grammar. If bewilderment demands, I will consult the wisdom of crowds, throwing the stumper onto Twitter, or putting out a plea during a regular radio spot. Another option is the Wiki reference desk, an online powwow of experts who latch onto language questions as keenly as piranha onto a paddler.

Back in 2012, I wanted to identify those inside-out phrases you hear in political speeches, where words from one half transpose to complete the other half. The classic example hails from JFK: 'Ask not what your country can do for you; ask what you can do for your country.'

No sooner had I pressed send on the Wiki site than a skulking maven called Markov replied with 'chiasmus', springing from the Greek *khiasmos*, meaning crisscross. Better yet, the query lasted several days, the posts spawning more examples, plus the kindred term of 'antimetabole', which sounds more like a laxative. Jokes aside, the service is brilliant, and brilliant is the service.

Language is just one of the Wiki desks. Pilgrims can also file their questions under maths or entertainment, computers or humanities. And if none of those scratch your itch, there's always miscellaneous, where our latest riddle landed in 2010:

A fire broke out in a prison. Most of the prisoners made it out safely, but they were severely injured, both physically and emotionally.

The king therefore decided to reduce the remaining time for each
of the surviving prisoners by half. Here's the problem: What about
the convict who was serving a life sentence?

The asker had the sexy handle of 75.33.217.61. A contributor called
mazca objected to riddles being lodged at the reference desk. The
sentiment was endorsed by WikiDao, who thawed somewhat by asking,
'Can you remember what book you saw it in?'

75.33.217.61 couldn't recall. The impasse attracted a regular named
Baseball Bugs, who reckoned the king should free the lifer a year before
he dies. In quick response, WikiDao underlined the idea's illogic, since
nobody can pinpoint the date of their death unless they're suicidal or
have a definite gallows booking.

Googlemeister was the next to weigh in. He suggested the king could
remove the prisoner's legs, sparing the half-man his full sentence. In
response, Buddy431 floated the idea of a partial pardon. The prisoner
could perhaps gamble on his longevity, nominating his final birthday
somewhere in the future, enabling the king to split the difference. Let's
say the inmate guesses he'll breathe his last at 75. Working backwards,
you could then bisect the interim, the prisoner taking his chances when
the king unlocks his cell, knowing he'll be topped should he outlive
his allocated date.

Despite the query being derided at the outset, the riddle certainly
sparked a merry forum. Nobody, not even an aloof expert, could resist
a riddle's appeal—assuming the query was a riddle at all.

The scenario runs closer to a Solomon conundrum, a teaser for
the logician rather than an evasive question with a predetermined
answer. Puzzle archives overflow with this subset, partial stories
needing the reader's deduction to complete them. A rope bridge, say,
has a maximum loading, yet Jungle Jim wishes to cross with surplus
cargo. Or a zookeeper can only count feet to calculate his population
of antelopes and ostriches. Maybe, just maybe, this prison puzzle had
no answer, since 75.33.217.61 couldn't cite the source, and two days
of sword-fighting at the Wiki desk had failed to settle on a strategy.

That's when APL joined the fray. Tongue in cheek, he spoke as
'King of the Internet', ordering WikiDao to be imprisoned for life for

A drum—referring to its bullock hide [Malagasy]

his churlish opinions. Somehow the ribbing loosened a thought. Barely a minute had elapsed before APL returned to his keyboard. 'Strike that—I'm using my royal prerogative to cut his sentence exactly in half. From this day hence User:WikiDao will spend every other day in prison, and every alternate day free.'

'Whoo!' typed another user a few hours later. 'That's the answer, APL! I feel excited!'

Yes, riddles can do that. That breakthrough moment is exciting, for playground kids and chatroom consultants alike. I'm not sure whether 75.33.217.61 shared the surge, but the wisdom of many had prevailed. Prisoner X was free to go, on the odd days anyway. What's more, he got to keep his legs.

⌐ 24 ⌐

Who is the great one that glides o'er the earth, and swallows both waters and woods?

Before *The Hobbit* there was *Hervarar Saga Ok Heiðreks*. To be clear, this Norse epic is not the prequel to the work of J.R.R. Tolkien, though the similarities are undeniable. Where else might you find blazing swords and wily dwarves? Several Middle Earth names echo the *Hervarar* saga, too, from Dwalin and Durin (the dwarves in question) to the all-purpose *mithril*, the rare ore used for Dwarvish corselets and Elvish rings. The metal was forged by the first epic, you could say, then reshaped by the second.

Should sceptics continue to doubt the parallels, then read the saga's small print. Soon you'll see that a certain Christopher Tolkien—the ringmaster's youngest son—translated the Norse classic in 1960.

Riddle-play is another overlap. In both yarns, *The Hobbit* and *Hervarar*, a scene revolves around a set of elusive questions. Tolkien's Bilbo must use riddles to mollify Gollum, a ploy to deflect the river-dweller's attention, preventing him from noticing that his precious

What's the ideal game for emos?

ring is missing. With Anon—the mystery Norse scribes—the riddles embody life or death, plus a god feigning to be human. Out of respect for elders, let's focus on the first *mithril*-moulder.

The epic arose during the 1200s, yet many of the stories bear the hallmarks of earlier folklore: proof that there's nothing new under the midnight sun. Boiled down into English, the title reads *The Saga of Hervör and Heidrek*. For her Facebook profile, Hervör might write: *Warrior queen, likes to cross-dress. Trying the quiet(er) life after so many battles, raising two gorgeous princes.*

One of those boys is Heidrek, whose profile would eventually go this way: *King of Sweden and parts beyond. Riddlemaster.* So masterful, in fact, that he dared any wrongdoer to gamble their neck via riddles. Though rather than the king doing all the asking, Heidrek dared any felon to conjure a brain-curler on the spot. Should the king duff an answer, then the convict was spared, all crimes absolved. Naturally the reverse applied too. Should Heidrek crack every puzzle you could muster, then you'd have no choice but to face the music, where the tune was a two-beat melody of *sweesh* (the sword) and *thunk* (your head).

One such sucker was Gestumblindi, a thane of dull wit and a Goth by birth. As part of a vanquished race, Gestumblindi was obliged to pay a monthly tribute to his conquerors. As you know, bills can be tough to juggle at the best of times. During one lean stretch, Gestumblindi fell behind a few kroner. His ruler wasn't impressed. Heidrek threatened the thane with prison, or the riskier option of running the riddle gauntlet.

On the eve of sentencing, Gestumblindi was beside himself. Desperate for a loophole, he slew a beast in the name of Odin, pleading with Valhalla's boss for insight. Odin went one better. Later that night a stranger called by Gestumblindi's house, if stranger's the right word. How else would you describe it—opening the door to meet a mirror image of yourself standing on the stoop? For the second time that night, Gestumblindi was beside himself, this time with a tinge more optimism.

The doppelganger was Odin in disguise. The deity rubbed his mortal hands at the prospect of a riddle showdown, sneakily bound in human form. Gestumblindi was quick to raid his wardrobe, dressing the god to complete the charade. Come the morning, Odin stood in Heidrek's court, seeming for all money the errant debtor.

Forlorn tennis

Dungeon or wordplay—what was the choice? The faux Gestumblindi opted to quiz his king. As a purist, Odin adhered to the *fornyrthislag* format, or old verse, the kind found in the Poetic Edda, a Norse anthology emerging during the same era as the saga. In lay terms, old verse observed a pause (or *caesura*) amid each line, the halves often unified by alliteration. Such subtleties can stray in translation. Nonetheless, to get the nub of Odin's delivery, here's his first teaser, the poem alluding to a very human vice:

> *That would I have which I had yesterday;*
> *heed what I had:*
> *Mind-whacker word-thwarter,*
> *and speeder of speech.*
> *Aright read now this riddle, Heidrek!*

The king was astute. He recognised ale as the relevant mind-whacker. The riddle was solved, and the *mithril* sword awaited. But the bogus Goth wasn't done. He posed more verses, about bridges and dew, about anchors and goldsmiths, each description laced with deception.

The Norse word is *kenning*, a poetic mode that distils its subject into a lyrical epithet. In Viking tales, say, a longboat might be labelled a sea-steed, while the warrior's sword is a wound-hoe. The *kenning* combines essence with evasion, a terse metaphor that only becomes familiar with usage, often in riddle bouts like the one we're witnessing.

No matter what verses Odin could finagle, the king found the poise to crack them. Riddlemaster was seeming a reasonable boast, even when Odin took a turn for the obscure:

> *Who is the great one that glides o'er the earth,*
> *and swallows both waters and woods?*
> *The wind he fears, but wights nowise,*
> *and seeks to harm the sun.*
> *Aright guess now this riddle, Heidrek!*

To lend you a fighting chance, wight is an archaic word for man. The noun derives from Old Norse, in fact, where *vettr* was the word for any living thing. As for nowise, that means 'no way', the verse implying

Why do lions eat raw meat?

that this mysterious Great One doesn't give a tinker's cuss for humans or the sun. Guess now this riddle, reader!

Heidrek managed. Did you? The answer is the all-swallowing fog that shrouds the sun and foils mortal plans, with only the wind its enemy.

The king said as much, causing the fake thane to dig deep into his repertoire again. By this point, readers must wonder whether Heidrek's internal haze was lifting. As able as he was, solving every riddle thrown his way, the king failed to see how borrowed clothes were screening the Great One himself. Or maybe that would be asking too much. Still, the saga did stress how Gestumblindi wasn't the brightest Goth in the borough. Surely the detail counts. A wiser ruler may have smelt a rat. Not Heidrek. His confidence only waxed as vanity blinded his judgement. For all his talk of fog and cloud, he couldn't pierce the deeper riddle that stood before his eyes.

That chance came in the final riddle, the cut-throat *fornyrthislag* that wrapped up a run of 36 straight. If the king wavered, Gestumblindi walked free. If the king swooped, so would his sword, removing the prisoner's imitation head. The riddle's importance was reflected in its focus:

> *Guess one more riddle, since wiser thou seemest than any other wight.*
> *What said Odin in Balder's ear before he was borne to the fire?*

To update Valhalla for you, Balder was Odin's second son, the god of light. According to the Edda, he was killed by a wayward spear, the kind to snuff out a deity and aggrieve a loving father. It was Odin's sorry chore to carry his son to the pyre. En route, he whispered something in Balder's ear, words the Edda refused to reveal, a private matter between kin. In short, nobody would know what Odin said . . . except Odin.

Suddenly the fog lifted, though Heidrek was the one who was truly blown away. He sat there mind-whacked, staggered to realise that the Great One was locked inside a convict's flesh, reeling off riddles like a regular jester. The king had barely found his tongue, stammering his suspicions, before the Goth magicked himself into a hawk and flew for a window. Or wind's eye, to use the *kenning*. One, two, three wingbeats and the bird-cum-god vanished into the ether, reminding Heidrek—the so-called riddlemaster—of his true place in the pecking order.

Because they can't cook

◖25◗

Why is a turnpike like a dead dog's tail?

Parasols were all the rage in New York City a century ago. In case the costumes in *Porgy and Bess* don't convince you, try page 38 of *Fun, Magic and Mystery*, a pulp volume published in that metropolis by Wehman Brothers in 1905. There you'll learn that a parasol carried aloft in the left hand implies a desire for acquaintance. If carried in the right? A signal to the male that he is too willing.

I'm shocked. Who knew this secret code? Did Knickerbockers get around Central Park with brolly and semaphore tables? Imagine the outrage if you were reading the wrong playbook. According to *Fun, Magic and Mystery*, a parasol furled in the left hand means, 'Meet me on the next cross-street.' Though I pity the wretch who takes that gesture as gospel, pressing his suit on the corner of 49th and Lexington, only to offend a damsel with a potential weapon in her hand —whichever hand.

Every mannerism is annotated under Parasol Flirtation, from tapping to twirling to swinging the prop in Chaplin style. The index is part of a suite of social cues. For the cover price of 10 cents, you could also learn how to flirt using cigars, pencils, whips and postage stamps. (Top left corner of the envelope = I hate you. Level with surname = Accept my love.) For the same dime you'll also have access to comical epitaphs, fortune-telling exercises and invisible-ink recipes.

Riddles await the reader, too, three full pages, sandwiched between card tricks and Ikey Isaacson jokes. One stands out for being in tune with the flirtation segment:

> *When is a bonnet not a bonnet?*
> *When it becomes a woman*

A good line to remember, gents, next time you're courting a Mennonite. Yet the same riddle betrays the collection's generic flavour. Nothing so loud and savvy as New York City suffuses the wordplay. Check out the

Two dead ones carrying a living one.

Big apple chunks

What should a clergyman preach about?
About half an hour

If a bear went into a dry-goods store, what would he want?
Muzzlin'

What was the first scene at the Chicago fire?
Kerosene

Why is there no such thing as a whole day?
Because every day begins by breaking

Why is a person reading these conundrums like a man condemned to
    undergo a military execution?
Because he is pretty sure to be riddled to death

riddles I've sampled above and you'll find a mix of puns and nudges that could belong in most meridians. For my money, only one captures the bedlam of NYC with the same sardonic wit as magazine cartoonists manage a century down the road. Who can't hear the gridlock blare of the Holland Tunnel on-ramp in this lost testament?

Why is a turnpike like a dead dog's tail?
Because it stops a-waggin'

The same wisecrack is tangible proof the Big Apple's problems haven't changed so much in 110 years.

Shoes [Spain]

◻ 26 ◻

Τι πιάσαμε, μας πέταξε μακριά.
Και τι δεν είχε πιάσει, κρατήσαμε.

What we caught, we threw away.
And what we didn't catch, we kept.

For all we know, Homer the poet may be as real as Homer the Duff Beer drinker, the animated confabulation of several storytellers. We know so little of the man—the Greek, I mean—even down to his Greekness. His dates are vague, his town of origin a blank. Was he blind? Was he female? Some three millennia later, all we have are theories and counter-theories, plus two masterpieces: *The Odyssey* and *The Iliad*.

Homer, the name, is a potential clue. The likely source is *hómēros*, meaning hostage. Think less in prisoner terms and more the notion of being bound to another. If Homer was blind, as goes the legend, then his days on earth, around 800BC, were likely at the mercy of a seeing companion.

Spot the irony? As his own enigma, Homer leaves us groping. When it comes to solid facts, we too are hostages, indebted to scholars whose guesses at least are educated. There's a reasonable chance that Homer is shorthand for a storytelling continuum, some meme aligned to the oral tradition that bears his byline. Nobody can rule that out. Though we can find solace in the epics he/she/they left behind.

The battles and the sieges, the Sirens and the Cyclops, the sea dragon and the Trojan horse. Jerry Bruckheimer is a sophomore compared with Homer, a poet who knew how to maximise any given action sequence. With image, with brio, with rhythm too, each story neatly bundled into dactylic hexameters.

Pterodactyl what? The method is the sexy six-beat of the ancient blockbuster. Recite a page of Homer's Greek, or a worthy translation, and you'll hear the sorcery charge the air. The formula places spondees (two long syllables) beside a dactyl (one long syllable, followed by two short), before closing on a trochee (a long and a short syllable in combo).

Who falls down the chimney every year?

Rather than explain it, let's hear it: 'He bound his sandals onto his comely feet, girded his sword about his shoulder, and left his room looking like an immortal god.' This snippet is lifted from Book II of *The Odyssey*, translated by Samuel Butler. The 'god' in sandals is Telemachus, Odysseus's son. Recite the words again and you'll eavesdrop on the pit-a-pat, as if the looping of leather enjoys its own *oom-pah* soundtrack.

Story and metre—Homer was a maestro. But that didn't mean he could govern his own narrative. According to folklore, the poet succumbed to riddle-talk while away from his manuscripts. Twice, in fact, the second time fatally.

The first lapse involved the Oracle of Delphi. The temple clung to the crest of Mount Parnassus, near Athens, a professed conduit between heaven and earth. Pythia was the blind seer in charge, a woman who knew better than to speak in plain Greek. So it was that when Homer wished to glimpse his future, the prophecy was perverse: 'The Isle of Ios is your mother's country and it shall receive you dead. But beware the riddles of young children.'

Not the message you'd expect in your average fortune cookie. And if that's what you copped, you'd boycott the restaurant. But the Old Greeks were made of sterner stuff. As a race they warmed to the gloom-and-doom register. Just like Homer, the ultimate Greek, who seemed to make a special effort to fulfil the prediction. Call me paranoid, but if some mystic chick foretold my death on an island called Ios, then I'd leave Ios off my itinerary. Maybe Homer had the same thought. Who knows? Perhaps he skirted the Aegean until curiosity won out. Or his guide was distracted and misread the ferry timetable. Whatever the route, we next find the poet digging his toes into the warm sand of Ios, a jigsaw fragment within the Cyclades group.

The cove was quiet. A fleet of boats skidded onto shore. Fishermen leapt down, their sacks heavy from the overnight haul. Not that Homer could see all this, but he heard the carry-on, the hubbub of labour, the grunt of boats being dragged. The voices approached, spurring Homer to ask, 'Catch anything?'

A few young boys were part of the crew. The cheekiest said:

What we caught, we threw away. And what we didn't catch, we kept.

Santa Klutz

Homer baulked. Here was the riddle foretold by Pythia, yet it made no sense. Stingray? Medusa? Nothing stood to reason. The celebrated brain responsible for the era's greatest yarns was lost in a whirlpool. His body slumped. He felt the sand's creeping chill through his bones.

And that's where the story leaves him: in reverie, in torment, huddled by an invisible sea, gnawing an *aenigma*.

The aftermath is guesswork. Maybe the boys loitered to relish the damage they'd done. (Boys can be like that.) In a perfect world they'd offer hints. Though why alleviate the old bugger's pain? This was sport. Naturally they knew the answer was lice, the parasites living in their thick Cycladean locks, yet they didn't share their catch's catch, for that would ease the agony. Instead they gathered their nets and reeled in their lines. They joined their fathers to lug up the boats and left the stranger to stew alone.

And die alone, the first man killed by a riddle, though not the last. The poet's body keeled to starboard. The weight of frustration, together with the knowledge of the oracle, his ebbing health, a sense of completion on a lost mother's island, was all too much for Homer, who succumbed to the sand.

As soon as the people of Ios figured out the corpse's celebrity, they made a fuss. They toasted the poet with wine and song. Trumpets blew and goats were slain. Elegies and sacrifices were made. Every villager turned out for the occasion, including those sea-brats, who must have thought twice thereafter about asking loaded questions.

According to *Certamen*, the Greek narrative to imagine the event, they buried Homer on a headland near the beach. Its view was the open stage of his stories. While the epitaph was plain, for all its hexameters:

Εδώ γη καλύπτει το ιερό κεφάλι
Από θεϊκός Όμηρος, τραγουδιστής των ηρώων.

Here earth covers the holy head
Of godlike Homer, singer of heroes.

What tune is loved by all?

⌐⌐ 27 ⌐⌐

Was ist ein Kannibale, der seinen Vater und seine Mutter gegessen hat?

What is a cannibal who has eaten his father and mother?

There's a riddle bouncing round cyberspace that doesn't quite add up. Indeed, numbers are its major flaw, or perhaps I've said too much. Maybe now's the time to wheel out the question and see if you cop the sucker punch:

According to Sigmund Freud, what comes between fear and sex?

At least that's how you should *hear* the riddle. Fact is, the Freudian pun is designed to work orally, which feels so right for a Freudian pun. On paper, however, the riddle reveals itself:

According to Sigmund Freud, what comes between vier *and* sechs?

Vier is German for four, while *sechs* is six, the even numbers creating a gap for the answer to penetrate. Sorry, that sounded filthy. Freud can have that effect.

So then, did you handle the hard one? Damn, I did it again. All of a sudden, every second word seems pregnant with subtext. If it's not innuendo, it's the unvoiced id, Freud's own term for the mind's sub-basement.

By the way, the answer is *fünf*—the German five—but let's get back to the basement.

The id is where the wild things are—the sexual beast and the murderer, the voyeur and the savage. The captor in this metaphor is the superego, the screw who keeps the trapdoor locked, the moral cop and parent. Meanwhile the tenant in this whole ménage is the ego, the realist wedged between contrary forces. The ego is the sense of self we project to the world. It's the ombudsman tasked to negotiate between the legislator and the Neanderthal.

Spying on these different selves can be delicate. An evasive organism, the mind is reluctant to slide under glass, resistant to light, impossible to freeze-dry.

Thus the power of unconscious mannerisms, as much as the words we let slip. In 2014, CBS anchor Rob Morrison labelled Prince William 'the Douche of Cambridge', a bungle that could betray a republican streak. Or then again, perhaps his tongue was struggling to separate duke from duchess. Only Morrison would know, assuming he consciously does.

One way we might tell is by listening to his jokes off-camera. This was one of Freud's quirkier theories, as if subdividing the psyche wasn't radical enough. 'Psyche', in fact, is a Freudian term, a word he drew from 'butterfly' in Greek. 'Analysis'—by the same token—is Greek for 'release'. Semantically, every therapy session in Dr Freud's rooms amounted to the freeing of vivid orange monarchs into the air—or anti-monarchs as the case may be. Jokes and riddles did a similar service, he reckoned. Not just the gags you favoured, but those that made you laugh. For Freud, humour granted a peephole into another's mind.

As with the mind, Freud split humour into three precincts. First, there is *der Witz*, which translates as 'joke'. This category covers scripted quips as well as spontaneous repartee. Here our cackles signal the release of energy we would have spent in keeping our emotions in check.

Next comes *das Komische*—the comical—which sounds the same, but applies more to the sphere of intellect. Clowning is a common example, where your laugh might reflect the performer failing to fulfil an action your mind has already anticipated. You draw an invisible line from Action A to Outcome B that the clown fails to follow. The deviation tickles the psyche.

The third style is *der Humor*, more a catch-all label than anything. *Der Humor* relates to the connection we feel when laughter becomes its own pleasure. A joy, if you like, which aptly translates as *Freud* in German.

From analysis to theory, Freud explored these ideas in a very readable—and funny—treatise of 1905, *Der Witz und seine Beziehung zum Unbewußten*, or *The Joke and its Relation to the Unconscious*. To propel his argument, of course, he needed samples, and many of the jokes fall under the Jewish umbrella, familiar scenarios starring disgruntled spouses, caustic rabbis and tavern pundits. Examples of *Rätsel* (riddles) are fewer, though a certain cannibal can brag a triple billing in one part of the work. Here's the opener:

What is SpongeBob called on Greek TV?

What is a cannibal who has eaten his father and mother?

Famished? Indiscriminate? A monster? Potential punchlines dance in the mind, yet very few guinea pigs I tested with this riddle managed to match Freud's answer of 'an orphan'. Seems so logical once you think about it, a little like the road-crossing chicken, but that's the Freudian point. He called this style of punchline *Verschiebung* (displacement), the train of thought jumping from one sense to another. In the cannibal's case, the superego is liable to take the reins, looking for the moral angle. Or perhaps the id hijacks the helm, desperate for perversity. In the end, neither outcome plays out. The riddle is funny for being matter-of-fact, refusing to buy into ethics or depravity. In a way the humour relies on our overreading of cannibal, at the cost of the question's rationality.

I mentioned that the man-eater won a triple bill. Now that your moral compass has been subverted, see if you can answer the other *Rätsels*:

And if he has eaten all his other relations as well?
The sole heir

And where will that kind of monster find sympathy?
Under S in the dictionary

Same place you can find Suppression, the very word that humour can defy. Or so said Sigmund Freud, our riddles the briefest jemmying of the basement door.

⌐ 28 ¬

What goes on four feet in the morning, two feet at noon …

Chances are you know the Oedipus story already—boy meets dad, boy kills dad, boy bonks mum—so I won't bore you with the blow-by-blow. But I wonder if you know the vital details? Riddle-wise, I mean.

Put it this way, the enigma sitting at the legend's centre is so devious it spawned a new brand of irony. This same riddle is also deemed the mainspring of all others, at least in the West: the riddle that demanded to be part of my 101. Bossier than that, the Oedipus story has seized two chapters, for reasons you'll soon discover.

Oedipus Rex, the Sophocles play, was written around 429BC, though the yarn had been circulating the agora long before the script emerged. Athenians could hardly resist. Revenge, sex, power—all the ingredients were there. Add a lion with nymphet breasts and you had the perfect sizzle.

But before we meet the monster and her monstrous question, let's meet the man. Oedipus had the world at his beckoning, or so he thought. As the alpha prince of Corinth, he could boast good schooling, good looks, all the palace perks. The only sticking point was the Delphic oracle, the same institution that brought Homer unstuck.

Before newspapers were invented, Greeks paid blind priestesses for their horoscopes. Fine and dandy if the news was good, but Oedipus felt cursed the moment he heard about the mother-and-father kinkiness. According to the oracle, the youth was fated to commit patricide and incest in one financial year. Imagine that for a moment. Last time I checked my stars the worst thing for Scorpios was a wasted opportunity.

Shattered, the youth returned to Corinth. He packed his bags and fetched his horses. To hell with blind seers and malign stars—Oedipus was taking control. He went to the palace to kiss his mum, Merope, chastely, and hug Polybus, his king and father. He told them he was travelling, without being too specific, knowing he needed to put distance between himself and home. Sadly, all he managed was Thebes, some 100 miles away, with an ugly bingle in between.

It happened in Davlia. Some arrogant old fart was playing chicken with his chariot and ran Oedipus into a ditch. Enough was enough. Oedipus saw red. He flew across the junction and pummelled the geezer to a pulp. A flurry of punches that left a lump in the dust, dead as mutton. And that is how Oedipus came to kill Oedipus Senior, not that Junior realised his kinship at the time. How could he? He thought Polybus was his dad after all, rather than his foster pop who'd claimed a baby stranded on a Theban hill.

Oaken vest, a furze peruke, a nettle cravat?

(We'll deal with these unlikely origins in a moment, but first let's return to Davlia where the dust was only just settling.)

Oedipus sluiced away the blood and righted his chariot. The sky was darkening. Thebes was close, a place to lay his head. The prince resumed his escape, the rhythm of the wheels soothing his spirits. Slowly the murder dissolved from his mind. He felt back in control again, the reins in his hands, only to meet a topless lion with a woman's head guarding the city's gates.

The sphinx also boasted a pair of eagle wings, though she wasn't flying anywhere. Terrorising Thebes was her full-time gig, teasing all comers with a riddle, and eating those who bungled it. Oedipus must have seemed one more treat on the menu, another fool for dessert.

He brought his chariot to a halt, keeping out of pouncing range. He unhitched his horses and tied them to a tree atop the cliff. Which makes me wonder: did he peek beyond the brink? Sophocles doesn't say. But if he did, he would have seen the bones littering the precipice's base. Such a sight might have stolen the young man's nerve. As it was, Oedipus returned to the monster to see what she was selling.

Life, in a word. One shot. Solve the sphinx's riddle and you were free. Get it wrong and you were supper. Why not, thought Oedipus. He'd had a long day. Besides, the oracle news lent him added courage. If he blew the riddle, the sanctuary of the monster's belly awaited him, far beyond the prophecy's reach. Then again, if he managed to crack the sphinx's code, then Thebes would stand to be his refuge. So it was he accepted the challenge, and the sphinx recited:

What goes on four feet in the morning, two feet at noon, and three feet in the evening?

One magic word—the answer—and his life would be spared. The sphinx waited, licking her chops. She had all night. Thebes was going nowhere, and she ruled the gate.

Oedipus knew the stakes. As a neck riddle, doom was always a flipside. But so was salvation. He chanted the question under his breath, at least the wording we've just heard, though other versions exist. The main obstacle in this regard is Sophocles himself. For reasons not made

Hedgehog [Irish]

clear, the playwright omitted the riddle from his script. Verbatim at least. Even the sphinx dipped out on a cameo.

In other versions of the riddle, like the one recorded by Apollodorus, a later scholar, the sphinx included a bonus element: 'What is that which has one voice and yet becomes four-footed and two-footed and three-footed?'

And if that's the beta version, then the gamma hails from Athenaeus, a grammar buff whose take was more singsong:

A thing there is whose voice is one;
Whose feet are four and two and three.
So mutable a thing is none
That moves in earth or sky or sea.
When on most feet this thing doth go,
Its strength is weakest and its pace most slow.

Same, same, but different. The voice ingredient might have helped Oedipus to dredge up the answer, but I have my doubts. After the oracle, then the hiccup in Davlia, the riddle was his least fear. Win-win, he could take a free swing at the *aenigma*. All his predecessors, men whose bones adorned the base of the cliff, had likely quaked in their boots, too panicky to find the answer. Not Oedipus. Thanks to the oracle, he could tackle the puzzle with a sense of impunity—a handy way to think in any situation. Shrug off the fear of failure and your mind is freed. Conquer anxiety and your imagination scampers loose. He drew a breath and blurted: 'Man.'

The sphinx did a double-take.

Oedipus went on to explain his answer, how babies moved on hands and knees, graduating into walking, etc., but the monster wasn't listening. The riddle was dead in the water. Man—the animal, and the answer—had won out. The scourge of Thebes said nothing, for the consequence was obvious. She lumbered to her paws and dragged her sorry leonine arse to the brink. Midair, she refused to flap.

The rest is destiny. Oedipus entered Thebes. Locals broke out in celebration. Praise and blossoms rained from every window. Children gathered on street corners to touch their hero. Yet the riddle was far

What did 0 say to 8?

from done. True, the sphinx was dead, but the deeper meanings behind her enigma would be slow to retract their claws. What paraded as the answer would serve to be a deeper riddle. To go there, we need another leg.

◰ 29 ◳

...and three feet in the evening?

Reaching the heart of Thebes, Oedipus was met by Jocasta, the city's queen, no less. She stood tall, holding out her arms, eager to embrace her saviour.

In quick time, love bloomed. The pair shared a natural rapport. Wedding bells were soon chiming, despite the widow-queen still lamenting her precious Laius, slain by person or persons unknown. Not that Oedipus realised himself to be culpable, the king having travelled incognito. In the same vein he knew that Jocasta was hot, but not that she was his mum.

Nor does the irony end there—the real sweet spot is the sphinx's riddle. For best effects, keep your eyes on knowledge as a central theme of the Oedipus tale. Not just the force of the Sophocles drama, knowledge is integral to riddling in general. Every riddle contest is an intellectual power play, where knowledge and ignorance go toe-to-toe. A solver needs inborn wit to nullify a question's trick, to parry the blow, and return the assault. Then there's a related branch of knowledge, what the Greeks call *anagnorisis*, the brain flash that burns off falsehoods, allowing you to realise how matters truly stand.

Oedipus had the first knowledge in spades, but sorely lacked the second. His fatal eureka would come in Act 3, of course. But right now Thebans presumed their new king to be wise, largely due to a single riddle which he'd solved with a blind swing. Regardless, praise for his smarts was sung at the altar on the day Jocasta wed her equally oblivious son.

Nice belt

For that's the tragedy within the tragedy, neither newlywed linking their happiness to a glum baby abandoned on a Theban hill. Just like the sphinx's riddle, the essence lay in the legs. Oedipus the name stems from *Oidípous*, or swollen foot, the handicap owed to an injury inflicted by Laius, who bound his son's ankles at birth. His motive was yet another blighted prophecy, predicting his boy would grow into a murderer. The minute Laius heard about these future atrocities, he tethered his newborn and left him for the ravens on a hill beyond the city. Shepherds came instead, finding him a royal home in Corinth.

Fast forward 30 years, and there we see Oedipus, king of Thebes. He stands proudly beside his Jocasta, the burble of their newborn munchkins surrounding them. Yet all is not well in the liberated city. Since the Laius murder, a pestilence has gripped the place. Foiling the sphinx proved a false dawn, as crops failed, cattle buckled and people died in the streets. Quarantine wasn't the cure. That's far too sensible for ancient Greece. Apparently the answer was cracking the Laius case. Unmask the killer and the plague would lift—but where to start looking?

Try Thebes, suggested the resident blindman, an ancient seer named Teiresias. Tapping his cane for dramatic effect, he said, 'The wretch who murdered Laius—that man is here.'

Still ignorant of his own role in the crime, Oedipus pushed the seer further on the matter. Sophocles' dialogue speaks to the heart of riddling:

TEIRESIAS: This day shall be thy birthday and thy grave.
OEDIPUS: Thou lov'st to speak in riddles and dark words.
TEIRESIAS: In reading riddles who so skilled as thou?
OEDIPUS: Twit me with that wherein my greatness lies.
TEIRESIAS: And yet this very greatness proved thy bane.

'Twit' in this context means to tease, and not the idiot we know today, though the two are related. The root lies in *ætwítan*, Old English meaning 'to accuse against'. Despite his blindness, Teiresias could see what no other Theban could. He knew the city's saviour was its scourge. Not that he said so. Instead he spoke in riddles to protect his own neck.

Why is B like fire?

Horror upon horror, the truth emerged in the final act, the blood-shed turning extravagant. The wailing. The mutilation. Jocasta found a curtain rod, the sturdier the better, and threw her weight into the void. On finding his mother hanging, Oedipus took a brooch from her body and used its pin to erase his sight, now that he could finally see. Meanwhile the plague vanished overnight.

Which leaves the riddle of the riddle itself and its symbolic role in the drama. Claude Lévi-Strauss, a man you'd expect to know all about legs, proposed a kinky theory about the enigma. The French philosopher viewed the sphinx's sequence differently. Four feet in the morning, according to most commentators, denotes a crawling child. Just as two feet at noon implies the mature biped, while the finale equates to the elder with a walking stick. Easy once you crack the metaphor, but Claude had a new angle. In his eyes the four feet translated as the sexual act, not a baby per se, which may well be the result. Slang dictionaries call it a knee-trembler, where the shagging is done between upright partners, four feet planted on terra firma.

Risqué, sure, but is the conjecture so important? Philosophically, yes. For if we can fathom the riddle, we can also imagine how the story came to be conceived. Sigmund Freud naturally swooped on the yarn, coining the Oedipus complex as the suppressed desire of a man to bed his mother. Going one step further, this same idea extends to bumping off the rival suitor, namely the father, which Oedipus achieved while heading for his mother's bedroom.

Observe the putz: Oedipus, the antihero, maimed by his father, vainly fleeing his own destiny, and all the while drawing closer to the fate he dreaded. En route he kills the man he longs to spare. He meets a female monster, naked and ferocious, asking a riddle whose answer is Man. Not Human, or Woman—but Man. Oedipus nails it and the she-devil is destroyed, opening the way to the boy's first lover, just as the blind priestess had predicted.

Some theorists suspect a sexist complicity, where three fey women conspire to trap the male, but that feels a leap too far. I'm keener on the legend's greatest irony, where Man was as good as Oedipus saying Me.

Think about it. The riddle was his bio in miniature, not his triumph. All the basics were there. Left to die on a hillside, the wretch had

Because it makes oil boil.

squirmed on all fours into the arms of shepherds, who found him a home in Corinth, a prelude of the royalty he'd inherit. Next, to cheat his fate, he approached the sphinx on his own two feet. And lastly, come the story's twilight, he walked the Theban court with his father's sceptre as his third lower limb.

If only he'd twigged at the time. If only he'd recognised himself to be the solution below the surface, he might have defied the monster by walking the other way. He might have tried cliff-jumping to thwart the oracle. But no, he tackled the neck riddle to save his life, he thought. Or end it sooner. To kill the sphinx, Oedipus said Man, never realising which man in particular. Hey presto, the gates opened. He entered the town a hero, embracing the destiny that would seal his ruin. To quote the ever-present chorus: 'Behold this Oedipus—him who knew the famous riddles and was a man most masterful . . . See him now and see the breakers of misfortune swallow him.'

Most riddles demand solving. While others, like the mother of them all, are possibly wiser left to lie.

◻ 30 ◻

Why did the girl kill her sister?

You need the backstory before you take a stab. A sad backstory, which obviously doesn't get cheerier, but I'm just reporting the facts.

We begin with a funeral. The girl who's about to kill her sister is attending the burial of her mother. (Fresh from the Oedipus outrage, you probably took that last sentence in your stride.) At the funeral, this same murderer-to-be meets a handsome guy she doesn't know. Straight away she's smitten by his charms and strength, his broad shoulders and calming voice. Yes, he's the one, she believes. This realisation prompts the girl to kill her sister a few days later. The big question being: Why?

Please, indulge me. I'm struggling with this one. Why did she do it? Your answer here: _____

Where does bad light fall?

Have you decided? Is it safe to move on? That depends on your response, for despite being known as the Psychopath Riddle, this is really a question that invites speculation rather than a correct solution. Your guess is as good as mine, unless your guess betrays you to be a murderous loon.

Law-abiding citizens are liable to say, 'I don't know.' A deflection, really, and not something a 'famous American psychologist' would accept. The inverted commas should sound a warning bell. Whenever 'famous' people are anonymous, you know there's fishy business. This same psychologist presented the funeral story to 'many arrested serial killers' to measure their responses. Apparently every felon guessed the same motive.

Namely, the girl killed her sister as she hoped the guy would attend this follow-up funeral as well. Nuts, I know, but that's why this meme gained momentum across social media in the early 2000s. The source and date are hard to pinpoint. The appeal is obvious, however—imagine a simple pop quiz to expose your own evil kink. But the test is phony.

Barbara Mikkelson, together with her husband Michael, blew the lid on the story in 2007. The pair are best known as Snopes.com, the online debunkers of urban legends, much as Adam and Jamie bust myths on television.

'As a quick 'n' easy way to separate the sheep from the murderous goats, it wouldn't work,' wrote Barbara. The verdict was swift. The clinical question had never been trialled—and wouldn't work anyhow.

Hard evidence was assembled by Kevin Dutton, a research fellow at the Department of Experimental Psychology at Oxford. In his 2013 book, *The Wisdom of Psychopaths*, Dr Dutton describes how he tried the story on genuine psychopaths and not one offered the 'second funeral' motive. As for why, one subject put his finger on the problem, saying, 'I might be nuts, but I'm not stupid.'

To run a secondary test, put up your hand if you pictured a bunch of deranged killers when reading the words 'genuine psychopaths'. That's the same flaw lying at the riddle's root. Hannibal Lecter may well be the poster boy for antisocial gourmets, but a psychopath is actually anyone in your circle who's ruthless, egocentric and devoid of empathy. One hypothetical is hardly going to diagnose the condition. As a foolproof measure, the funeral yarn is pretty idiotic.

Besides, who's to say that other responses were any less calculating? I could imagine the girl killed her sister in order to score a larger slice of the inheritance. Or is that just me? I maintain that the handsome soulmate was a total red herring.

Asking around, seeing if I have any emotional vacuums as friends, I heard a few people presume Mr Right was the sister's new boyfriend, making the killing an act of jealousy. Though why she didn't ask for the goss, or check the condolences book for a phone number, I'm at a loss to tell you.

There's good news, however. Well, for me. I can't speak for you. While digging up this urban legend I visited Dr Dutton's own website (www.kevindutton.co.uk). There, to reach the homepage, you need to run a gauntlet of character statements, a far shrewder measure of your personality. For example, where do you stand in light of these claims:

> Rules are meant to be broken.
> Driving fast cars, riding a rollercoaster and skydiving really appeal to me.
> If something better comes along it's okay to cancel a longstanding appointment.

In each case, do you: disagree strongly, disagree, agree or agree strongly? I jumped through the hoops to discover that I was unlikely to be a remorseless bastard, managing a modest 16 out of 33. Lucid proof, in case my wife's reading this, that I have the capacity for empathy. Then again, it's more your score I'm worried about.

Where do reindeers live in Paris?

Anti-riddles

They act like riddles and sound like riddles, but are they riddles?

(And if you're expecting a tidy answer, then maybe this is the last place to look.)

◄⅃ 31 ⌐►

What's red and bad for your teeth?

Most people guess it's cordial. Other stabs include raspberry sorbet or tomato sauce—but you think beyond the kitchen. Though I wouldn't think too long, as the answer is absurd.

Antisocial, even. It's certainly anti-riddle, holding the genre in disdain, which is their signature. By and large, even if riddles are racist or ribald, they stick to niceties. I pose the crafty question and you rummage in your imagination for the answer. Keeping to the etiquette, the answer will be recognisable by its wit, or sense: an arc to span the spark gap the question leaves open.

Anti-riddles spit on that protocol. The punks of pundom, they disregard wordplay and the entire boom-tish pact that Oedipus and his like had fought hard to establish. Ample reason, you'd imagine, to avoid these scofflaws, but I hold the opposite view. Rivals can tell you much about the forms they oppose. Study the sceptics to grasp the idealists. Define the technophile and you'll flesh out the Luddite.

Even the fact that you're about to meet a platoon of anti-riddles says something about the subgenre. Clearly there are several ways to misbehave. Some are puerile. Some are questions parading as riddles. And damn, some are funny too.

Like our first example, the red dental hazard. Care to have a guess? Enough think-time already. The answer is a brick.

Crunch! You've just been hit by the self-evident. Not for the first time, either. Cast your mind back to 1847, when a certain chicken traversed a particular road, and you'll realise anti-riddles are stayers. Raiding my own riddle memory, I realise how one of my first and favourite riddles as a kid was actually an anti-riddle in drag. Perhaps that's why I liked the big red rock-eater, as it seemed such a lawbreaker, serving to 'satisfy' the question:

Which travels faster: heat or cold?

What's big, red and eats rocks?

A typical anti-riddle, delighting in the bleeding obvious—or the bloody injurious, in the case of a brick. Here's another example:

Why did the old woman put roller skates on her walking frame?
She had dementia

See, you thought it was going to be punny, or imaginative, rather than biographical and sad. Your mind was off-leash, playing in a generous space of free associations, rather than treating the information as a police report.

What sport does a vampire avoid?

Give yourself a pat if you guessed *lacrosse* or *garlic football*. Both do the business in an orthodox way, honouring the riddle manifesto. Compare that quip to this brute:

What dessert do vampires love?

Blood oranges, maybe. Blackforest cake? Neither. Try this for size: *Vampires aren't real.* Unfair, you yell, and with good reason. The anti-riddle eases you into a game-playing mode, only to breach the agreement with servings of sobriety. Worse than that, they resemble an adult who's midway through a role-play with a child, pretending they're exploring the galaxy together, only to call a halt and tell the little astronaut her space gun is just a stupid feather duster.

Sometimes the anti-riddle is a stand-alone groaner:

What did the farmer say when he lost his tractor?
Where's my tractor?

Or the genre prints a licence to be perverse:

What would Winston Churchill do if he was alive today?
Scream and scratch on his coffin lid

Scorning the undead one minute, then reversing a famous death the next: anti-riddles are rebellious to the marrow.

Heat—you can catch cold

Antitheses

How do you confuse a blonde?
Paint yourself green and throw forks at her

What starts with E, ends with G and contains everything?
Everything

What did one lawyer say to the other lawyer?
'How was your weekend?'

What's worse than finding a worm in your apple?
The Holocaust

⌐ 32 ⌐

Why can't you tell secrets to a cornfield?

Go on, yell it out. You know the answer. 'Because it has too many ears!'

Feeling better now? I'm sure you've heard the pun a dozen times. But there's a reason I chose this particular chestnut to tell the story of a famous piece of birch.

We begin with Frank Epperson, an accidental inventor, aged eleven. One bleak winter night—as bleak as California can get anyway—Frank left his soft drink on the porch, a wooden stirrer sitting in the cup. Come morning, the liquid had turned to ice, or what Frank went on to call an Epsicle.

Almost two decades on, in 1923, Frank took his icy treats to Neptune Beach's funfair, where a craze ignited. The Epsicle had arrived, even if the eponym didn't last long. A few months into the boom, Frank dumped the name for the more popular Popsicle—an American icon on ice. Indeed, during World War II, the Popsicle image was chosen by the 8th Air Force Unit as the quintessential symbol of Americana. Not too shabby for a cup of soda left out in the weather.

What's the best way to burn 1000 calories?

Serendipity may have sparked an empire, but several tweaks have since ensured the Popsicle's appeal. If it's not the spectrum of flavours, from bubblegum through to watermelon, then it's the riddle imprinted on each birch stick. That is, the riddle on the exposed end, while the answer is buried in the ice. If you can't lick the question, then you need to lick the Popsicle.

Collectors are mad for them. Cyberspace is littered with stained examples, each one exposing a corny line. For a taste:

Who do all inches follow?
Their ruler

Risky, right? To load a painful pun into a product that already threatens brain freeze. Yet the same little stick can act as America's yardstick, better than any imperial ruler. In a quick time-scurry you can see how language and culture evolve. You hardly need dates to sense that this list is chronological:

What was a trick that the loaf of bread taught the dog?
Heel!

Why was the baby comforter so sad?
It was a little down

What did the golfer name his son?
Chip

What kind of music sticks with you?
Taped music

Why couldn't the elephant use the computer?
He was afraid of the mouse

Five riddles on five sticks, like relay batons across the generations. Though you'll never guess the sidetrack that two consumers took, inspired by the Popsicle tradition. Even if you knew the cornfield answer. Or thought you knew . . .

Jason Kreher and Matt Moore are the renegades involved. The pair work for an ad agency called Wieden+Kennedy in Portland, Oregon. During their spare time, when not finessing campaigns for clients, they turned their minds to schadenfreude—the joy derived from the anguish of others. With a few deft strokes, the German term was converted into the satirical trademark.

Imagine a childhood treat combined with a dose of bleak adulthood. 'I don't think either of us is cynical,' said Kreher, or Moore, responding to a Q&A in April 2014. 'But it's fun to take something innocent and make it profane. There's nothing wrong with pondering life's greatest tragedies while enjoying a nice snack.'

A mental snack, at least, since SchadenFreezers aren't available on the shelf at this stage. Instead, users of Tumblr can see these grim ice blocks played out as GIFs on http://schadenfreezers.tumblr.com, quick animations that melt before your eyes. Puns don't play a part in this array. There's no scared elephant or pigs talking swine language—just the heartache of living inscribed on birch. Click on any GIF to see the bright block (with its innocent riddle jutting out) become a lurid puddle, so exposing the stick's emo answer. Here are Exhibits A to D:

Why did the river cry?
Because her parents were getting a divorce

What did grandma say to the frog?
Something racist probably

What did the soldier forget?
Nothing. Not one thing.

Why did the circus close?
A long chilling list of animal rights violations

While the bluebird is always sad in Popsicle-Land, the sad labourer gets a meaner treatment in SchadenFreezia:

What makes a janitor happy?
It doesn't matter

Meanwhile, the riddle that you'd expect in either domain gets a very different answer at the hands of Kreher and Moore:

Why can't you tell secrets to a cornfield?
Because the corn will tell everyone your awful secret

My house has one beam and two doors.

⊐ 33 ⊑

Knock, knock!

Despite all the comings and goings in *Macbeth*, the Porter only has a cameo. He's nameless for starters, along with a Sergeant, a Scotch Doctor, an Old Man and three Witches. What's more, the Porter only crops up once, tending the gate in Shakespeare's tragedy, and even then he's on the grog.

His role is twofold—opening the gate, and lightening the mood. Shakespeare was canny that way. There's only so much gore an audience can digest without a spot of levity. The murder of Duncan, King of Scotland, is the scene before the Porter's moment in the drama, oblivious, tipsy, wondering who the hell is banging on his postern: 'Knock, knock, knock! Who's there? Faith, here's an English tailor come hither for stealing out of a French hose: come in tailor here you may roast your goose.'

The knocker is no such thing. Knockers plural, for Macduff and Lennox have come to visit their thane, Macbeth. Despite the palaver, neither nobleman is an English tailor nor goose-poacher. The Porter's conjecture is the product of a pickled brain, with a riddle variation the possible hangover.

Notice I said 'possible', as there's no less conjecture about the source of knock-knock jokes, the pun-loaded format that operates as a riddle in reverse. Keeping to the Scottish Play, first staged in 1606, let's revisit how the routine works:

A: Knock, knock!
B: Who's there?
A: Thane.
B: Thane who?
A: Thane is the river in Parith.

Unforgivable, in many ways, but that brand of corn is integral to the knock-knock gag. The offered 'caller', so to speak, is at the forefront of a pun. The dialogue allows the wordplay to reveal itself in the final

The nose [Hawaiian]

No-bell prizes

Knock knock! Who's there?
Irish Stew who? (Irish stew in the name of the law)
Nana who? (Nana your business)
Xavier who? (Xavier breath and open the door!)
Euripides who? (Euripides jeans, you pay for dem)
A pile-up who? (Pewww)
Yah who? (I prefer Google)
To who? (No—it's to whom)
Suspense who? [silence]

response, the riddle's answer if you like, despite the fact that the listener has no chance to guess.

Some knock-knocks (see box) are more agonising than others, yet can we really blame the Bard for this crime against good taste? While the Porter's schtick establishes the format's template, there's no sign of the pun extension that has come to distinguish the modern version.

Joke historians, seriously, argue the likely genesis to be a game called Buff, first noted in a 1929 book, *The Games of Children: Their origin and history*. According to its author, Henry Bett, the game involved a stick for thumping the floor, a cue for the call-and-response as follows:

Knock, knock!
Who's there?
Buff.
What says Buff?
Buff says Buff to all his men, and I say Buff to you again.

If nothing else, Buff embedded the dialogue pattern in popular memory, an important ingredient of the whole formula. Just as riddles need their respondents, the knock-knock hinges on the quick interplay of caller and asker. There's no show without Punch—or Judy. Buff soon evolved on the strength of bad puns, the kids exchanging Buff for new words, recruiting their listener to play straight man.

What do you call a dyslexic geneticist?

Between the wars the joke's spread accelerated, reaching the heights of the American Pomological Society, a fancy mantle for apple-growers. In a 1933 newsletter called *Proceedings* (these people couldn't resist), comes the following speech extract: 'Now my time is up, the king of all fruits and I are saying—Knock, Knock, Who's There? Apple. Apple who? Appalachian brand, Apple Growers and American Pomological Society member; greetings.'

Whatever the causal link—the king of fruits, or the King of Scotland—the knock-knock format has made its mark across the world. The French know the routine as *toc-toc*, the Dutch as *klop-klop*, and in South Korea you play *kon-kon*. So next time you're assailed by some pun-toting four-year-old loaded with Ivana Wee-Wee and cash-who nuts, then simply say Armageddon.

Armageddon who?
Armageddon outa here.

◱ 34 ◲

I turn polar bears white
and will make you cry . . .

In full the riddle goes:

I turn polar bears white
And will make you cry.
I make guys pee
And girls comb their hair.
I make celebrities look stupid
And normal people look like celebrities.
I turn pancakes brown
And make your champagne bubble.
If you squeeze me I'll pop.

DAN

If you look at me, you'll pop.
Can you guess the riddle?

Chronic web-surfers will know this riddle already. Polar bears may live at the pole, but nasty conundrums like this specimen thrive in cyberspace. Despite the layout, it doesn't rhyme. Despite the mishmash of imagery, there's an alleged link. And in spite of the verse's inanity, the enigma is known as The Harvard Riddle.

The reason is due to the customary postscript. If the riddle doesn't fry your brains, then this little kicker does the job: '97 per cent of Harvard graduates can not figure this riddle out. But 84 per cent of kindergarten students were able to figure this out. In 6 minutes or less.'

Or said another way, 'Nah-nah-nah-nah-nah.'

Be my guest if you want to find the solution. Quite a few pre-schoolers have managed the feat, apparently, but I have my doubts, built on my journalism training. Show me the data to verify the statistics. Who are these kindergarten students? I want names. And which particular Harvard grads were tested? Give me degrees, academic records and SAT scores.

Then you have those grammatical slips. Small potatoes, but it all adds up, with 'can not' (*sic*) in the final taunt, the whole message ending on a truncated sentence. Throw these elements together and you quickly get a hoax vibe.

The riddle itself bobbed up online in 2005, launching a decade of bewilderment. Either those kindy kids are drinking Smart Milk, or the conundrum is a crock. Undaunted, a few brave souls have grappled with the verse, coming up with several possibilities:

Pressure—the atmospheric kind, as well as peer pressure (the kind to make you cry), and the ravages of stress.
Time—from evolution to mourning the dead, from bladder cycles to life cycles.
Air—cold air and hot air, plus airtime and effervescence.

Honourable attempts, but the actual answer—assuming there is one to find—may well hinge on the closing jeer. No matter how shrewd, toddlers wouldn't offer any of those answers above. Atmospheric

Soldiers without souls fight without pay.

pressure? Please. So ask yourself what they would say, given the verse's final line: *Can you guess the riddle?*

That's right—to solve this ludicrous non-rhyme you need to absolve yourself of any understanding. Yes or no: do you know the answer? Harvard smarties may well squirm over such a blunt challenge, as opposed to the sandpit brigade that brags far fewer letters after their names.

'Do you know why the grass is green and the sky is blue?'

'No,' says the child, who genuinely doesn't.

'Correct.'

⌐35⌐

Which came first, the chicken or the egg?

Not a riddle, you say. Not even an anti-riddle. And you're right on both counts. This question is more a debate trigger, an evolutionary oldie. What's it doing in a book about riddles—or anti-riddles for that matter?

The same reason GEGS (a clichéd rebus for 'scrambled eggs') must appear in a cryptic crossword history, as it's the knee-jerk example many outsiders nominate when it comes to symbolising the art form. When I told people I was documenting riddles around the planet, they typically suggested one of two chickens: the road-crosser, and the egg dilemma. So I felt beholden to bung it in, if only to highlight its unsuitability.

Yet before we go there, maybe we should solve the enigma. Better now or never, our minds supple after so many convoluted questions already. Looking past semantics, I vote we use our riddle mojo to solve an eternal riddle that's not.

First, we should clarify: what sort of egg do you mean? If you mean a snake egg, for instance, or a turtle egg, then (b)—the egg preceded the chicken by aeons, since chooks were relative latecomers to the jungle. However, if you mean *chicken* egg, that's a different can of worms. The dilemma has been dubbed the granddaddy of all causality questions,

Chesspieces [Mongolia]

Egg box

When it comes to folklore, the egg wins the frequency race at a canter.

A little house absolutely entire. (Lamba people, Zambia)

There is a place where a white store sits in which hangs a yellow mask. (Amuzgo people, Oaxaca, Mexico)

God's little bag, its stitching can't be seen. (Malagasy)

A white house full of meat, but no door to go in to eat. (Afro-American, traditional)

A long white barn, two roofs on it, and no door at all, at all. (Ireland)

There is no place to attach a string. (Turkey)

bugging the hell out of ancient Greeks as much as modern geneticists, not to mention theologists.

Ask any hard-core Christian and a chicken wins the day. Day Five, in fact, according to Genesis, back when God was converting the cosmic blank into earth. 'And God said, "Let the water teem with living creatures, and let birds fly above the earth across the expanse of the sky."'

Hang on, chickens can't fly. Try the next verse: 'So God created the great creatures of the sea and every living and moving thing with which the water teems, according to their kinds, and every winged bird according to its kind.'

There you have it, from the mouth of God. One god at least. Take the problem to a neighbouring temple and Hindus will push the egg idea, since their universe was hatched from the Brahmanda, or the creator-egg, the celestial version of a Kinder Surprise.

But let's skip religion for now. Where does science put its faith?

Opinion is no less polarised. One camp favours the chook, due to a protein called OC-17, the compound responsible for making eggshell.

What can be swallowed, as well as swallow you?

You can't make an omelette without eggs, just as you can't make eggs without OC-17.

Ask the rival school and they'll recite the Gospel According to the Proto-Chicken. This rare bird was a long-lost cousin of today's Orpington, an egg-layer by anatomy, yet not a true chicken as we know chickens. Just because it walked like a chicken and clucked like a chicken didn't mean it was gallinaceous. A good parallel is the wolf–dog evolution, where epochs stretch between proto-dog (wolf) and the lovable spaniel next door. Anyhow, this prehistoric hen did the wild thing with a proto-rooster, resulting in an ovoid output no different from any other proto-chicken egg, except this was zoological history in the making. Inside the shell was a genetic breakaway, a zygote mutation we've come to call *Gallus gallus*, alias the chicken. Ergo, egg won the race.

But where's the applause? Despite a winner being named, the grandstand sounds like a morgue. The simple reason being that humans don't really want a winner. Deep down, the question is beloved for lacking an absolute answer. That's how idiom has adopted the phrase, applying the chicken-and-egg mystery to any cause-and-effect loop. The mystery is embraced; the circle has no starting point.

Which sets the conundrum apart from your typical science problem. Despite its farmyard imagery, the singsong cuteness of its language, the question acts as a perpetual engine. The moment you favour one team in the race—the egg gang or the chicken brood—the counterview is there to push against your verdict. A small propeller starts to spin in your brain, whirring between two magnetic poles.

The spiral is called a virtuous circle, the feel-good counterpart of the nastier cousin. One begets the other, begets the other, begets the other: but who begat whom? In the history of tricky questions, it must be the catchiest Catch-22.

A classic dilemma, but not a classic riddle. A Roman statesman called Sulla put his finger on it. The *aenigma* was already doing the rounds back then, around 80BC, just as Aristotle had voiced the puzzle in the agora three centuries earlier. Sulla saw the quandary much like a tool, 'rocking loose a great and heavy problem, that of the creation of the world'.

Pride

And he's right. The question is a coded means of asking how the earth came to be. Our latest evidence points the finger at The Big Bang, the mega-explosion that generated a zillion particles and atoms. Fine for cosmology geeks, but riddle nerds can't help but notice that the ultimate letters of The Big Bang just happen to spell EGG.

◱ 36 ◳

There are five houses painted five different colours

Let's keep on the scientific bent, turning to Einstein's Riddle. A dubious name, all things considered, as Albert Einstein quite possibly didn't invent it, and second, it's not really a riddle. The poser is still worth airing, however, a chance to spotlight a breakaway school of puzzles that found momentum in the 1850s. The prime mover was Lewis Carroll, a mathematician we've already met. Most know Carroll's frenetic rabbit and his disappearing cat, but few realise that the novelist developed his surrealism via drafting a series of brain games. Despite the puzzles banking on cold logic, Carroll used them to paint fantasia:

All dragons are uncanny.
All Scotchmen are canny.

From these two propositions a rational mind can conclude that all dragons are not-Scotchmen and all Scotchmen are not-dragons. A cakewalk compared to the muddle the genre could create. Taking a giant stride towards the surreal, Carroll extended the formula into this kind of caper:

No shark ever doubts that it is well fitted out.
A fish that cannot dance a minuet is contemptible.
No fish is quite certain that it is well fitted out,
    unless it has three rows of teeth.
All fishes, except sharks, are kind to children.

From within, silk scattered.

No heavy fish can dance a minuet.
A fish with three rows of teeth is not to be despised.

Hold these statements to the light and you'll likely see Wonderland's lobster quadrille as a watermark. But what's the answer? Well, it's manifold and messy, as the solver scores brownie points for every valid deduction he can draw from the details. Irrefutable stuff, such as: if not a shark, then kind to children; if despised, then no three rows of teeth, and so on. You must be cautious in your language. You need to separate solid data from presumption—a golden rule of maths and physics.

Hence the Einstein association. Frontier science demands that you extrapolate from the sprinkling of knowns; a field like quantum mechanics is its own colossal logic puzzle. As you'd expect, Einstein pushed the genre as far as it would stretch, presuming he devised this quasi-riddle we're about to meet. Quasi? Anti? You be the judge:

> *There are five houses painted five different colours. A person with a different nationality lives in each house. The five house owners each drink a certain type of beverage, play a certain sport, and keep a certain pet. No two owners have the same pet, play the same sport, or drink the same beverage.*

If the data seems incomplete, then your instincts are sharpening. A long list of assorted facts—fifteen in total—append the five-house scenario, telling you such crucial tidbits as:

> *The Dane drinks tea.*
> *The person who plays football rears birds.*

I won't reproduce the whole list here, as you'll only want the solution too. Besides, the answers are multiple, depending on whether you're tasked to name the baseballer, or the fish-owner, or the nationality of the yellow homeowner's neighbour. Other books take that road, where even the shortest answer accompanies a slab of calculations, much like the chain of deductions that go into solving a difficult sudoku. Let's leave the equations to the experts and focus instead on the riddle's origins, leaving the maths department for the history.

Clouds [Kazakhstan]

Suspiciously, Einstein's Riddle first appeared in *Life* magazine in 1962, seven years after Einstein's death. Unless the father of relativity managed to invent time travel as well, I'd say the puzzle's alleged creator is merely that—an allegation. Editors at *Life* claimed the enigma had been crafted by Einstein as a boy, the riddle found in the great man's papers, but there's no hard evidence supporting such a claim.

So it is the riddle preserves a deeper riddle. For a genuine bid at genius status, a solver must do more than pinpoint the milk drinker, or rumble the volleyballer, but identify the true author as well.

⊐ 37 ⊏

The cock crew, the sky was blue ...

James Joyce had a deep-seated fear of hyphens. Compatriot—the word—seems pedestrian compared with the zest of fellowcountryman. Things like streetorgans and meatchoppers were likely to clutter a Joycean auctionroom, while commonplace meals were usurped by menus of warmbubbled milk, crustcrumbs, jampuffs and plumpudding. This joy for invention alone makes *Ulysses*—his 1922 masterpiece—truly ground-breaking. Sorry, groundbreaking.

Early in the novel there's even the oddity of ghoststory. The plea comes from a group of rowdy schoolboys, begging their history teacher, Stephen Dedalus, to tell a creepy tale. The tactic is twofold. Every Irish lad loves a fright. Then there was the bonus of distracting Mr Dedalus from his deadboring history.

Stephen is obstinate. After, he promises. He does his best to teach his boys about Pyrrhus, the ancient Greek whose victories came at a cost. But the lads are restless, and Stephen is miles away. He's only recently lost his mother, and the grief gnaws at him. The guilt too. She'd asked him to pray at her bedside and he'd welshed on his promise.

Herein lies the beauty of the scene: the paradox of being in control (as a teacher) and being unmoored (as a son). The contradiction deepens in Joyce's repeated use of 'pedagogue', a word once applying to a Greek

How do you call a meerkat?

slave, a servant who led boys to school, yet now embodying master, the same man trying to subjugate his pupils.

Until hockey at ten, anyway. The boys remind their teacher that it's Thursday, a half-day, so Stephen closes his book. Time has got away. But then he remembers the story he pledged. If he can't honour his mother, he can at least be faithful to his brats.

'Who can answer a riddle?' he asks.

The boys bundle their books and pack away their pencils. But wait, is Mr Dedalus reneging on his ghoststory, or is the riddle his ghoststory? Either way, Pyrrhus is history as sir tells his riddle:

The cock crew
The sky was blue:
The bells in heaven
Were striking eleven.
'Tis time for this poor soul
To go to heaven.

The rhyme falls flat. The boys beg to hear the riddle again. Stephen obliges and the boys give up with little fuss. With an itchy throat the teacher answers his own riddle, 'The fox burying his grandmother under the hollybush.'

If that was the answer, it was tripe. Oh well, time for hockey anyhow. The boys cram their satchels and break asunder, stranding Stephen as the one laugher in the room, despite his riddle's failure to add up. Yet a non-answer differs from a meaningless one. Literary sleuths have dined out on this episode. The deeper you dig, the sooner you see why. The boys had begged for a ghoststory. Dedalus gives a nonsensical piece of folklore instead. Or did some reason lie in the rhyme he offered?

Professor John Rickard, a Joycean from Bucknell University in Pennsylvania, unravelled the scene in his 1997 paper, 'Stephen Dedalus among schoolchildren: The schoolroom and the Riddle of Authority in *Ulysses*'. The fox riddle was a remix, as Rickard reveals in his essay. The original ditty belonged to Irish folklore, commandeered by Joyce and given a decisive tweak. In the original, the non-answer was 'the fox burying his mother under the holly tree'.

C'meerkat

Notice the makeover? The grieving son had altered the punchline. For reasons mindful or subconscious, a mother had become a grandmother, just as the holly had altered from tree to bush. 'Stephen distorts the authority of language for the purpose of evading an unpleasant memory,' writes Professor Rickard. By corrupting the standard response, Dedalus had turned a meaningless answer into the opposite, one simple act of denial transposing an anti-riddle into a doggerel with significance. The history boys had expected a ghoststory. Slyly, unwittingly, they got one, their teacher burying his unspoken guilt that came alive in riddle.

⌐ 38 ⌐

What lake can fly?

Go on, guess: what lake can fly? Lake Titicaca sits high in the Andes, roughly 4 kilometres above sea level, as high as any twin-engine Cessna reaches. Could that be the candidate?

Then there's Kobe Bryant, who slam-dunks like a bird, but he's a Laker.

Swan Lake seems eligible, too. Swans fly, of course, while the ballet version is alive with jetés.

Or feel free to take the easy option: kick the brain into neutral and wait for the chapter to make the reveal. So far that's been the book's protocol. Why should things change? Unless you know the answer off the bat, I can't blame you for biding your time as the paragraphs accumulate. Bide your time and the solution will arrive on a platter.

'I don't know,' as I might say to a pesky nephew. 'What lake can fly? Tell me.' Because deep down there's an appetite for the answer, a key difference between riddles and humdrum questions.

By comparison, if I asked you for Lake Titicaca's deepest point in metres, you'd be forgiven for checking your fingernails. Either you know the answer as a full-time limnologist or you don't give a flying rat's. Questions of that stripe focus on what trivia you've managed to retain, the brain lint, the eclectic knowledge.

What should you keep after giving it?

I can recite African republics or Q-words in Scrabble because I find that stuff interesting in a nerdy kind of way. Perhaps you could retaliate with the six noble gases, or the last 20 Man Booker winners. Fair enough—we each have our patch. Trivia celebrates memory, mania and a dash of intuition.

Other questions seek other responses, from the state of your health to exercises in reason. It's hard to be too general about the rogatory mode, as questions are grouped, though riddles stand out for punching different buttons in the brain. They tease in want of satisfaction, often via a surprising bypath.

So then, what lake can fly? At face value, the answer's there to seize, no diploma required, as long as you're sufficiently resourceful. Since that's the other difference—riddles summon the wildcard of creativity.

What lake can fly?

Do lakes have wings? Is there a bird with lake in its name? Your brain starts raking through the riddle's elements, looking for a missing link.

Maybe now's the right time to fess up. Promise you won't hate me. Keep in mind that this specimen is filed under Anti-riddles. I'm almost too scared to admit that this riddle has no real answer. Not in English anyway. I came across the teaser—in a foreign anthology—and saw the potential of testing an idea, first on my website, and now on the page.

Until now, more or less, *Riddledom* has delivered Q-and-A. This chapter is a field test to see what Q-without-A can unlock. Some readers, I reckon, have skipped to the next chapter already, or tossed the book in disgust. My heresy has breached some unwritten contract. Others, like you, want to see where this flying-lake baloney is leading. Please, remain in your seats: it's worth it.

Back in 2013, I placed the riddle on my blog with full disclosure. I then offered a prize for the best suggested answer, meaning that players were both dared and enticed.

Suggestions flowed, from Lake Skywalker to snowflake, from Dragonfly Lake in Singapore to Russia's 'Mere' Space Station. Dove Lake in Tasmania earned a jersey, in league with John Lake, a *Newsweek* sportswriter who vanished into thin air in 1967. There was Aswan Dam in Egypt, Reindeer Lake in Saskatchewan, and the Mexican cactus fly called cochineal, which gives us the dye known as crimson lake.

Ultimately a pun took the cigar. A player named JB suggested Loch-Heed Aircraft and flew off into the sunset with his loot. The game was over, but its value still resonates long after the deadline. Unlike orthodox questions, riddles can unshackle the mind. Throwing your brain into a spin may not end world poverty, or decipher whale song, but it will prepare the mind for the unexpected.

As for the actual answer, I've slipped in a few clues along the way. The 'lake' you're chasing is perching in paragraph 4 of this chapter, though hanging is a truer description. The language you need, as I hinted, is the principal language heard on the shores of Titicaca. Indeed, the minute you convert the riddle into Spanish, the payoff approaches:

Qué tipo de lago puede volar?

The Spanish word for bat, the flying kind, is *murcielago*. Lake in Spanish is *lago*, the same four letters that end the airborne animal. Can you see how the wordplay operates? Almost every culture has riddles like this. In English we might ask:

What sort of key climbs trees?
A monkey

What kind of bat somersaults?
An acrobat

After the online mania, these prescribed solutions seem, well, prescriptive. Reduced to a finite answer, each gag becomes binary, depleted, which explains my urge to widen the horizon. A boy from Bolivia may know the flying-lake routine by heart. Doubtless, what began as a thinking exercise has long since fossilised for the *muchacho*, seeming more a mechanical call-and-response, an old script to memorise rather than a curiosity to consider.

But that limitation vanished the moment I negated the punchline. Placed in a new language, the riddle lost its knee-jerk answer, converting the solver into a thinker, an inventor. There was no cliché to recall, no easy exit; every newcomer is challenged to guess the unguessable.

The master of riddles lies in a puddle.

Suddenly a ravine crossed your pathway, and your bridging materials were the stuff of free association. A tall order, but the exercise triggered a creative storm when thrown to the crowd. No doubt having a prize up for grabs was important, as the reward incited a contest. The equivalent in the realer world might be a lucrative patent, a profit jump, a miracle cure, perhaps even escape from disaster, assuming your team is ready for the problem—which seldom owns a ready-made answer.

The tongue [Latvia]

Letters & Numbers

Not a game show, but its own mindplay genre, where riddlesmiths dabble in the alphanumerical.

Whichever hemisphere you prefer, prepare for a musical number about numbers, a famous letter involving letters, and other oddities.

⌐ 39 ⌐

As I was going to St Ives,
I met a man with seven wives ...

Grab a calculator. In case the full verse has escaped your memory, here it is:

As I was going to St Ives,
I met a man with seven wives,
Each wife had seven sacks,
Each sack had seven cats,
Each cat had seven kits:
Kits, cats, sacks, and wives,
How many were there going to St Ives?

Step by step we have 1 + 1 (the narrator + the polygamist) = 2.

So far so good. Now comes the tricky part, where multiplication enters the fray. Taking in the wives etc., here's the breakdown:

Wives = 7
Sacks = 7 × 7 = 49
Cats = 7 × 7 × 7 = 343
Kittens = 7 × 7 × 7 × 7 = 2401

Crunch them to get 2800, plus the opening pair, reaching a grand sum of 2802, the number of people, felines and receptacles bound for St Ives.

Or wait, before we lock it down, maybe the total is 2800, keeping the husband and narrator out of the final sum, since the riddle only specified kits, cats, sacks and wives.

No, hang on. Who's counting sacks? That's ridiculous. You may as well count whiskers and buttons. Sack the sacks. Subtract 49 from the last aggregate, and confirm 2751 (or 2753, if we include the surplus pair).

How do you get an actor off your porch?

Then again, skip every feline and go with nine—the wives and the other twosome. Or eight, if we discount the narrator. Or possibly seven, if we single out the humans from the verse's riddle, namely the womenfolk, assuming the narrator isn't female, which creates its own complication.

On second thoughts, the rhyme neglects to say which direction the polygamist and his harem are travelling. Ergo the number going to St Ives could well be one, namely the poet, while the other mob can't flee St Ives quick enough.

Unless, of course, the wives/sacks/cats/kittens are awaiting the polygamist at home, rather than escorting him to or from St Ives. Reread the riddle and you'll see how it subtly omits to state whether that extra rollcall is in physical attendance or not. That same ménage could well await the master once he gets home, before or after he visits St Ives, unless of course he lives in St Ives, among the females and felines. Therefore the answer is two, or conceivably one, depending on the travellers' directions.

Pedantically, another answer could be zero, as the speaker is St Ives bound, but all those others mentioned in the question might be heading the other way, or any damn way, or not even travelling.

I don't know about you, but I've lost count of plausible outcomes. What say we round it up to ten?

It's no wonder the English ditty has flourished since the early 1700s, the riddle yielding more conceivable answers than it owns lines. Egyptians were smitten by the kitten multiple, too, opting for mice and grain over sacks and baby cats. The variation was found in the Rhind Mathematical Papyrus, dating back to 1650BC. (Rhind, by the way, is not on the Nile, but is the Scottish enthusiast who purchased the scroll in Luxor.) Among the papyrus's tables and calculations—giving modern buffs a rare glimpse into early maths—was Problem 47, a riddle-like inventory that prefigures the St Ives travelogue by some 3000 years. Boiled to its bones, the problem reads this way:

There are seven houses;
In each house there are seven cats;
Each cat catches seven mice;

Pay him for the pizza

Each mouse would have eaten seven ears of corn;
If planted, each ear would have produced seven hekat of grain.
How many things are mentioned altogether?

Grab an abacus . . .

⌐ 40 ⌐

One

Supermodel Tyra Banks was no budding babe in her tweens. Back then her aunt invented the nickname of Lightbulb Head, her niece's noggin being 'small at the bottom and bigger at the top'. For Tyra, the name was taken as an endearment. Besides, the whole lightbulb issue vanished as soon as those other vital statistics arrived.

The anecdote is incidental in terms of world history, but fundamental in terms of stereotypes. Supermodels are frivolous: that's the perception. They like to talk about themselves. They take pains to underline how normal they are, just like you and me, aside from their perfect legs and faces and bodies and curves and hourly rates. Keeping to the clichés, the nickname story could afford to be vainer. Your typical model is vain, right? Still, few of us bother to hear the subtleties, the grace notes in a familiar riff, not where stereotypes are concerned. At our worst we judge a person for their job, their race, their religion, and we stick to what we presume.

Add a lightbulb and the deal is sealed. The format is versatile, combining one bunch of archetypes and the household task of replacing a bulb. The riddle always centres on the number of such people needed to fulfil the chore, with bureaucrats requiring a steering committee to allocate delegates, while know-it-alls need zero, as they're never in the dark. Over the years the gag has thrown together the most unlikely housemates, from protozoa . . .

How many amoebae does it take to change a lightbulb?
One. No, two. Make that four. Wait, eight. Hang on, sixteen . . .

What do you call a fat psychic?

. . . to genre authors:

> *How many mystery writers does it take to change a lightbulb?*
> *Two. One to screw it almost all the way, and the other to give it a*
>   *surprising twist at the end.*

Folklore mavens struggle to isolate the lightbulb moment, the inspiration that sparked the original riddle. Early traces stem from the late 1960s, most poking fun at ethnic minorities. Think Poles (or Polacks) in the States, the Dutch to the German mindset, or the Irish to the English. Pick any page in the atlas and I'll show you one race mocking another. At least with lightbulbs, the rib-jabs are mainly gentle—almost light, you could say:

> *How many Polacks/Friesians/Irishmen does it take to change a lightbulb?*
> *Three. One to hold the light and the other two to rotate the ladder.*

> *How many Marxists does it take to change a lightbulb?*
> *None. The bulb contains the seeds of its own revolution.*

In linguistics, the format is dubbed a snowclone, a term coined by Glen Whitman in 2004. A whimsical take on snowcone, where any ice flavour can perch in the cone, the snowclone is a phrase or saying where a keyword is interchangeable. 'X is the new black', say, where any colour (or food or fashion) can fill the breach. Examples are many: 'the mother of all Xs'; 'have Y, will travel'; 'my kingdom for a Z'.

What gives the lightbulb snowclone added appeal is the minor variations you can make to the template itself, opting for the verbs 'screw', or 'change', as these two classic tangents illustrate:

> *How many cops does it take to screw in a lightbulb?*
> *None. It turns itself in.*

> *How many psychiatrists does it take to change a lightbulb?*
> *One, but the lightbulb must want to change.*

Getting back to Tyra Banks, Little Miss Lightbulb Head:

> *How many supermodels does it take to change a lightbulb?*
> *Two. One to mix martinis, the other to call an electrician.*

A four-chin teller

Or my favourite, in light of the debate I had with my editor putting this chapter together:

> *How many pedants does it take to change a lightbulb?*
> *Don't you mean light bulb?*

So firmly cemented in social repertoire, the format can cope with absurdity as well. This next specimen is a tweet from English quipster James Martin (@Pundamentalism):

> *How many clowns does it take to fix the creepy flickering lightbulb*
> *in your attic?*
> *Just one. And he's up there already.*

While our last example—well, you should know its source already:

> *One.*
> *How many psychics does it take to change a lightbulb?*

⌐⌐ 41 ⌐⌐

Aso ko sa pantalan, lumukso ng pitong balon, umulit ng pitong gubat, bago nagtanaw dagat

Even in English the riddle bamboozles:

> *My dog jumped from the wharf over seven wells, jumped again over*
> *seven forests, before it saw the sea.*

You crave the answer—or I did on finding *A Little Book of Filipino Riddles*, as collated by US anthropologist Frederick Starr. For a little book dating back to 1909, it carries plenty. Try 400-plus riddles from the 7107 islands that make up the Philippines.

Just as fascinating, there are different riddle themes depending on which sector of the archipelago you visit. Locals on Luzon imagine the mouth as a creek filled with shells. On the island of Cebu, the hand

When does time go back and forth unchanged?

Manila folder

I throw the eggs; they crow immediately.
Firecrackers

What creature made by Lord God walks on its back?
A boat

No tearful eyes walking without feet.
A pen

Running and running, but it cannot go away.
A hammock

Leaf of a banana become wider; leaf of a coconut become longer.
A road

It loads and loads but never unloads.
A cemetery

entails five brothers with only one pillow. In Mindanao a grasshopper has a horse's face and bamboo wings. While north in Palawan, the moon inspires this story:

Adda pisi a dalayap nga incalic; tal-lo a papadi dina macali.
I planted a half-lemon; three priests cannot dig it up.

Superstitions are equally eccentric. Orthodontists would go broke in Manila, since crooked teeth foretell wealth. Lightning is attracted to geckos, and repelled by vinegar. If you sleep parallel to the roof's ridgepole, you will suffer nightmares. Should you hear a horse neigh in the first hour after midnight on 1 January, you will become poor. And please don't wave a ladle at a fisherman, unless you wish him to come home empty-handed.

Another taboo, which takes us one step closer to cracking our chapter's riddle, concerns the playing of tops. Kids can spin their toys all year, except early January. The problem is their noise—*gutum, gutum,*

When it's noon

gutum. The sound goes too close to the Tagalog word for hunger, repeated over and over, and thus predicts famine.

Father José Sanchez soon came to realise that the Filipinos had their own perspective on things. The Spanish Jesuit kept a journal of his time on the islands back in 1692, noting such details as sleeping mats and children's games. By that point the nation was under Spanish rule, thanks to the arrival of Ferdinand Magellan a century earlier. Indeed, the Spanish flag flew above the islands for almost 500 years, a reign reflected in so many trappings of Filipino life, from Catholicism to architecture. All the same, there remains a strong residue of the colony's previous incarnation. You see that embodied in a bowl of jellied pineapple, the indigenous fabric, the pockets of animism—and of course the Arabic footprint.

Before Magellan lobbed in 1521, parts of the archipelago had adopted Islam, influenced by the rise in Arab traders of the late 1300s, and the Arabs' consequent dealings with places such as Java, Brunei and Malaysia. Mosques bloomed across Manila, along with a custom known as *sungka*, which Father Sanchez described in 1692.

The word translates as autumn-and-winter, which only counts as a distraction. The board game is more to do with strategy than seasons. The Arabic name is *mancala*—or نقلة—springing from their verb 'to move'. Travel to the outer reaches of the Arab world and you'll see a dozen variations of the game, under numerous guises, from *bao* in Zanzibar to *toguz korgool* in Kyrgyzstan. When Father Sanchez saw the diversion for the first time, the game was played with stones as movers, though tiny shells are now more common.

Before we crack the riddle, let's take two jumps back. Imagine an egg carton with two parallel rows of seven sockets. A larger hollow, like an ashtray, juts out from either end. *Sungka* boards are typically carved from mahogany, the ritzier models resembling snakes or sea-dragons. No dice are rolled. *Sungka* depends on quick counting and tactics.

Rules vary, of course, the game having as many offshoots as seashells, some 49 per player. To start, you fill your seven houses, as the sockets are known, with seven movers each. In the Filipino version, the frenzy moves anticlockwise. Both players start at the same time, emptying one of their seven houses and 'sowing' the shells as their hand circles the

A smallish girl. On her head, a bundle of ashes.

board, dropping one shell per hole, including into your own store (the ashtray) down the end, but not the one at your opponent's end. And so it goes, with rules applying to empty houses and captured shells, the game a kind of speed-chess played on an abacus.

A theory behind the autumn-and-winter name relates to the idea of storing food in the leaner months, though somewhere like the Philippines can be too fertile for its own good. If not the volcanic soil, then the national imagination. How else to explain the *sungka* metaphor of dogs jumping off wharves, swerving among wells and forests before returning to the sea? Or even the second *sungka* riddle I found, separate from the Starr collection:

> Saro an lawas, duwa an payo, katorse an ngimot; kun
>   minakakan nagagadan.
> *One body, two heads, fourteen mouths; when it eats, it dies.*

Whichever metaphor you prefer, the game of *sungka* has been unveiled in a riddle: two exotic diversions for the price of one.

⊐ 42 ⊏

Red nuts and gin

The crossword was invented out of desperation in 1913. The man responsible was Arthur Wynne, a native of Liverpool, England, though his moment of inspiration struck in New York City, three sleeps short of Christmas.

Wynne was working for the *New York World*, filling a nagging gap in the children's section of the paper, the deadline pressing on his neck. His diagram mimicked a diamond, hollow in the centre, with 31 clues listed below the grid. He called it a word-cross, a term that flip-flopped in step with the puzzle's revolution.

Because revolution was the word. Nearing 1920, there were crossword scarves, crossword sweepstakes, crossword songs on Broadway, even a

A hookah [Punjabi]

crossword divorce in Chicago. The fever climbed to contagious levels, threatening to cross the Atlantic.

England resisted for a time. London headlines warned of the fad's potency, its threat to novel-reading and industry. Despite the hoop-la, the Yankee gimmick soon found its niche in Britain, too, the virus mutating into an exotic strain known as the cryptic. The pioneer in that regard was a poet-cum-translator named Edward Powys Mathers. He viewed the dictionary-like clues of Wynne as limited, preferring to craze his work with a few more cracks. Here's a taste:

> Evil does not change for the better = VILE
> The highest and great part of a bridge = RIDGE
> Demonstrator from on high = SHOWER
> A deadlock that may break a wedlock = STALEMATE

Note the formulas on display: anagram, concealment, double meaning, pun. If they sound familiar, they should, as *Riddledom* has been meddling in similar trickery. Rather than invent a new breed of crossword, Mathers was actually furthering the wordplay tradition of folklore and riddle that his culture already celebrated. Cryptic clues, you could argue, are essentially an offshoot of riddles.

The link was foreshadowed by *A New Collection of Enigmas, Charades, Transpositions, &c.* The book hit the streets in 1806, some 120 years before Mathers debuted for London's *Observer*.

Say the number quickly—120—and the interim seems a blink. Truth being, the gap is likely wider, as many of these riddle styles were already emerging before *A New Collection* reached the shelf. The lull displays the importance of Wynne's grid. In essence his diagram was a cupcake tray, a symmetrical block of spaces preserving the established tidbits of British cookery.

Look for yourself. *A New Collection* overflows with rookie clues. First, you have the bald challenge of the anagram:

RED NUTS AND GIN

Not an authentic riddle, of course, but a deception sitting in a riddle book awaiting the right interloper to jumble the letters, so forming a

What's round at both ends and high in the middle?

thirteen-letter word. While I let you figure out the answer, let's see how the trick is reborn in Mathers' work:

Arising out of NTN case

Hardly stylish, but this clue marks a major evolutionary step from the bald anagram 'riddle' to the polished cryptic clue. In the first phase, a solver was given no insight into the answer's definition. Presuming a phrase was sought, RED NUTS AND GIN could well result in SUDDEN RANTING or DAUNTING NERDS. Who knew? A solver lacked a sign-post. Likewise, TINSEL could turn into SILENT or LISTEN, or maybe ENLIST, or even INLETS. A solver had no compass bearing to confirm the answer's direction.

By contrast, Mathers' pioneer clue supplied two chances of reaching the target. First there was the letter batch in need of jumbling—'NTN case'. And second, a handy synonym of the answer: 'arising'. Mix the first and you'll define the second, this NASCENT clue laying down the etiquette for future clue-mongers to observe.

As we'll see in Chapter 62, the riddlesmiths of yore would slowly head in that classier direction, customising words to act as their own hints. (MAN'S CRISIS, say, might point to NARCISSISM, or MASCULINITY could well be clued as AIN'T I MUSCLY.) But before that sophistication arrived, the best that old riddle books could manage was RED NUTS AND GIN.

Basic, no question. But in 1806, such naked anagrams were the general understanding of how the formula operated. (Look twice at that last sentence, and you'll grasp your 13-letter solution.) More time would need to pass before the recipe could evolve into the elegant sport we know today. More time and less tolerance for any old random offering. The changes would first arise in the shape of sleeker riddles, a new genre emerging in the mid-1800s. And then, some decades later, away from the riddle page, the game would be codified in THE WORDY WASP DREAMS of Edward Powys Mathers.

⫍ 43 ⫎

Cry, foe! Run amok! Fa awry! My wand won't tolerate this nonsense.

Crucio promises pain, and *lumo* light. Then there's *confundo*, the bringer of bamboozlement, while *descendo* guarantees a sinking feeling. Each spell is taught by Hogwarts School of Witchcraft and Wizardry—the kind of spelling most of us associate with J.K. Rowling, creator of the Harry Potter cosmos.

But her bestselling series is also distinguished by more orthodox spelling, namely the business of N-A-M-E-S. Make that one name—the one that shan't be spoken, Mr You-Know-Who, alias the dark lord.

Enough beating round the bush—I speak of Voldemort, Harry Potter's nemesis. On the off-chance you've been trapped in a cave for the past decade and still hope to enjoy the Rowling series fresh, then skip the next few paragraphs. Though I'm guessing most of you will know which riddle I'm nearing.

Correct—it's riddle with a big R, as seen in Tom Marvolo Riddle, a previous student of the magic academy. To kickstart your memory, let's arrange that name differently:

The name is a cover-name, conceived by anagram. If you juggle the sixteen letters correctly, help by throwing your source in a circle, you'll reach the declaration: I AM LORD VOLDEMORT. Tom Riddle is the dark lord's actual name, just as Anakin Skywalker is the true identity of

What escapes a savannah fire?

Darth Vader. (Watch out—I'm in the mood for blurting out franchise secrets. Maybe you should skip this whole chapter if you wish to experience any film or book from scratch.)

The Voldemort trick is nifty wordplay for Rowling's many English-reading fans, but what about the other millions depending on translations? That's where the real riddle began. Linguists from Albania to Romania were forced to conjure a Tom Riddle variant to veil the evil Voldemort, or a name of comparable menace.

The efforts made were impressive (see box), with Frenchman Jean-François Ménard the standout among translators. His solution to the Riddle riddle was dreaming up Tom Elvis Jedusor, yielding the anagram: *Je suis Voldemort*. But Ménard's feat didn't end there. Not only does Elvis make an unscheduled cameo at Hogwarts, thanks to Voldemort's makeover, but the new surname Jedusor mimics the French expression *jeu du sort*, or 'fate riddle', making the dark lord a Riddle within a riddle.

Before we *evanesco*—the Hogwarts cue to vanish—we should focus on a final brainteaser, one that Rowling tweeted in October 2014. The message read like a curse:

Cry, foe! Run amok! Fa awry! My wand won't tolerate this nonsense.

More than a few thousand among Rowling's 3.8 million followers suspected an anagram, but stirring the Tom Marvolo Riddle was a cinch compared with these 54 letters, with little by way of handrails. The only hint J.K. added in an ensuing tweet was: 'Something to ponder while I'm away. X'.

Errant guesses over coming days prompted the author to relent. No amount of *ascendo*-chanting was going to help Potter fans rise to the challenge, not before the author hinted she was working on a screenplay about Newt Scamander, her old monster-minder from Hogwarts, and a sporadic pseudonym for herself. The cryptic tweet, she confirmed, mixed the opening sentence in the film's synopsis. Her tip set off a deluge, with one devotee going close:

Newt Scamander's History of New York Fauna. One town, my tale.

Others were miles off:

A bald spot where no grass grows [Masai]

Newt Scamander went on the mysterious way of Flannar Rook.
I brung bick Harry. U glad. Me go wurcke now. No speak.

Actually, that last one was Rowling's own wayward bid, illustrating what the sentence wasn't. Shrewder suggestions came in, proving to J.K. that 'other people love puzzles, riddles and anagrams as much as I do!' After a few more nudges, green-lighting the New York tangent, plus the use of Newt's full name, a PhD student from Sheffield—Emily Strong—cracked the code:

Newt Scamander only meant to stay in New York for a few hours.

Her prize? Instant media fame, and a direct reply from the sorceress of Hogwarts herself, with J.K. Rowling declaring Emily to be The One True Hermione of Twitter.

Tom Riddle reborn

Spanish:
Tom Sorvolo Ryddle > *Soy Lord Voldemort*
    (I am Lord Voldemort)

Icelandic:
Trevor Delgome > *Ég er Voldemort*
    (I am Voldemort)

Norwegian:
Tom Dredolo Venster > *Voldemort den store*
    (Voldemort the Great)

Russian:
Tom Narvolo Reddl > *Lord Volandemort*
    (Lord Shuttlecock-of-Death)

Why don't sharks eat lawyers?

⊐ 44 ⊑

Mostro son io più strano è più difforme . . .

I am a monster, stranger and more alien . . .

IS SMAISMRMILMEPOETALEUMIBUNENUGTTAUIRAS:

(a) an Incan god;
(b) a middle-ear infection;
(c) an anagram veiling the moons of Mars; or
(d) an anagram veiling the rings of Saturn?

If you answered (a) or (b), then you don't know the twisted mind of Galileo Galilei, the father of modern science. To those who circled (c), you've stolen a leaf out of Johannes Kepler's playbook. When Kepler, the Royal Astronomer of Prague, received this 37-letter anagram from Galileo, a younger astronomer based in Padua, he thought the code hid news of Mars. The message was in Latin, he sussed that much. He begged his penpal to be more explicit, or give some hints at least.

Back in 1610, wordplay like this was frequent. Patent law was only taking baby steps, meaning a scientist had to keep his discoveries on the down-low. Kepler knew the anagram related to a novelty Galileo had found in the sky, as that's how the jumble was couched in the letter—but what exactly?

Torment caused the Czech to fudge a few vowels and transform the odd consonant, emerging with the phrase:

Salve umbistineum geminatum Martia proles.

Translated, the stab reads: *Be greeted, double knob, children of Mars.* Logically, Kepler concluded that Galileo had used his homemade telescopes to realise that Mars owned two moons, the so-called double knob. But Kepler was wrong—and right.

Quite by fluke, Mars does have two moons—yet neither man knew this cosmic truth. Phobos (Fear) and Deimos (Terror) weren't spotted for another 250 years, when Galileo's primitive tubes were superseded by American giants in the 1870s. Kepler's guess then was a cute piece of clairvoyance, but about the wrong planet. Rather than Mars, Galileo had been gazing at the furthest known body of that time, the distant orb of Saturn:

Altissimum planetam tergeminum observari

So ran the anagram's answer. Or said in English: *I have observed the highest of the planets three-formed.*

Before you accuse Galileo of doing his own fudging, this was a time when Latin *u*'s could double as *v*'s and vice versa. The triple formation he mentioned in his solution referred to the rings that surrounded Saturn, though Galileo's lenses were too weak to verify their shape or nature.

So why would a famous astronomer send the anagram to another famed astronomer? Seems kind of risky, flaunting a breakthrough in broken Latin, given that your rival might crack the code and claim the discovery as his own. But that's the genius of the move. The anagram created a buzz across Europe. For Galileo to resort to scrambled letters only served to prime the rumour mill, implying that the Paduan had plumbed another secret of the night sky. In effect, the puzzle confirmed a breakthrough, at the same time protecting its particulars. Besides, even if Kepler was to unsnarl the code, his eureka would only be validating Galileo's discovery, unless his hunch hit on the wrong planet.

So much secret talk made Galileo an inveterate code-monger. Among his journal's many cosmic sketches was the occasional riddle. His best ignores the heavens altogether. To spare you the agony Kepler suffered, I shall tell you the next riddle's answer in advance. Are you ready? That way, as you read the verse in translation, you can see how the man who unravelled the universe defined the riddle itself:

I am a monster, stranger and more alien
Than the Harpy, the Siren, or the Chimera.
Neither on land, in the air or in the sea is there
A beast whose limbs can have so many shapes:
No one piece of me conforms with another,
Any more than if one is white, the other is black,
A band of hunters often follows behind me

What do you get if you sit on the moon too long?

Looking for the tracks made by my feet.
I live in the darkest places, and if I pass
From the shadows into bright light,
My soul quickly slips away with the onset of day,
And my tired limbs fall away, and I lose
My being with my life and my name.

⊏⅃ 45 ⌐ㄴ

Which is easier to spell,
fiddle-de-dee or fiddle-de-dum?

'Spell pseudonym,' said the host.

'P-S-,' I started.

'Wait. Let me use it in a sentence: It is totally lame for a crossword-maker to use a pseudonym. Pseudonym.'

The crowd cackled at the slur on my profession. The audience was only small, about 50 people wedged along the bleachers, enough to test the nerves as I stood in the spotlight, trying to stop my name from being M-U-D.

Once the laughter ebbed, I spelt pseudonym. The crowd seemed crestfallen. Where was the fun in seeing success? The show's biggest lure was schadenfreude, a much tougher word to spell under pressure.

The venue was a tin shed on the campus of Macquarie University, in Sydney. The indie musical was *The 25th Annual Putnam County Spelling Bee*. Early in Act 1, the host-cum-actor dragooned three volunteers from the audience. By conspiracy, those three suckers just happened to be the co-hosts of *Letters and Numbers*, a TV game show that prided itself on spelling, among other old-fashioned skillz.

Luke Brattoni, the evening's emcee, had been a contestant on our show. He did pretty well but had never won his way into a second episode, making this musical his chance to inflict revenge.

Asteroids

'Spell strabismus.' This grenade was aimed at Richard Morecroft, my telly colleague, who coped manfully with the eye condition. Lily Serna was next, my sister in numbers, who nailed googolplex with ease. (If you're listening to *Riddledom* as an audiobook then I mean ease, as in comfort, and not *e*'s the vowel, since googolplex only has one.) Under blazing lights, we'd all survived our first humiliation, but then the words turned nasty.

Because English can get that way. Pity the new speaker who has to pronounce cough, dough, through and bough. In a word, tough, which makes five variants, and I'm not even being thorough by including lough.

Tested under pressure, schoolkids can quickly come to fear spelling just as much as adults. In a public forum it's easy to grow timid, resentful. Just utter the sequence of pea-pear-pearl and you appreciate how spelling can seem one haphazard incantation you'll never hope to master.

Consequently, it should be no surprise to learn that there's a whole swathe of riddles poking fun at spelling. After all, humans will try to belittle anything they dread. Though a curious side-effect of so many alphabetical riddles (and there are so many) is that they actually help you to spell. For instance:

> *Why should the male sex avoid the letter A?*
> *Because it makes men mean*

> *Why is a cedilla like a pearl?*
> *Because it's found under the C*

> *Why is O the noisiest vowel?*
> *Because all the rest are in audible*

Next time you have to spell inaudible, omit the O. It's a handy mnemonic, which happened to be my second word to spell. I coped, though my fellow conscripts toppled with quinquefoliate (Richard) and calcareous (Lily). By this stage the show was itching to proceed with its mainstay cast, the plan somewhat hamstrung by a hanger-on who needed ousting.

'Spell *patwang-fweeee*,' said the host, adding his sample sentence: 'In *Mad Magazine*, Issue 265, the sound of a branch flinging baby Tarzan into the air was *patwang-fweeee*.'

Twenty men with white turbans.

Damn Don Martin, the cartoonist behind such cockamamie sound effects. The *patwang* part was obvious, leaving me to guess how many *e*'s occupied the whiplash bit. I guessed five, being one too many, allowing the show to continue among those who knew the script. Taking my seat, I gleaned that fiddle-de-dum might seem simple in theory, yet fiddle-de-dee can be spelt with a lot more *e*'s. (And yes, listeners, I did mean the other kind this time.)

⌐⌐ 46 ⌐⌐

My first is in riddle, but not in little . . .

Startling is a startling word. Here's why:

STARTLING

STARTING

STARING

STRING

STING

SING

SIN

IN

I

Shedding a letter per step, the leftovers never need to readjust, spelling a new word every time. Startling is also notable for breaking into fragments, giving you START at the start and LING (a fish) at the tail, just as NOTABLE can be split into NOT/ABLE or NO/TABLE.

In cryptic-speak, this last device is called a charade. Rather than rearrange a word, which the recent chapters expected, this formula sidesteps the Mixmaster for the chopping block. But in order to make the dissections work—turning REARRANGE into REAR/RANGE—the charade riddle had to number the answer's segments. Try this head-scratcher from 1806:

My third is under my second and surrounds my first.

Fingers and toes [Fiji]

If you think that's slippery, then good luck with this poser from the same era:

My first's a prop, my second's a prop, my third's a prop.

What makes both riddles extra tough is their lack of context. Were the answers edible? Musical? A species of flower? Wiser in hindsight, since I peeked at the answers, I can make your job easier. The two solutions you're aiming for are both common nine-letter nouns, the first from the wardrobe, the second a piece of furniture.

Give in? No shame. You were desperately seeking a WAISTCOAT and a FOOTSTOOL. Parsed into plain English, a waistcoat is under a coat around a waist, while the body's prop (a foot) can join a sitter's prop (a stool)—and pouffe!

Later in the 1800s, such popular fracturing took a curious step inward. Instead of snapping words into pieces, the riddlers of the day sensed the potential to get more molecular, just as scientists were unlocking the components of blood samples and gnat wings in the same period. Here's a specimen from 1864:

I am composed of seventeen letters.
My 14, 3, 10 is a weight.
My 6, 11, 4, 13, 15 is a place of abode.
My 2, 16, 8, 14 is to stop.
My 12, 15, 10, 1 is a part of an encampment.
My 5, 7, 17, 9 is a product of the sea.
My whole is part of the Decalogue.

For the sake of apostates, the Decalogue is the fancy name for the Ten Commandments. To determine which law is being enlisted, we need to crunch the numbers. To show you the routine, let's convert RIDDLE, say, to 123456. By so doing, we could then report that 526 is a fiction (LIE), and 4216 is DIRE. Doing the same with the seventh commandment— THOU SHALT NOT STEAL—we can plunder the required cargo of TON, HOUSE, HALT, TENT and SALT. Given fresh coordinates, you can also pluck SLOTH, LOATHE and TOOTHLESS, but why spoil a good homily?

Despite what God demanded, plenty of intellectual theft applied to the charade formula around the 1850s. The biblical sample above was

What goes into the forest facing home?

soon superseded by more elegant approaches, like this next anonymous gem from the same era. Here you'll find a riddle that skips through its answer letter by letter, all in the bars of rhyme:

My first is in riddle, but not in little.
My second is in think, but not in brink.
My third is in thyme, but not in time.
My fourth is in mother, but not in brother.
My last is in time, but not in climb.

This new recipe requires careful sifting, in true riddle fashion. The task of the solver is to isolate the letters that vary between the two offered words. Once sifted, the answer dances below the surface of these possibilities, reading downward:

RD
TH
HY
M
TE

Can you spot a word emerging from the mire? Scramble mire and you'll have the answer's homophone. That's right, RHYME. Thankfully, this sift-and-pick method, complete with rhyme, became the default setting for the micro-charade of coming decades. Thankfully, as the 'waistcoat' style was far too stiff, while the Decalogue mantra contributed to an Eleventh Commandment: *Thou shalt not splinter long, random phrases into multiple random words, with neither reason nor rhyme.*

⌐ 47 ⌐

Perhaps the solvers are inclined to hiss ...

What links Edgar Allan Poe, Queen Victoria, Vladimir Nabokov and the Book of Lamentations? Not a riddle but a trivia question. Given that the queen never wrote about nymphets, and Lamentations lacks a raven, your wiser answer is the acrostic. For those who don't know this puzzle type, here's a taster:

An axe on your shoulder [Russia]

Marvellous
Understanding
Makes my lunches

That's a relic stuck to my sister's fridge—the MUM in question. The acrostic is a common device for primary schoolers (like my niece) to paint word-pictures, using the topic's individual letters as starting points for each line. Not just young kids, either; Old Testament scribes also dabbled in the acrostic. The word derives from Ancient Greek, where ἄκρος means highest, and στίχος verse. Here the 'high' refers to the foremost letter, as opposed to the genre's exalted status, the acrostic an alphabetic skeleton for authors to flesh with imagery.

Speaking of MUM, Poe wrote a nine-line poem spelling out ELIZA-BETH (the name of his mum, as well as his mum's mum), for the *New York Evening Mirror.* He then enriched the formula in 1846, crafting a 20-liner for the same publication. This time the first letter of the first line, second of the second, and so on, revealed the writer's affection for FRANCES SARGENT OSGOOD, a friend's wife—which seems a little creepy in the Poe-tic tradition.

Less risky, *The Sydney Gazette* published an acrostic puzzle on St Andrew's Day 1804. Call it strange, or call it SAD (the initials of St Andrew's Day), but the purple doggerel spelt out a man who wasn't Andrew:

Darling Sons of Freedom, still
Unto Thee shall Gallia bend;
Neptune's 'tis, and Pallos' will
Conquest shou'd they Arms attend.
Advance! The Fates will have it so:
Not leave unpluck'd one Laurel from the Foe.

Good luck to anyone in the 21st century solving that who-am-I without the six initials giving the game away. Unless you know your British history, you may have missed the allusions to King DUNCAN, the mediaeval saviour of Scotland.

Which goes to raise a second question: is the acrostic a true riddle? Umpteen books from the last few centuries teem with verse published under the umbrella of riddles. So why should acrostics differ? The fact that the answer is embedded in the lettering, as well as the allusions,

How do trophy wives get minks?

should only underline its riddle status, you would think. Let's entrust this rarity from 1888 to settle the matter:

Perhaps the solvers are inclined to hiss,
Curling their nose up at a con like this.
Like some much abler posers I would try
A rare, uncommon puzzle to supply.
A curious acrostic here you see
Rough hewn and inartistic tho' it be;
Still it is well to have it understood,
I could not make it plainer, if I would.

Greg Ross, a former editor at *American Scientist*, shared the poem on his superb Futility Closet site. The ditty was crafted by a mystery figure named 'Maude' for the *Weekly Wisconsin*. Before I type the answer (or your eye beats me there), how would you classify this thing: as a poem, riddle, puzzle, code or diversion? Perhaps all five combined. Ignoring the buried letters, there's a fair chance you can arrive at the answer, solely using the lyrics—a much fairer chance than the DUNCAN doggerel anyhow.

According to Ross, 'con' in Line 2 is short for contribution, though con as in trick goes nearer the mark. Obviously this Maude had the confidence to try this higher form of 'highest verse', embedding a method that's seldom seen in the genre. If you can't spot the answer, consider every initial *couple*. Strung together, you will solve one peculiar acrostic, whether it's a riddle or not.

⌐ 48 ⌐

The century's wonder—a raree-show . . .

Bloody cheek, that last chapter. Apparently Queen Victoria was an acrostic-maker, or so this Astle joker reckoned, but we never got to see her handiwork. Fine then, to make up for such double-talk, this sequel chapter offers two bits of Victoriana—the queen's genius, and her genus—both in the realm of the double acrostic.

The same way minks get minks

I wasn't fibbing. The monarch was indeed a fan of riddles plain and poetic. Victoria held the throne for 64 years, roughly two-thirds of the nineteenth century. During that reign she had eight children, ensuring that the palace halls were alive with pitter-patter and the fireside was kindled by games and wordplay. The queen herself devised conundrums for the older ones, including the so-called Windsor Enigma.

The teaser appeared in 1861, the jewel within a collection entitled *Victorian Enigmas; or Windsor Fireside Researches: Being a Series of Acrostics Enigmatically Propounded.* The book's editor, Charlotte Capel, emphasised the publishing coup by adding the shout-line on the flyleaf: *Encouraged and Promoted by the Royal Precedent and Example.*

All up, nine clues were listed just after the preface, each one owning a geographical bent. Quoting the instructions, 'The INITIALS of the following places form the name of a town in England, and the FINALS (read upwards) what that town is famous for.'

More puzzle than riddle, almost a crossword precursor, the clues went from merciful-if-vague (*A city in Italy* = NAPLES) to cruel-if-not-impossible (*A town in Bothnia* = TORNEA). Clearly the heirs apparent to the throne were versed in the atlas. Once solved, the nine answers could then be stacked to meet the monarch's own instructions. See if you see what one saw:

NAPLES
ELBE
WASHINGTON
CINCINNATI
AMSTERDAM
STAMBOUL
TORNEA
LEPANTO
ECLIPTIC

Skim the heads down, and the tails up, your round trip going to spell NEWCASTLE, the city of COALMINES.

Double acrostics, a fashionable variation of the 1850s, were not always as bare as the queen's creation. While the Windsor Enigma was artful, adhering to the geo-theme, the more poetic efforts gave solvers a riddle bonus. This fancier approach was split into the segments

What cheese is made backwards?

of 'The Letters' and 'The Words'. The first entailed a bank of clues, like the ruler's city list, yielding answers that camouflaged the solution. The second section was more riddle-like, a quatrain foreshadowing the answer you were after.

One stylish example ran in *The Illustrated London News* back in 1856. Just as modern cartoonists portray today's affairs in the press, so too did riddlesmiths play with current events in the Victorian era. In spring that year a small seed had made a sizable impact on London's imagination, the occasion demanding a double acrostic. Part 1 was the standard bank of clues, the format in many ways foreshadowing the crossword 57 years later. Rather than grapple with their quaint wording here, let's fast-track to the thirteen answers below, including the incomplete pair that opened the original list:

The Letters
VENGEANC[E]
INDUSTR[Y]
COUNTY
TIMES
OUTCAST
ROXANA
IDYL
ASP
REGINA
EEL
GAMA
IONIC
APPLE

There's your challenge. Either unearth the news topic from the words, reading their extremes from top to bottom. Or take the braver option and see what you make of this baffling riddle that escorted the table of clues, Part 2 of the acrostic:

The Words
The century's wonder—a raree-show
Design'd from a leaf out of Nature's book.
If you guess my two words, you then will know
How the one from the other existence took.

Edam

A raree-show is a genteel way of saying freak show. All the way from Guiana, this particular rarity was on display at London's Kew Gardens. Can you guess its freakish nature, using both words and riddle in combo?

How green is your thumb, dear reader? I wouldn't dwell too long on the conundrum, if you want my advice. The marvel we're chasing has the Latin handle of VICTORIA REGIA, literally the royal Victoria, a coinage devised to honour the long-ruling queen. As for the raree itself, the tropical plant bloomed that summer in Kew's hothouse pond, drawing hordes to see the jaw-dropper first-hand.

Supplied enough humidity, the *regia* pod could sprawl into a pad some 3 metres in diameter, sturdy enough to support a young girl standing on its heart, or so the period sketches suggested. Hearsay asserts that the girl was Alice Paxton, the daughter of London gardener and architect Joseph Paxton. The detail is delicious, as the veins radiating across the mammoth lily were also said to have inspired the strutwork of a glass palladium that Paxton designed in Hyde Park during the same decade. The palladium of course was named Crystal Palace, the second covert column in your acrostic letters, and the place where the *Victoria regia* would soon be relocated, the venue the cosier for the Guianese native. Botany, geography, architecture—the world coming curled in one majestic offshoot of the riddle.

⌐⌐ 49 ⌐⌐

'Twas whispered in heaven, 'twas muttered in hell . . .

Lord Byron didn't do it. Despite what some anthologies say, the great Romantic poet was not responsible for this next riddle. Rather the perp was a dilettante named Catherine Maria Fanshawe, born in 1765, the middle child of a Surrey clerk.

We know so little of this poetess, as was her calling card. In short, we're told she was an admirable letter-writer, an avid reader and 'a designer in almost every style'—quoting the *Dictionary of National*

Why does Father Time wear bandages?

Biography. She dabbled in watercolours, drew, etched, travelled south for her health, and eventually died childless in 1834, joining her parents under granite in Chipstead.

Her poems lie in a smattering of collections. The pick is a posthumous volume, *Memorials*, a book arranged by the Reverend William Harness, who'd declined the offer of being Fanshawe's sole heir. Scroll through the e-version and you'll see how the etchings dwell on children, while the poems have the shape and scansion of Wordsworth, the other great Romantic of the day.

There in *Memorials*, on page 41, is the famous riddle—or a clever poem wrongly attributed to a famous man. The opening line runs at odds to this chapter's heading: *'Twas in heaven pronounced, and 'twas muttered in hell* . . . Clunkier, you have to admit, compared with our chapter's heading that survives. The change was allegedly made by a parodist named James Smith. The rest of the riddle is all Miss Fanshawe. Bearing in mind that this section is called Letters & Numbers, see if you can snare the answer, studying the poem's full chapter and verse:

'Twas whispered in heaven, 'twas muttered in hell,
And echo caught faintly the sound as it fell;
On the confines of earth 'twas permitted to rest,
And the depths of the ocean its presence confessed.
'Twill be found in the sphere when 'tis riven asunder;
'Tis seen in the lightning, and heard in the thunder.
'Twas allotted to man from his earliest breath;
It assists at his birth, and attends him in death;
It presides o'er his happiness, honour, and health;
Is the prop of his house, and the end of his wealth.
In the heap of the miser 'tis hoarded with care,
But is sure to be lost in his prodigal heir.
It begins every hope, every wish it must bound,
It prays with the hermit, with monarchs is crowned.
Without it the soldier and seaman may roam,
But woe to the wretch who expels it from home.
In the whispers of conscience 'tis sure to be found;
Nor e'en in the whirlwind of passion is drowned.

Because day breaks and night falls

'Twill soften the heart, and though deaf to the ear,
'Twill make it acutely and constantly hear.
But, in short, let it rest like a beautiful flower;
Oh, breathe on it softly, it dies in an hour.

My hunch, Byron would be proud of it. The polished piece was assembled overnight, thanks to a language debate that had raged earlier that day. As an added clue, that debate was held with a certain Mr Hope of Deepdene, Surrey. The topic concerned the creeping misuse of a letter. Has the penny dropped? Dropping is another clue, for that droppable letter is H, your answer.

Hooray for her handsome hymn, hey? Hands down, it's heroic handiwork, with every line carrying H in some way. The poem won ample admirers, including Byron's groupies, plus a Welsh colliery owner called Horace Mayhew, who exacted a Cockney revenge in 1850, a few years after Catherine's death. 'Ere's an 'ilarious sample:

I resides in a Hattic, and loves not to roam,
And yet I'm invariably absent from 'Ome.
Though 'Ushed in the 'Urricane, of the Hatmosphere part,
I enters no 'Ed, I creeps into no 'Art.

But that's enough men stealing the Fanshawe limelight—the poets and the coalminers. Let's end with Catherine's other talent, namely her own ear for lampoonery. Perhaps the spinster herself sensed the Wordsworthiness of her unsung poetry, if not in subject matter, then in execution. Why not test her worth, and turn her words against that other big Romantic? To complete the stunt, the riddle-writer ditched the alphabet to focus on a lakeland stream in one almighty piss-take of the era's nature poet. I swear if Miss Fanshawe was alive today, she'd be an A-list satirist:

There is a river clear and fair,
'Tis neither broad nor narrow;
It winds a little here and there,
It winds about like any hare;
And then it holds as straight a course
As, on the turnpike road, a horse,
Or, through the air, an arrow.

A delusion letter under the pillow.

🔲 50 🔲

What's the difference between a dasher and a haberdasher?

If you said 'haber', then you win second prize. After reading so many riddles, you've clearly grown wise to verbal skulduggery, though there's a better answer out there. Maybe not as funny, but certainly astuter.

Astuter? Not a word, says autocorrect. Possibly not, but that never curbed a certain clergyman who owes his stature to his unique entangling of English. Of course I refer to Reverend William Archibald Spooner, the long-time dean and divinity lecturer at that notable college—or coatable knowledge, as Spooner would have said.

We've met the man very briefly in our Wonderland chapter, and we've seen his signature slip-up used to solve Lewis Carroll's raven riddle. (Remember the bird that's a pest for wrens?) So famous did the reverend become for his bird-watching (I mean word botching) that spoonerism even reached the *Oxford Dictionary* during his lifetime, early in the twentieth century. Allegedly his sermons and lectures were marbled with flip-flop phrases, converting a loving shepherd into a shoving leopard, or twisting Lot's wife into a philosophical riddle.

As an extra turkey quail (sorry, quirky tale), Reverend Spooner was also the likely inspiration for Wonderland's White Rabbit. Charles Dodgson, alias Lewis Carroll, was an Oxford cohort, the tenures of both men running parallel for many years. While no journal entry confirms this link, the odds seem short that Spooner, a short-sighted albino who was forever tearing between lectern and pulpit, was the rabbit's prototype.

One legacy beyond question, however, is the genre of riddles that celebrate the Spooner curse. Thanks to the man's letter-swapping, a scad of riddles have been whelped in the reverend's name. Classically the blueprint is presented as a question of contrast, such as in these examples:

A dream [Mongolia]

What's the difference between a manic rabbit and a counterfeit coin?
One's a mad bunny, the other is bad money

What's the difference between a savant and a deviant?
One's a smart fella, the other's a . . . (you get the idea)

As you'd guess, the Spooner style is ideal for smut, or speaking in the 'Morse code', shall we say. Just one tweak and a shining wit can be undone. What tweenager hasn't delighted in the perils of fire truck and pheasant plucker? Then again, in a breakaway variation, there's also the wholesale swapping of words, a mix-up in the Spooner vein, such as:

What's the difference between a jailer and a jeweller?
One watches cells, the other sells watches

What's the difference between a shepherd and a student?
One minds his stock, the other . . . (you're a fast learner!)

Which leads us to Will Shortz, the Puzzlemaster on America's National Public Radio, as well as the crossword editor at *The New York Times*. Back in 2011, Shortz was eager to learn whether there existed any fresh spoonerism riddles. Rifle through most joke books and the usual suspects appear under the Spooner banner, from the clean cat-flap to the dirty West Bank. Hair the well was the new material? Shortz put the challenge to the airwaves, inviting listeners to invent their own examples. An avalanche ensued. Two entries involved dogs:

What's the difference between a dog and a marine biologist?
One wags a tail, the other tags a whale (from Marcia Kenley)

What's the difference between a good handyman and a bad dog?
One is busy doing chores, the other is busy chewing doors (from Tom Simard)

Meanwhile the winner, from Michael True of Virginia, needs an American accent to make it work:

What's the difference between a wedding chapel and a restaurant's daily specials?
One's a marrying venue, the other a varying menu

Coconut trees above a pond.

A nifty effort, as was the offering from Ottawan crossword-maker Gary Disch, who picked up third prize. Even the question is elegant, enough to inspire envy in any Oxford lecturer:

What's the difference between a dasher and a haberdasher?
One has short spurts, the other sport shirts

⌐ 51 ⌐

101 × 5

Bill Hawks, the British prime minister, agrees to be the guinea pig. He steps forward from the crowd and enters a steampunk phone booth. Doctor Stahngun, the booth's inventor, squashes in beside him. He throws a lever, presses a few buttons, and that's when things go pear-shaped. Nothing amiss about the time machine—that works fine. Too fine, in fact, the damn apparatus hurling Stahngun and Hawks ten years into the past.

The crowd is left aghast, yet not clueless. Two of the guests—a dapper archaeologist and his juvenile sidekick—are seasoned detectives. Together they've cracked the strangest cases, from the golden apple of Baron Reinhold to the deadly Elysian Box. What's one more mystery to solve? This whole time-machine fiasco has the feel of another case for Professor Hershel Layton and his protégé, Luke Triton.

Plus a crossword-maker, as I was also roped into the case. Here in Australia anyway, the publicists behind Nintendo enlisting my puzzle profile to help flog the latest Dual-Screen (DS) game—*Professor Layton and the Lost Future*.

The overlap was deduction, I guess. Layton is a master of clue-cracking, and I make crossword clues for a living. Where the professor travels to St Mystere to find an apple, I shuffle GANZIPARM on national TV to uncover AMAZING, or even better, MARZIPAN. The role was part of a game show called *Letters and Numbers*, a *Countdown* spin-off that ran for eighteen months on the SBS network, from 2010 until 2012.

The eyelashes [Hawaii]

By default, the gig foisted the mantle of Wordplay Ambassador on my shoulders, a title that sits snugly to this day. Ten times more snug than Master Logician, say, which I'm not, though that's exactly what I had to impersonate for a week in November 2010, flogging the Layton game.

Think about it. For a Japanese engineer to make a point-and-click adventure of 168 mini-puzzles, he'd hardly limit those puzzles to language, or taint the inventory with any semantic business at all. The apple hunt, for instance, otherwise called *Professor Layton and the Curious Village*, outsold Mario Kart Wii by the truckload in 2008, both in Japan and around the world, and you don't boast those numbers by dabbling in anagrams or double entendres. The common language had to be logic, spatial challenges and numbers, mazes and sliding blocks: the dialect shared by multiple markets, from Urdu to Pashto.

In Japan, such word-free puzzles boomed in 1966, when Akira Tago, a Tokyo psychologist, released *Atama no Taisou*—or *Head Gymnastics*. The book sold millions across the subway crowd, triggering some 22 sequels, each title loaded with wayward triangles, broken vases, matchsticks and chessboards. A close comparison, in terms of literature, would be IKEA instructions, where language is stripped to its minimum and your role as reader is to translate the fragments into a chair.

Or in my case, a hot seat, dolled up for cameras and swearing by the virtues of the Layton experience. For the record, I enjoyed the game. Any smart rival of Mario Kart Wii deserves publicity. The DS series, developed by Akihiro Hino, and built around the famous head-games of Akira Tago, is a refreshing antidote to knifing zombies or stealing Chevrolets. Instead of reflexes, you need cool reasoning to move through the narrative. Unless you happened to be a Wordplay Ambassador with a penchant for spoonerisms who blew his help-coin budget a few equations short of Act 2.

Sure, I travelled back through time with Luke and Hershel. I decoded clocks in the antique store. I fathomed the bus timetable after 'clicking' with Florence, the old lady who was waiting on the kerb. Yet the further I entered the adventure, the more assistance I needed. A different story if the pivot points were verbal—English-verbal anyway. Or if every logistic conundrum was a riddle in the purer sense, dealing in meaning and metaphor. But this was maths, more or less.

Which has more legs: a horse or no horse?

Machine logic. Geometry. As it was, nearing the pointy end, I had to store each unsolved puzzle at Granny Riddleton's cottage, forcing the poor darling to camp on the porch.

My bacon was saved by Puzzle 034. Just as well, since Nintendo was hosting Sydney's press corps for high tea in the Stamford Hotel, a block above Circular Quay. The launch resembled Doctor Stahngun's demo, minus the phone booth, and double the champagne. And just like Stahngun's debacle, the high tea threatened to lapse into low comedy as I duelled with a journo called Nicole in a DS puzzle-off, seeing who'd be crowned as Master Solver: the crossword king, or a 22-year-old lifestyle reporter from *K-Zone* magazine?

Nicole won. I can't lie. Her spatial awareness in the Crazy Keyhole challenge was a thing of beauty. Still, I managed to steal my moment with the Layton stumper that ran closest to riddlehood. The puzzle was called The Mysterious Memo. The professor had returned to his apartment to find a note lying on the table. The message was terse:

101 × 5

Happily I spotted the gimmick straight away. The writer of the note, the professor's flatmate, was clearly in trouble. Can you see why? As a bonus clue, a calculator was also part of the screen shot. Nicole struggled. She suspected the puzzle to be 100 per cent numerical whereas I sniffed the alphabet. Riddle or not, this was my territory. Back at school, taking maths as far as I could tolerate, I devoted far too many hours to morphing figures into letters, seeing what words I could render on a calculator.

Turns out quite a lot. Did you know that 55178 is BLISS in disguise, once flipped over? Or that 98275 and 78075 can capsize to spell SLEIGH and SLEDGE? Just as 35009 hides an upside-down GOOSE, like the dyscalculic crossword-maker who flunked General Trig.

Obviously Layton's friend was in crisis. Quintuple 101 and you get SOS, upright or standing on its head. So many wasted years fiddling on a Casio had finally paid off. If only Mr Smith were alive, my maths teacher, the man who said, 'Astle, the calculator is made to calculate and not turn numbers into the ABC.' He'll be turning in his grave this very moment, all the better to read Luke Triton's mayday.

A horse has four legs, but no horse has ten

Lost & Found

*A trove of riddles involving lost treasure, absent
answers, missing maps or a found prince.*

52

In the fields grazeth a calf whose body changeth hue thrice in the space of each day

Glaukos was last seen playing with a mouse before he disappeared. King Minos, his father, was worried sick, as was Queen Pasiphaë, both parents ordering servants to search under Crete's every stone. All in vain. The boy was gone.

If Minos could summon his own father, namely Zeus of Mount Olympus, then he'd beseech the supreme god to reclaim his child. But that hotline was shut. So he turned to the Kuretes, a cultish troupe of nine male dancers who worshipped Rhea, the ancient fertility goddess. Maybe they knew the boy's hiding place. They didn't, but they were kind enough to render the king a riddle:

In the fields grazeth a calf whose body changeth hue thrice in the space of each day. It is first white, then red, and at last black.

This riddle is very old, and very strange—I'm telling you now. Putting a date on Minos is next to impossible: the king belongs to antiquity. Homer mentioned the ruler in both his epics, while the Greek historian Thucydides labelled Minos as the first man to own a navy. Suffice to say, this potentate goes way back. Even Minos, the name, is Cretan for king, making King Minos a living tautology, assuming he ever lived in the first place.

Real or fabulous, the same ruler has left us two enduring legends—the bull-man monster of the Minotaur that marked his reign, and perhaps the oldest riddle known to man. Maybe. Who knows? Myths tend to muddy the water. As an artefact, the verse differs according to which mythologist you ask. The lines above are courtesy of Apollodorus,

House full, barn full, but you cain't git a spoonful.

translated from the Cretan original via Greek, muffling the riddle even further.

By chance, Minos did have a three-toned calf in his stable. Just as the fey dancers described, the calf began the day with a white pelt which turned red by noon, then jet black nearing nightfall, much like a bovine mood ring. The beast was doubtless a curio, yet barely the instrument that would bring back Glaukos—or was Minos missing the point?

Afraid that might be true, the king called for Polyeidos, a Corinthian seer whose name alone seemed a promise. Broken down, *poly-* means many, just like that polychromatic calf in the stable, while *eidos* relates to idol, both words denoting form, or thing.

If anyone could grasp what meaning lay in a kaleidoscopic calf, it should be the seer. Modern readers will detect how the colour-shift whispers the Oedipal trilogy of legs, where one creature (man) changes his make-up depending on his age. Polyeidos was alert to analogy as well, likening the colours to a ripening mulberry, and therefore a child by association. Bite into the immature fruit and the flesh is white. Over time, that colour deepens to a young blush, soon to arrive at the rich black of adulthood. Tidy work, but the correlation failed to rescue Glaukos.

What did work is about to stagger you. Later in *Riddledom*, we'll see how the rebus ran amok during the 1800s. Known as a picture puzzle, it puts a pat of butter beside a teacup to denote 'buttercup'. Simple enough, compared to the miracle Polyeidos was about to pull, solving his own rebus in 3D.

Still searching for Glaukos, the seer sat pondering in the palace gardens. Suddenly a loud hum caused Polyeidos to notice an owl, pursuing a swarm of bees. By daylight, what's more—a double strangeness. The bird was flushing the bees from a wine cellar. The seer put two and two together. He linked the night-hunter with darkness, the owl an infamous agent of the gods. In the same breath he apportioned sweetness to the bees—or *glukus* in the Greek. Somehow the answer was obvious. Polyeidos sprang to his feet and dashed into the cellar. One by one he prised open the honey barrels to find young Glaukos, the fruit of Minos's loins, foetal inside the last—drowned.

Air [Ozark Mountains]

Riddle-cracking was not the seer's only gift. Polyeidos revived the boy with special herbs from the garden. Glaukos was saved. Minos was elated. He asked Polyeidos to linger for a while, urging the prophet to teach his son the basics of divination, perhaps to have a riddle-solver closer to home for the next crisis.

⌐ 53 ⌐

Sounds like where a robin or eagle might keep their money

Hollenbeck Park sits below the giant letters of HOLLYWOOD. Just over 20 acres, the place has a trout lake, a skate bowl, playgrounds and picnic shelters. Spend an hour wandering and you're sure to encounter joggers and squirrels, families and tourists. Unless you visited in early June 2014, when pandemonium ruled.

Back then, a horde of Angelenos fumbled shrubs and sifted tanbark. They frisked seesaws and groped the ivy. They checked under benches and shook palm trees, everyone hoping to find a bubble-mix canister. Inside was more than just detergent, or a plastic wand. According to the Twitter feed of @HiddenCash, there was also money in the mix.

The message that launched the frenzy asked, 'LA: Are you ready to play with bubbles today?' Seems the answer was a resounding yes. While @HiddenCash was only a week old, the fad was already ablaze. That will happen, if someone plants money in public spaces. In its first week the Twitter account boasted half a million followers, despite nobody knowing the donor's identity.

The few details the press could glean were only those Mr X chose to share over social media. Apparently his fortune derived from real estate investment, his @HiddenCash idea a playful way of giving back to the community. Beyond that, the bio was blank. Not that citizens were overly fussed. The good people of LA were too busy rumbling Hollenbeck for bottles of detergent.

Why did they make Courteney Cox?

The first drop was the weekend before, late May, up in San Francisco. On that occasion the hunt clue was a riddle:

You're usually feeding them but today they're feeding you.

Pigeons? Goldfish? The teaser was elusive. Maybe babies fitted the description, but where did that leave you? In the end it was a fluke at ground level that unlocked the riddle. Two or three envelopes were found downtown, full of cash. The wads were taped to parking meters, those urban things we feed around the clock. The stunt drew hundreds to the street, where thousands were there to be collected.

Word soon spread. People took selfies with fans of banknotes. TV bulletins relished the mayhem—and the mystery. Days after the meter-mania came the bird riddle:

Sounds like where a robin or eagle might keep their money.

This time the focal point was LA, specifically the media precinct known as Burbank. (Say the name sloppily and you've solved Mr X's riddle.) But now the swarm of early adopters had swelled into stampede proportions. Fortune-seekers parked in loading zones to maraud the Empire Center, a shopping complex off the Golden State Freeway, rooting through bins and skips, groping merchandise, frisking clothes racks. Traffic hit a standstill. One building site was forced to suspend operations until the madness had abated.

Similar bedlam struck Whittier, a city southeast of LA, where crowds went hysterical in a park, pursuing the next lead. Fences were trampled, plants squashed, a sprinkler system uprooted. Day by day the @HiddenCash craze was at risk of self-destruction, though Mr X was quick to pay for damages, urging seekers to play nice.

His other plea was philanthropy. He wished the joy of riddles, the thrill of the chase, to inspire players to share what money they uncovered, to give to those in greater need. While many did just that, the bigger outcome was a slew of copycat hunts across the country. Mr X tried to distance himself from his imitators. But in the end there's only so much control a faceless millionaire with a passion for grand-scale games can wield.

That's one reason Jason Buzi removed his mask. The entrepreneur from Palo Alto was keen for the fun to continue, on the proviso that the

Because Lisa Kudrow

riddle-solvers acted responsibly. Over July, the games reached Houston and Chicago, Mexico City and London, the escapade climaxing with a curious incident on Coney Island in early August.

Pez dispensers were the canisters this time, from Superman to the Green Lantern, filled with money and buried just below the sand's surface. At least, Buzi and his team had peppered the beach on the hunt's eve, announcing the game the following morning:

> *The superheroes can't see.*
> *They are buried below*
> *Where the earth gets soft*
> *Between your toes.*

Hours later came the Instagram, the picture of a lifeguard chair supplied to orientate the hunt. The hordes descended on Coney Island, but the sand was empty. Overnight, as happens on most summer nights, the beach was ploughed by New York City workers, unknowingly scooping the treasure into the vehicle's cage or burying the dispensers out of reach.

Yan Budman, the @HiddenCash co-founder, was the real superhero. The moment he heard of the broken promise he bought another 38 dispensers and planted them across Brighton Beach in Brooklyn. The subsequent hunt was just as fun but something of the lustre had been lost.

Of course, I'm only guessing on that, since the New York stunt was the last in a series. Speaking to the *LA Times*, Buzi said, 'This does not mean we are abandoning our mission of bringing people together in a fun or positive way, or of giving back.' Or said another way, after ten weeks of civic rumpus, the @HiddenCash bubble might have burst.

⌐ 54 ⌐

Basin Street Banquet

Edward Nigma was a lost cause from square one. As a kid he won a puzzle book by swindling classmates in a jigsaw contest. Outside in the playground he fleeced all suckers with coin tricks and other

What did the balloon say to the pin?

sleight-of-hand scams. Only to graduate to a carnival stall where his chiselling increased, skimming Joe Public with Chinese knots and similar flimflam. His banner said it all:

Match wits with E. Nigma the Puzzle King

Nobody could. Edward made sure of that. Cheating was his bread and butter. Soon the shyster owned a chic apartment in the city, complete with puzzle decor, from concentric mobiles to crossword rugs. But somehow the pickings felt too easy. The man wanted more in life—a worthy challenge, a smart opponent. In short, Nigma needed a nemesis.

Batman was the obvious choice. And if dressing up was good enough for Gotham's guardian, then Edward would follow suit, so to speak. A bodysuit, in fact, lurid lime from wrist to ankle, the whole ensemble stencilled with question marks. In one quick makeover, The Riddler was born.

The official birthdate was 1948, nine years into the Batman saga. A holy grail among collectors, *Detective Comics #140* was The Riddler's debut, the classroom rat evolving into a supervillain before you reached the staples. As would be his trademark, his maiden heist came with a riddle.

Quirkily, the three words were delivered on a billboard, meshed into a simple crossword for onlookers to solve. The lone clues went this way:

1 Horizontal—a water utensil
2 Vertical—a public way
1 Vertical—a formal dinner

Relax—the answers combine to spell this chapter's heading:

Basin Street banquet

Puzzle-wise this riddle is intriguing. Firstly, in the same year, another superhero was struggling with a crossword clue, namely Superman in a radio play called *The Crossword Puzzle Mystery*. Secondly, despite the crossword format being 34 years old, The Riddler still relied on old-school terms, using Horizontal and Vertical, rather than your everyday Across and Down, the lingo entrenched before the war. Either Eddie Nigma was old-fashioned, or the artistic trio of Dick Sprang, Win Mortimer and Charles Paris had yet to get the memo.

Watch it, Buster!

Whichever the case, Batman and Robin unravelled the billboard and made a beeline for the gala dinner on Basin Street. That was their first mistake, taking the solution to be a neutral message, rather than a riddle in its own right. Blunder #2 was arriving at the Basin Street Hotel, where a civic function was being held, providing The Riddler with a plum opportunity to empty the vaults.

Which vaults? you ask. Please, don't tell me you fell for the felon's chicanery too? After all my warnings, honestly! The crossword answer was not a communiqué but a homophone. Said aloud, 'banquet' becomes 'bank wet', as that was the devious plan—The Riddler blowing the precinct's water main to flood the bank's underground strongroom. The ruckus allowed the robbers to scuba through Gotham's sewers, pilfering the loot at leisure.

Fortunately, the Basin Street Hotel was a few doors from the Basin Street Bank, a symptom of The Riddler's psychosis. Here was a cheat hard-wired to be semi-helpful, dropping off riddles as if courting his own undoing. This time round the caped crusaders arrived too late, the vaults gutted and the gang gone. Maybe next time, as there was never any doubting—from comic sales alone—there'd be a next time, with more handcrafted clues to second-guess.

More rampant riddling—all from *Batman* #179 (1966)

How can one get into a locked cemetery at night?
With a skeleton key

Can you tell what nationality Napoleon's parents were?
Cors-I-can

Why is the letter A like honeysuckle?
Because a bee follows it

When does 10 added to 10 equal 10?
At 9.50 (or 10 to 10)

My house is large but the door is small.

⌐ 55 ⌐

In the morn, when I rise, I open my eyes . . .

What bird works in Hollywood?

Gee, let me think: Ryan Gosling, Ethan Hawke, Timothy Robbins, Dame Maggie Smith, Teri Hatcher, Taylor Swift and Russell Crowe (who's also a Kiwi). Walter Pidgeon was there for a while, as was Peter Finch. Johnny Depp played Jack Sparrow, Gregory Peck portrayed Atticus Finch, while Jodie Foster won an Oscar for Agent Starling. The list goes on. That's the benefit of brain-storming, or the byproduct of a riddle that's open-ended: too many answers can fly.

What's twisted in the kitchen?

A jar lid, a pretzel, a corkscrew, a wet cloth, a daiquiri lime . . . Any solution seems to work. The syndrome is common in riddledom, thanks to the question's inbuilt block. Under pressure, humans may find alternative routes, several if the looser parameters so allow. But what about a riddle that has five quatrains? Surely the wiggle room is minimised by packing so many details into 20 lines.

You'd think. But then again you've never messed with Eliza Hurst's riddle. The quatrains were unearthed by a second empress of enigmas, Faith Eckler, the co-publisher of *Wordways: The Journal of Recreational Linguistics*. She and her husband Ross have been responsible (some would say culpable) for launching alphabetical anarchy over the last 35 years. Forget pretzels, the *Wordways* quarterly is one twisted journal. To get a feel for this American wonder, try these articles from recent issues:

'218 Color Names Used in Palindromes'
'Dvorak Typewriter Words'
'Anagram Sudoku'
'Coincidental Synonym Chains'
'Seesaw Alphanumerics'

Cosmo it ain't, but the topics are tackled with kindred verve, including a long-lost riddle Faith dug up in a library backroom. The oddity was tucked away in an English almanac called *The Ladies' Diary*, dated 1831.

A simple timeline as far as riddles go, until readers started delving deeper, tracing the enigma back further to *The Ladies' Diary* from 1782, again attributed to Mrs Eliza Hurst. And just to jolt your bearings further, the verse also bobbed up in *Dickson's Balloon Almanac* of 1801.

If you're feeling flummoxed, beware. This chapter is just warming up. Hot-air ballooning is almost risk-free compared to the bruising your brain may cop in coming pages.

Helmet snug? Seatbelt fastened? Let's do this.

At first glance, no solution was on offer, despite the riddle's multiple sources. The ideal challenge for a smart audience, reckoned Faith, who ran the poem in *Wordways* in August 1981. Long-winded I know, but you need to digest all 20 lines before we enter the labyrinth. Take it away, Mrs Hurst:

In the morn, when I rise, I open my eyes,
Though I sleep not a wink in the night;
If I wake e'er so soon, I still lie till noon,
And I pay no regard to the light.

I am chaste, I am young, I am lusty and strong,
And my habit oft change in a day;
To Court I ne'er go, am no Lady or Beau;
Yet as frail and fantastic as they.

I travel abroad, and ne'er miss the road,
Unless I am met by a Stranger:
If you come in my way, as you very well may,
You will always be subject to danger.

I have loss, I have gain, I have pleasure and pain,
And am punish'd with many a stripe:
To diminish my woe, I burn Friend and Foe,
And the ev'ning I close with a pipe.

How many men can wallpaper a feminist's house?

I live but short time, and die in my prime,
Neglected by all who possess me:
If I say any more, to what's gone before,
I fear you will easily guess me.

Readers responded in fits and starts. Ross Eckler himself fancied fame to be the answer. The logic felt seaworthy. After all, a reputation never sleeps; it travels near and far; for all its strength, one misjudgement can make it frail. As for the stripes in the fourth quatrain, think prison stripes, the cost of ruining one's name. While the troublesome pipe in the same stanza could be the bagpiper marking a dignitary's funeral. Tenuous, no question, but the opening bid incited a volley of ideas.

Greed was the next suggestion, the greed for money in particular. Greed is restless, lustful, borderless. The stock market is a tale of pleasure and pain. No investor is immune. The pipe is a symbol of the brooding plutocrat, while the stripes could be the milling on a coin's edge . . .

Even from here, I sense you turning tepid. Greed the answer feels more like blind hope. One reason is the tangible 'nouniness' of folk riddles. Traditional solutions are seldom abstract. You know yourself, after so many waterlilies and cherry stones, period enigmas tend to own tactile answers. Greed and fame feel like modern takes on old metaphors. While the London stock market was alive and dangerous in 1780, both early bids seemed errant speculation.

So what happened to the actual answer? What did Mrs Hurst intend?

This story is no less knotted. A researcher named Jeff Grant, spurred by the mystery, dived into the *Collection of English Almanacs for the Years 1702–1835* to find that the critical document was a gap in the record. Clouding things further was the general nature of almanacs: yearly publications that withheld a riddle's solution, forcing readers to shell out in twelve months' time. Add to this a slapdash sense of continuity, and you'll understand how material might stray in transit.

Initially Grant believed he'd found the answer—an oven—until he realised that this was one of six answers intended to satisfy the previous year's dozen riddles. Some answers went click, matching their riddles perfectly. Others, like the work of Mrs Hurst, still seemed orphans.

Eight if sliced thinly enough

Lastly, to make this saga the full snake pit, we have a pirate called Thomas Carnan to consider. Almanacs were big business in the 1780s, encouraging chancers like Carnan to cannibalise several editions into a rival publication. Consequently, *The Ladies' Diary* was a bootleg makeover of *The Woman's Almanac*, a more credible banner, with neither periodical taking the trouble to unlock Mrs Hurst's poem.

Mind you, the oven detour mobilised a new theory. Jeremiah Farrell, the current editor of *Wordways*, contemplated fire as the outcome, a very folksy kind of solution. Think it over: a fireplace is stoked through the night; its character fluctuates depending on fuel; it can be fragile or fantastic and always dangerous; the stripes could apply to the griddle it serves, while the tobacco pipe also fits neatly.

There it was. After 130 years, the enigma was conquered. Readers of *Wordways* were free to return to the comforts of phonetic synonyms and synthetic phonemes, until Jim Puder, a regular contributor, presented Plan Bee.

Puder was convinced that the insect was the missing ingredient. Bees have no eyelids and therefore can't sleep a wink; asexual worker bees are chaste by default; they travel abroad—from flower to flower—and don't deviate unless a stranger intervenes; the stripes speak for themselves, along with the danger, leaving Puder the pipe headache. This last hurdle was cleared after consulting apiarists. Apparently the queen bee and her workers can often emit a sonorous hum overnight, an eerie sound the keepers had come to call piping.

Bingo. The bee was the key. But this riddle wasn't done. From 2011, no *Wordways* felt complete without fresh conjecture erupting on the Letters page, as if the ghost of Mrs Hurst haunted the quarterly. Her spirit was refreshed by Ronnie B. Kon, a reader who had travelled from Los Gatos, California, all the way east to the Rare Book and Manuscript Library at the University of Illinois. According to records, this archive was the only vault on earth to hold the 1832 sequel to *The Woman's Almanac*, and Ronnie was prepared to drive the 3300 kilometres to get the better of a riddle.

He came, he saw, he was underwhelmed. The answer allegedly was a candle. A candle? The fire dimension was covered, but how do stripes punish a candle exactly? That's when Ronnie sussed the small

Why did the fly fly?

print and realised that a candle was the pick of the readers' suggested answers, since the intended solution was missing in action.

The story ran cold for a time until Faith Eckler was back on the case. All this talk of fire and candles had turned her mind to the riddle's 1801 cameo in *Dickson's Balloon Almanac*. There it was, the answer staring back from the archive.

As a sport, ballooning was starting to balloon. Just two decades before, the Montgolfier brothers had sent a sheep, a duck and a rooster into the clouds, the only injury befalling the rooster, due to the sheep kicking the bird a few minutes before lift-off. The craze was rising in both senses, sweeping up Mrs Hurst perhaps. Why else would a specialist gazette, filled with news about aeronauts, run a riddle that had no bearing on the pastime? The answer had to be a hot-air balloon. Look for yourself—the dawn rising; the newborn envelope; its frailty and wonder; its travel and trajectory depending on the brazier's burn. And the pipe? Maybe the overnight storage, the balloon dying after only a day of life.

Seven answers later—or maybe eight—the riddle was beaten. Eliza Hurst had her chance to rest, only for the debate to resurface. I kid you not. In a final bid for closure, Ronnie B. Kon returned to the fray, armed with a new theory. Not a balloon this time, or a bee, but the American flag. That's right, Ronnie's last shot for glory saluted Old Glory herself.

You probably don't need to refer to the poem to do the checklist again. A flag is raised every morning after its mock sleep; all of 25 years young at the alleged time of the riddle's creation, the USA was lusty and strong; it no longer recognised the court of England; weathered cloth makes it frail; the stripes are evident, more than the punishment they inflict, while the pipe is possibly the empty pole as the emblem is lowered.

Ovens and candles, greed and bees—did Mrs Hurst foresee the chaos she'd sown? Each tangent has its merits, though possibly there's a ninth idea ready to break the deadlock. Whichever answer you care to salute, let's be grateful for some familiar Q&A in coming chapters, if only to counter the pleasure and pain of this remarkable Q&AAAAAAAA.

Because the spider spied her

⌐ 56 ⌐

Se pareba boves, alba pratalia araba

In front of him he led oxen, white fields he ploughed . . .

I'm bashing out this manuscript on a keyboard, the letters marching across a white screen, the flashing cursor waiting for the next sentence. Okay, author, what now, what now, what now . . . ?

A far cry from AD800, when 'manuscript' honoured its Latin roots, a word deriving from *manus* (hand) plus *scribere* (to write). Back in the day, the cursor was a quill tip, the screen an expanse of parchment, the keyboard the craft the writer possessed.

As a rule that writer was a monk. A valued artisan, the scribe was responsible for shaping scripture, though the job's long and ill-lit hours came at heavy personal cost. The point wasn't lost on Florentius of Valeranica, a scribe of the 900s, who wrote, 'If you want to know how great is the burden of writing: it mists the eyes, it curves the back, it breaks the belly and the ribs, it fills the kidneys with pain, and the body with all kinds of suffering. Therefore, turn the pages slowly, reader, and keep your fingers well away from the pages, for just as a hailstorm ruins the fecundity of the soil, so the sloppy reader destroys both the book and the writing.'

Gothic engravings show various monks in the act of writing. Often the man is hunched like a cyclist, adding colouring to hollow letters, or dipping his quill into the inkhorn held by his assistant. Such is the scene, across European monasteries, that backgrounds our next riddle:

Se pareba boves
Alba pratalia araba
Albo versorio teneba
Negro semen seminaba.

The verse appeared in the margins of a Visigothic prayer book known as the *Verona Orational*. The author is unknown—most likely a Christian monk from northern Italy, his nose to the parchment around AD800. Translated, the quatrain reads:

When things go wrong, what can you count on?

In front of him he led oxen,
White fields he ploughed,
A white plough he held,
A black seed he sowed.

Should you be considering a farmer, then the nameless monk has tricked you, for the answer is the monk himself. The *boves* (or oxen) are his fingers yoked into servitude, ploughing the white page with his white quill, its point planting black ink as the hand traverses. Scholars are divided over the riddle's placement in the manuscript and whether the monk was testing his nib, in the same way as modern scribes doodle to awaken a ballpoint. Or possibly the riddle was born of boredom, the kind you might suffer after a glut of Visigothic prayers. Who could blame the guy? The *Orational* was 254 pages after all, jammed with liturgical antiphons which are as deadly boring as they sound.

But wait for the irony. Our nameless hero spent a year or so producing the volume, avoiding smudges, spacing the script, aligning the serifs, only for his marginalia to be the real darling of posterity. The monk may blush in hindsight, but his slapdash riddle on the periphery has grabbed centre stage in the present. The crux is language. While the folios are dense with old-school Latin, the quatrain flits between two worlds, showing glimpses of modern Italian in a Latin glaze. Vulgar Latin is the academic label, the spoken type versus the sort that fills the *Orational*.

The verbs, in particular, mark a breakaway. If the poem was pure Latin, then *tenaba* (held) would be *tenabat*. In Italian, the equivalent word is *teneva*, just the odd quill stroke shy. Likewise plough, the noun, is *aratrum* in Latin, as opposed to the riddle's *versorio*, which also happens to be Veronese dialect to this day, 1200 years on. Linguists can split hairs over the rhyme's ratio of new to old, but there's no doubting that the Veronese riddle is among the first documents ever written in embryonic Italian, and it's not even the primary document itself, but a quill test in a snooze-fest of Latin antiphons.

Your fingers

⌐ 57 ⌐

Why should the Captain of a vessel going to Woolnorth leave here with a good appetite?

Kudos to Smoke and Fudge. And lest we forget, Nellie and Wander. These were the Australian riddlesmiths of 1877 who shook off the shackles of British japes to forge a distinct colonial humour. Using puns and local colour, fauna and flora, headlines and homophones, these wits dragged a European medium into a new meridian. A very southern meridian, in fact, some 42 degrees south of the equator.

Tasmania, to be precise. The riddles arose from a fishing nook on the island's northwest edge going by the name of Stanley. You might have seen the town most recently as a key location in the film *The Light Between Oceans*. Before electric light, however, before celluloid, the town's foremost dilettantes held their Sixth Annual Literary Committee, seeking poems and prose of digestible standard, plus a modicum of riddles to enliven the anthology.

Fudge responded. As did Fragments and Nellie, Wander and Anon. Should you question why contributors opted for pseudonyms, you only need browse the 48 riddles that made the cut. I don't wish to disparage trailblazers, but many witticisms struggle on the page. Or let's be kind. Let's agree that five-star material of its day can lose a little twinkle in the fullness of time.

What metal do you get from clouds?
Silver—because every cloud has a silver lining

Hang your head, Smoke. The gag is laborious, but perhaps I'm being harsh. Fudge does no better:

What thing that boys play with is like a little animal?
A bat

What do you call a homeless sheep?

Stanley, please, was this truly the pick of the crop? But then something wonderful happens. The moment the focus swings from the generic to the specific, the collection shimmers. I'm not saying the humour lifts, but the spirit of place. Moving away from try-hard punchlines, you enter the writers' habitat, hearing and seeing the age:

> *How is it that Mr William Hannan can make his way through the bauera scrub better than his brother?*
> *Because where there's a will, there's a way*

Ferdinand Bauer, the Austrian botanist to lend his name to the native flower, was part of Matthew Flinders' crew to circle the continent in 1801. Amazingly, this history is launched by one simple riddle—though don't ask me to identify Mr Hannan. His details remain lost in the wilderness.

> *Why is the* Argyle *a most unfortunate steamer?*
> *Because every week she's in a strait*

The strait is Bass Strait, just off Stanley, the *Argyle* a regular steam service that negotiated the choppy waters.

Keeping things at sea, more history pulses through our final riddle, an original piece of work from Nellie. To fathom her teaser is to uncover a pirate map of distant archipelagos and brutal winds:

> *Why should the Captain of a vessel going to Woolnorth leave here with a good appetite?*

My favourite word in this question is 'here'. I love the brazen sense of home where X marks the spot, and any outsider must realign their compass.

'Here' is Stanley, of course, a fishing port protected by a black volcanic plug known as The Nut. Stuck on the edge of Bass Strait, the town has dug its knuckles into the earth, clinging on for dear life. The Roaring Forties, as the gales are dubbed, can blow an oilskin inside out. Hence a captain plying west to Woolnorth, at the top-left corner of the Tasmanian wedge, would be wise to hug the shoreline, keeping alee of Tin Kettle Islands. If you're still not convinced, Woolnorth has been renamed since this riddle first saw daylight, reverting to Matthew Flinders' opinion of the place: Cape Grim.

Alley Baa-baa

Go there now and you'll be stalked by the chopping blades of 60 turbines. The Woolnorth Wind Farm has prime position, harnessing the gales that howl across the Southern Ocean. The average blasts are cataclysmic. Hang on to your hat if you visit, as the wind seldom dips below 30 kilometres per hour, owing to the open run the air enjoys across the oceans. Like a long-range missile, the wind skips Africa altogether, hurling its energy onto the first landfall in 10,000 kilometres.

A seasoned captain approaching the cape would aim for the Tin Kettles. The proven route of 1877, according to Nellie's riddle, threaded between two granite islands within that archipelago, home to muttonbirds and metallic skinks. The islands resemble two steamed dumplings floating on the water, accounting for Nellie's quip, and answer: A Captain should be hungry when heading for Woolnorth, as *he will have to get through two Doughboys*.

I've checked Google Images, and the likeness resonates. The islands are twin chunks of the same loaf, both wearing frills of Bass Strait foam. Who needs a treasure map to confirm such gold, when a riddle selected by Stanley's Sixth Annual Literary Committee (1877) does all the navigation for us?

⌐ 58 ⌐

I'm the sweetest of sounds
in Orchestra heard . . .

'Primate' can apply to monkeys or bishops. Both uses spring from *primus*, or 'first' in Latin, since apes, etc., are deemed the upper reaches of the animal tree, just below humans, while a bishop is considered *el supremo* of the clergy.

Nonetheless, Samuel Wilberforce, appointed the Bishop of Oxford in 1845, wasn't happy with the implication, this whiz-bang theory of Charles Darwin's aligning *Homo sapiens* with chimpanzees and their other hairy cousins. Pshaw, he thought, and made no secret of

If two's company and three's a crowd, what's four and five?

his opinion. His wrath flared in 1860, opposing biologist Thomas Henry Huxley—grandfather of writer Aldous—in a slamdown debate at Oxford a few months after Darwin's treatise went to press.

No script of the stoush survives, though Wilberforce did publish a lengthy denouncement in the weeks preceding the debate. As for Huxley, nicknamed Darwin's Bulldog, his stance was no less staunch. Put the two in close confinement and fur was sure to fly.

At one point in the evening, Wilberforce was heard to ask whether it was to Huxley's grandfather, or grandmother, that the biologist owed his monkey ancestry. (The actual quote has been lost to history, but this was the snipe's gist.) Huxley gave a zinger in reply, admitting that he was happy to embrace his own apishness, but would be ashamed to be related to anyone whose oratory obscured the truth.

Boo-ya—or boo, depending on your particular colours.

The Oxford event was colossal, attracting thousands to the campus and generating editorials nationwide. For better or worse, after a life of devoted service, Wilberforce would come to be best known for his denial of evolution—plus a riddle he left among his papers in 1873. In an odd way, the Orchestra Riddle bears a connection to the Oxford slugfest:

> *I'm the sweetest of sounds in Orchestra heard,*
> *Yet in Orchestra never was seen.*
> *I'm a bird of gay plumage, yet less like a bird,*
> *Nothing ever in Nature was seen.*
> *Touch the earth I expire, in water I die,*
> *In air I lose breath, yet can swim and can fly;*
> *Darkness destroys me, and light is my death,*
> *And I only keep going by holding my breath.*
> *If my name can't be guessed by a boy or a man,*
> *By a woman or girl it certainly can.*

Nature, as you can see, lies at the riddle's heart, just as it permeates the great creation riddle, though at least Darwin had the decency to provide a possible answer. Wilberforce reneged, however, just like Mrs Hurst before him. The answer to his Orchestra Riddle has been lost, or was never issued.

Nine

Matters were in stalemate for half a century until a theory was floated by Sphinx, the alias owned by Henry Dudeney, a noted logician and puzzle-maker of the early 1900s. The AWOL answer, he argued, was a bubble.

The argument has substance. Bagpipes in quaint slang are known as a bubble, a nod to their air bladder. You'd scarcely find bagpipes in an orchestra, so that detail was sound. Second, a bubble's iridescence strengthens the plumage idea. Then there's the popping potential of land or water, natural threats to the bubble, just as the captured air (its held breath) lends sense to that allusion. Meanwhile, darkness, by virtue of its inky qualities, destroys all vision of the bubble, though the same could apply to most answers. As for womenfolk being better suited to guessing the solution, Dudeney put this down to 'bubble' being a vernacular breast.

Ironically, the bubble theory resisted popping for decades. The suds felt solid, until nature interrupted with one almighty splash. The counterblow was the killer whale, or whale in general. Again, the argument is persuasive.

To follow the riddle's logic, orca is integral to orchestra, the word, while the animal is a natural singer (though this truth would have eluded Darwin in his day, let alone Wilberforce). The gay plumes could be the blowhole's spray, producing rainbows midair. In addition, land and sustained immersion would imperil the beast.

So what about darkness then? Herein lies the theory's coup, for darkness loomed as a whale's new predator, the impetus for widespread killing as man was intent on harvesting the monsters' oil for candles and lanterns.

Are you still in Team Bubble? Then consider the homophone, where a wale is a raised rib of fabric, akin to the ridge in corduroy, a word stemming from *vala* in Old Norse, or 'knuckle'. In the sexist tradition of 1873, that term was deemed a piece of female dialect, needlework versus proper work, and thus an allusion open only to 'woman or girl'.

Whichever punchline applied, the Orchestra Riddle is an accidental soundtrack for Samuel 'Soapy' Wilberforce. (The nickname came courtesy of prime minister Benjamin Disraeli, who described the bishop as unctuous.) The man occupied the Oxford pulpit for 25 years,

A cup of milk spilled over the countryside.

preaching the word of God, yet his strongest after-image stands to be his opposition to evolution. Where Darwin and his followers preached the inner logic of nature, from whales to primates, Soapy Sam spouted froth that light would eventually destroy.

⌐¬ 59 ⌐¬

Fifty is my first, nothing is my second . . .

'You know, it's a pity you're not interested in doing a children's book,' said publisher Tom Maschler, back in 1976. 'Because you could do something that could really change the world. It would be magnificent.'

The words lingered with Kit Williams, a reclusive painter from Gloucestershire. 'They burned in me,' he told a BBC documentary team. Until then, Williams had worked mainly within the frame, creating narrative painting that lay outside the box. He loathed the sense of duplication a book would demand, repeating faces and costumes on every page, heeding some A-to-B format. But then a brainwave struck. He'd make a book like none other, a puzzle book with pictures, a riddle book with buried treasure. Three years later, the world knew the masterwork as *Masquerade*.

The treasure was a golden hare, its delicate filigree encrusted with ruby and turquoise, citrine and moonstone. Before *Masquerade* hit the shelves, Kit sealed the hare in wax to thwart metal detectors. He placed it in a ceramic casket, safe from the brunt of shovels, and buried the prize under the gaze of television quizmaster Bamber Gascoigne. Lastly, to camouflage the tampered earth, Gascoigne poured on a fresh cowpat from a Tupperware box. By cover of night the two men retreated, the quest in readiness.

Maschler was right. *Masquerade* changed the world. Leastways, it revolutionised children's publishing, forging a new genre and a worldwide frenzy. Hundreds of thousands of copies were sold. On the surface the story was magical but simple—a romance between the moon and the sun. A diffident beauty, Ms Moon wishes to give the glorious

Moonlight [Burma]

Sun a token of her love. She chooses Jack Hare to be her courier, but the animal is reckless. He races from Tara Tree-tops to the old fiddler, from meadow to High Street, and by the time he plunges into the sea the love token is:

Fifty is my first
Nothing is my second,
A snake will make my third,
Then three parts a cross is reckoned.
Now to find my name, fit my parts together,
I am all your past, and you fear me in cold weather?

This is the book's final riddle, a letter-by-letter charade that announces the amulet as LOST. But Jack Hare's strife is only a sliver of the reader's travails, presuming they wish to find the actual treasure. Not a crossword person, Williams knew he had to create a unique puzzle to keep the prize in situ for a while. He did that in spades, since no spade went anywhere near the cache for years.

Masquerade is not only an exquisite artefact, but its sixteen paintings are just as meticulous as the book's inbuilt subterfuge. The LOST riddle above is low-hanging fruit measured up against the messages hiding in the friezes that border each painting. Beyond that level lies another puzzle that only two physics teachers—Mike Barker and John Rousseau—managed to decipher, three years after publication. I won't spoil the conundrum, in case you'd like to wrestle with Williams' genius, but I can say that the quest was derailed by a gentleman with the alias of Ken Thomas.

The latter sent Williams a map of the suspected location, a crude sketch with ground zero circled in pen. By this stage, pummelled by the book's success, Williams felt relieved to confirm the hunch, inviting Thomas to proceed digging. The casket was duly found, the hare sold at auction for a tidy sum, and the frenzy seemed old news.

Not quite. Seven years down the track, Thomas's own masquerade was exposed. Rather than unlock the book's central riddle, he'd merely gleaned intelligence from Williams' former girlfriend. Or so ran the allegations. For her part, Veronica Robertson denied the account. Even though nothing scurrilous was ever proven in the wash-up, the

Eyeless, I lead the blind.

press smelt a scandal. Indeed, Williams himself confirmed that once, while picnicking with Robertson, he'd used a marker to pinpoint a noonday shadow on the vernal equinox, an action Robertson may have mentioned to the opportunistic Thomas, whose real name was Dugald Thompson.

All in all, a tarnished finale to a brilliant puzzle, but the marvel of *Masquerade* survived the squabble. Williams could resume his passion in imperfect anonymity, painting in private, the hare found, the monkey off his back. A few custodians in the Cotswolds were likewise soothed, since fortune-seekers had been burrowing rabbit-like across the length and breadth of Haresfield Beacon ever since that damned amulet was LOST.

Tom Maschler certainly had his faith repaid, while thousands of children around the world still cherish the story, quite apart from any murmur of loot and infamy. Of anybody, Messrs Barker and Rousseau, the lone solvers of the book, should feel the most aggrieved at seeing the treasure fall into fraudulent hands. Physics teachers too, ironically, the very breed to tell you that a solution is only as good as the solver's ability to show all workings-out, which the so-called winner never managed.

◪ 60 ◩

في قلب من حجر ولدت منذ فترة طويلة

In the heart of a stone, it was born long ago . . .

Lughayza is an Arabic word you won't need on your next trip to Iran, unless you nurse a fervid interest in field mice. The word applies to that animal's burrow, a maze of tunnels radiating from a central pocket, the easier for the mouse to flee its predators.

Lughaz, the root, means deviating, or turning something away from a straight path. A close match in English is 'delirium', which stems

Walking stick [Ukraine]

from *de lira*, or 'off the furrow', a daydreaming ploughman leaving the straight and narrow.

Keeping things curly, *lughaz* is also the Arabic word for riddle, as the courtly poets of Persia, a millennium back, had an aversion to stating the obvious. In old Iraq a jar of beer could never just be a jar of beer, not if the poets had their say. Their passion was for metaphor. Even better, a stretched metaphor, almost as long as the name of the poet responsible for this next piece of wordplay. I refer to the image-master Abū Yaḥyā Ṭāhir b. Fazl b. Muhammad b. Muhtāj, who converted his foaming lager into a lover around AD992:

> *A belle with a dark complexion and a small mouth*
> *who increases the joy of young and old.*
> *If you make her naked by taking the veil from her head*
> *she will be enraged, throwing froth from her mouth.*
> *If you desire to give her kisses*
> *she will laugh and make you cry.*

Cheers to that—a sensuous homage to Heineken. Though I ruined the surprise by telling you the answer in advance. Persian poets would rather tantalise you with their verses, seduce you down false paths until the light of realisation flickers. That insight might take time—a few seconds, perhaps several minutes. There was no rush. Muhtāj and his brethren took pleasure in composing long and convoluted poems, as tangled as the field mouse's maze.

Come the eleventh century, the poems would only lengthen and turn more riddly. The shift was signalled by the word *chīst-ān* (what is it) serving as the opener. Here's one I prepared earlier:

> *What is it that has neither trousers nor shirt?*
> *Yet you can place on her lap whatever you wish;*
> *Although she has no tongue, she speaks the truth,*
> *With a dragon, a scorpion upon her neck.*

The answer is a pair of scales. Though for all my queries I still can't confirm what the dragon and scorpion are doing there.

What does a mother-fixated architect suffer?

Nevertheless, as the century rolled on, the scales tipped in favour of the extended form, the court's chosen poets amusing sultans with a series of veiled metaphors. And when I say extended, I mean harem girls had only seven veils; the new-wave *lughayza* might own eighteen verses, each verse a different analogy, or a new facet of the same analogy.

Despite the excess side-trips, the answer might still remain a mystery, the poet keeping shtum until the sultan had lodged his guess. Though at least the potentate had a fighting chance, since the answer was often counted among the ruler's own possessions, or perhaps a quality he displayed. In 20 lines, say, Abū 'Umar 'Uthmān b. 'Umar Mukhtārī Ghaznavī made a riddle of the king's ambition, ending with the couplet:

> *Just as the sun leaves its traces in gold,*
> *The traces of him are found in the sun.*

Over the top? You bet. But the fawning was crucial to a poet's livelihood. Flattery in fact was a form of life insurance in Persia, keeping your head attached to your neck, or your sorry self from the jailhouse.

Unless you happened to be a poet facing conspiracy charges, like Mas'ūd Sa'd Salmān. The poor sod spent 20 years behind bars, earning the nickname of the 'prison poet'. Thankfully his verse-mongering shortened his sentence, though I'm prepared to cancel his parole altogether, thanks to a 34-verse headache he created. The poem is loaded with just as many metaphors, generous to the point that nobody can nail the answer, not even the Sultan Mahmūd, who supposedly had some personal link to the solution. Most literary detectives suspect that the sultan's sword fits the bill. Yet a rival camp is convinced by fire.

To save a tree I won't reproduce the *lughaz* in full. Instead, let me salvage a few lines that embody the ambiguity. That way, royal reader, you can choose which topic your private poet is outlining—the fire or the sword:

> . . . *in the heart of a stone, it was born long ago.*
> . . . *sometimes it is a ruby like the purple wine.*
> . . . *sometimes it is yellow, like the saffron flag.*

Edifice complex

It does not reveal its form to the touch.
. . . it is the essence of power . . . it is the essence of life.
If you offer it black stone in barter, it gives you red jewels in return . . .

What's your verdict, sire? Are the red jewels the blood of victims, or the flames dancing on coal? Is the heart of stone a flint's spark, or a sword's ore? Treat each metaphor with care, as it's liable to cut. Or burn.

Who whittles light sabres?

Uncle Jedi

War & Peace

*A few pages short of the Tolstoy version, this War & Peace
toys with conflict on the colonial and domestic fronts.*

*The hard-won truces, too, celebrating a Nobel Prize
winner, skipping games and a banana tree.*

⌐ 61 ⌐

Let us look at it quite closely,
'tis a very ugly word ...

'Horrible news from India: massacre of Europeans at Delhi, and mutiny. I have no apprehensions for our Indian empire; but this is a frightful event. Home; but had no heart to work. I will not try at present.'

Thomas Babington Macaulay wrote these words in his journal back in 1857. The Delhi killings he cited were savage, the bloodshed spilling across India. Clashes erupted in Uttar Pradesh up north, Bihar on the Ganges—nowhere seemed safe from the sepoys.

Macaulay—a poet and historian—'had no heart to work' because the sepoys were the men he'd helped to train as secretary of war 20 years beforehand, young Indians groomed to defend the Raj, not turn against it.

The mutiny only worsened as the year wore on. English men and women and their children were bludgeoned down in Calcutta markets. Knives flashed at Sunday sermons. The death toll multiplied.

And for what? The impetus would have seemed ludicrous if the situation wasn't so dire. The rub was the Enfield rifle, the British gun entrusted to the natives. To fire the damn thing, the sepoy had to bite open the cartridge, freeing the powder to pour into the chamber, and guess what grease coated the cartridge? Tallow. Beef fat. Heresy for a Hindu. So widespread violence and manslaughter was somehow the solution.

The stink first arose in Dum Dum, the munitions factory near Calcutta where the hollow-point bullet would come to be made. Radical clerics declared the grease a blasphemous sacrament, their ruling causing the senseless deaths that followed, the riots and the sieges.

A child's porridge is delicious.

Thirteen months. That's how long the uprising lasted. The body count was incalculable. The battle of Cawnpore alone reached 100,000, according to some estimates, the vast majority on the Indian side.

By the time the mutiny was quelled, Macaulay himself was close to death. He'd only last another six months, falling to a coronary in 1859, but not before the poet penned a riddle in lament of the colony he'd left behind. The verse is long, but to give you a meat-free taste of Lord Macaulay's Last Riddle, as it's known, here is the opening:

> *Let us look at it quite closely,*
> *'Tis a very ugly word,*
> *And one that makes one shudder*
> *Whenever it is heard.*

With ten more quatrains to follow, the riddle is too lengthy to reproduce, though the answer is worth revealing. As a clue, this ugly word has twelve letters, the marriage of two words that coalesced during the 1300s. For a bonus hint, the answer appears in this chapter's opening page lines, a crime lying central to Macaulay's dirge. One more verse:

> *But only see the consequence!*
> *That's all need be done*
> *To change this mass of sadness*
> *To unmitigated fun.*

The ugly word is manslaughter, a compound almost Joycean in its architecture. One split betrays the source—man/slaughter. Yet were the knife to fall a letter later, then the outcome is man's laughter, or unmitigated fun. The contrast is painful.

Among his last papers, Macaulay begged his readers to embrace the kinder of the two divisions, for:

> *It clears off swords and pistols*
> *Revolvers, bowie-knives,*
> *And all the horrid weapons*
> *By which men lose their lives;*
> *It wakens holier voices—*

Sleep [Swahili]

And now joyfully is heard
The native sound of gladness
Compressed into one word!
Yes! Four and eight, my friends!
Let that be yours and mine,
Though all the hosts of demons
Rejoice in three and nine.

⊐ 62 ⊏

Truly he'll see war

Remember that clumsy anagram from 1806—RED NUTS AND GIN? If not, then have a second peek at Chapter 42 and you'll recall the answer to be UNDERSTANDING, a laboured anagram that bears no connection to its source. Of course, it's a different ball of wax if you craft the same 13 letters into a more fitting phrase, reflecting the answer. Far more satisfying might be: STUNNING DREAD. Or: TURN AND DESIGN. Not quite there, but at least the reshuffle aspires to prefigure the answer.

That trend strengthened deeper into the nineteenth century, random jumbles becoming cognate anagrams. Cognate here means related, such as Christianity hiding in the new-wave sample: IT'S IN CHARITY. This stylish effort stemmed from 1826, two decades after those awkward red nuts cropped up in a puzzle book. Of course, cognate anagrams existed prior to 1800. It doesn't take Shakespeare to spot the ripeness of LUST in SLUT, or the clandestine twins of ANGERED and ENRAGED. Likewise, James I of England, otherwise known as JAMES STUART, was blended by a courtier in the early 1600s to reveal A JUST MASTER, which might well have earned a dukedom, if not a niche in the Anagram Hall of Fame.

Technically, yes, the anagram recipe is not a riddle in the strictest sense, yet riddle books capture the groundswell best. The day that TELEGRAPH was converted into GREAT HELP was the moment the

How do you spell mousetrap in three letters?

Masquerade mixtures—what are the single-word answers?

1. THE WAR
2. THE LAW
3. TO LOVE RUIN
4. TIS YE GOVERN
5. O SOUR HOPE
6. BEST IN PRAYERS
7. THERE WE SAT
8. SPARE HIM NOT

message was sent to future puzzle-makers. Call it a commandment: Thou shalt make thy mixes reflect their roots. Any other option was fool's gold.

By far the richest vein of cognate gems lay in a compendium from *The Masquerade* magazine published in 1826. Other samples may well predate this cognate batch, but *The Masquerade* collection was the earliest lot my sleuthing has uncovered. Little else exists of this magazine—a British annual of 'enigmas, logogriphs, charades, rebuses, queries and transpositions'.

No mention of anagrams, you'll notice, which went by the alias of transpositions. Single words were the common target, turning ENIGMATICAL into MAGIC IN TALE. Though now and then a notable name would enter the grinder, such as George Tierney, a Whig politician of the era with several Treasury roles while in power. This last aspect was reflected in the *Masquerade* transposition of his surname: I RENT YE.

Head and shoulders above Tierney, both in stature and mixture, was the Duke of Wellington. As the hero of Waterloo, the veteran

ANSWERS—1. Wreath 2. Wealth 3. Revolution 4. Sovereignty 5. Poorhouse 6. Presbyterians (and not Britney Spears!) 7. Sweetheart 8. Misanthrope

commander and former prime minister (1828–30) inspired a statue in Park Lane, a Tennyson ode, a thousand pub shingles and his own cognate anagram. At least his birth name did, Arthur Wellesley: TRULY HE'LL SEE WAR.

⌐ 63 ⌐

E rau lewe rua ndau vala tiko ng aka senga ni mundu . . .

A war is raging in Fiji as you read this sentence, one that began centuries back and shows no sign of relenting. Translated, the chapter's heading says as much:

There are two always fighting, their strife never ending . . .

Always and never—the riddle doesn't lie.

Why else would museum types go to such lengths to collect riddles, making trips to other latitudes to souvenir the quips and proverbs? For dinner parties, sure, but also for insights into the culture that crafted them. Humour is just one element on show. Any nation's riddle hoard can also convey how that civilisation sees the world, how they live, how they think. Fiji is a neat example, where one country's riddles testify the local faith and diet, dress and weather, trade and flora—and its warfare.

On a map, Tonga seems too remote for a Fijian canoe to reach. My thumbnail proposes the gap to be 800 kilometres, roughly the distance between Sydney and Melbourne, a fickle ocean intervening rather than a four-lane highway.

No sweat. Fijians have been visiting their neighbour for centuries, and we don't need Thor Heyerdahl to confirm that truth. All we need are riddles:

Au kakasivi tu nga ka yatho ki Tonga. *(I spit all the way to Tonga.)*
Ai nima *(The baler)*

What do Eskimo detectives rely on?

Au tutu thake tu nga ka yatho ki Tonga. *(I stand all the way to Tonga.)*

Ai vana *(The mast)*

Au suasua tu nga ka yatho ki Tonga. *(I am wet all the way to Tonga.)*

A uli *(The rudder)*

Travel brochures declare Fiji to be one idyllic destination, an island chain of coconut palms and tranquil beaches. That's the hype at least, what the ads try preaching. But turn to riddles and you'll see how the locals really pass their days and nights. Read between the punchlines and you'll sample the beauty and the drudgery, the colours and the seasons.

Better than brochures, a riddle acts as a snorkel, allowing you to dive below the surface of a culture, to float across the habitat and see the details up close. You can handle the hermit crabs (*I enter a house and run away*) and the ocean sponges (*I squeeze it in my hand and it's hidden*) without any risk of disturbing the environment. Though one Fijian riddle does the disturbing all on its own, presenting a living cowrie shell, as well as the missionary imprint on the islands. In English, the riddle goes this way:

A Catholic priest in a long black coat. When we go to see him he takes off his coat.
(The white cowrie shell)

For days I struggled to make the link, until I swapped my breathing tube for YouTube. There you can see how the sea snail inside the cowrie shell quickly retracts when a diver's shadow falls across the reef. In a flash, in a riddle, the animal goes from rubbery-black to cotton-white, just like a cleric shucking his vestments.

The reef, in fact, is where one war rages in Fiji. The waves edging the atoll are described as a 'band of warriors that fight day and night'. Tough for canoes to cross, but this is not the strife that opened proceedings. Closer to home, on terra firma, the machetes are flashing in a fight for survival. Here's the riddle in full:

There are two always fighting, their strife never ending. One of them gets the better of the other for a long while. But at last there comes a day when he falls asleep. As he lies sleeping his blanket is very thick and heavy. Then comes his enemy whom he used to conquer and seats himself upon him and oppresses him and triumphs over him.

Beware: if you find beheading offensive, then look away now. The war in question is hot and sweaty, with occasional blood, but only if the homeowner's clumsy. You know both opponents well, though under the Fijian sun the 'enemy' is ten times more potent, for the war is pitched between man and the island's *nyi* grass. Week in, week out, a farmer must wage war against the weed or stand the risk of seeing his crop overrun. The fight is backbreaking, unrelenting, the bush-knife's swish a constant pulse. Until one day the man will breathe his last. He'll fall asleep, as the riddle predicted, blanketed by the earth—and that damned *nyi* grass, his unsleeping nemesis, will hold dominion over his grave.

⌐ 64 ⌐

¿Por qué verdaderamente ganó Rigoberta el premio Nobel?

Why did Rigoberta really win the Nobel Prize?

When Pedro de Alvarado rode his horse into Guatemala, his first skirmish was against the Quiché nation. His second skirmish, too. Damn, the conquistador never really stopped skirmishing against those defiant Mayans, a fearsome people who knew the jungle backwards.

Eventually, by weight of numbers and musketry, the Spaniard won the day. A truce was struck, the hatchet buried. Only for Alvarado to double-cross the Quicheans, burning their leaders alive and razing their city of Quetzaltenango to the dirt.

Jouez-vous Nintendo?

More recent history suggests old habits die hard in this neck of the woods. Ever since the Spanish invasion, harmony has been hard to find, the country pitched in numerous wars against itself. Over time, conquistadors traded places with plutocrats. Colonisers became plantation owners, as the Mayans continued to suffer at the hands of those in power. From 1960 onward, the military kept the Quiché people under the cosh. In true warrior style, the Mayans pushed back, amassing a guerrilla force to counter the oppression with sabotage and surprise raids. The violence intensified. Villages burned, as the spectre of genocide grew realer by the day, with some 200,000 Mayans killed during a decade of shame, plus more than a million displaced.

In part we know these things due to a coffee worker named Rigoberta Menchú Tum. Just 23 years old, this Quiché woman fled her mountain home for Mexico. The year was 1982, her nation's darkest in terms of body count. By then, Rigoberta's own father had been killed by security forces in the capital, Guatemala City. She'd also lost her mother, and a brother, both having been tortured before meeting brutal ends.

Imagine Rigoberta's despair. The boiling injustice. Her story needed telling, but she lacked sufficient schooling to find her voice, shape her sentences. Enter Elizabeth Burgos, a Venezuelan who'd married into French academia. (Her husband at the time was cultural philosopher Régis Debray.) Together, over many meetings and patient interviews, the two women compiled a book, as Rigoberta remembered and Elizabeth wrote. More than a book, this ghosted memoir would serve as a tourniquet to stanch the republic's blood.

Slowly, it must be said. Disgrace might travel quickly, but peace often crawls. Fourteen years elapsed from the time *I, Rigoberta Menchú* made the shelves until 1996, when the UN Security Council reached a shaky accord in Mexico's neighbour. During that time—in 1992—Rigoberta Menchú won the Nobel Peace Prize, quite a feat for an under-schooled coffee harvester orphaned by the war around her.

The honour was one more step towards Guatemalan harmony. It's hard to ignore a global award, or the sight of a rainbow-wrapped

Quichean taking the podium in Oslo, dedicating her prize to her slaughtered compatriots.

Back in Guatemala, the award's impact is most visible in riddles arising from the period, little barbs of jealousy and suspicion forged by the ruling elite. When your rival gains the upper hand, you strive to bring them down. Whatever it takes: a counterblow, false charges. Or you slander them in the form of jokes, the kind crafted in municipal halls and haciendas across the capital.

American anthropologist Diane M. Nelson catalogues the snipes with grim efficiency. Each riddle a small grenade, Nelson recorded the corpus in her own civil war account, *A Finger in the Wound: Body politics in quincentennial Guatemala*. The so-called jokes fill an entire appendix, throwing mud at Menchú's looks and sexuality, her morals and her sloppy Spanish, her fame and her perceived commercialisation. Even her traditional costume copped a dressing-down:

> ¿Por qué verdaderamente ganó Rigoberta el premio Nobel?
> *Why did Rigoberta really win the Nobel Prize?*

You can taste the sour grapes from here, the whiny cynicism implicit in *really*.

Forget the laureate's courage. Her grievous losses. Her enforced exile. According to the riddle, Rigoberta won the Nobel Peace Prize because *ya es una indita muy desenvuelta*. That is, because she's a little Indian woman who's very articulate.

On the surface, the rejoinder seems a compliment. But enemies are seldom disposed to dish out flattery. The catch lies in the wordplay, since *desenvuelta* also means unwrapped, a swipe at the wraparound Mayan skirt that requires a belt to cinch. Hence *envuelta*, or girt, is Guatemalan slang for an indigenous woman, just as in English anorak denotes a trainspotter, or bluestocking a female intellectual. In one pun, splicing eloquence with looseness, Rigoberta Menchú is discredited. The aspersion aims to cheapen the prize, as if her silver tongue was her only saving grace, as well as to suggest that she's dropped her Mayan-ness to reach the limelight. Hurtful words, but a Quichean woman with warrior blood has suffered far worse in her time.

Two sisters: one black, one white

⊒ 65 ⊑

Pana visu vingi lakini mpini mmoja tu

There are many knives but only one handle

When it rains in Zanzibar, it pours. Wet season, or *masika*, can stretch from March to May, whipping the Indian Ocean into a surge, closing roads and sending locals to huddle under noisy roofs with a big pile of little to do.

Cue the cry of '*Kitendawili?*' Which literally means 'Riddle?', but more closely translates as 'Who's up for a war of wits?' Old English riddles display a matching challenge in their singsong prelude of riddle-me-ree. '*Tega!*' goes the African chorus. 'Go ahead', in the dictionary, but streetwise is the phrase 'Bring it on!'

And on it's brought. Swahili is vivid with riddles, most abiding by the African style of fractured metaphors. As the wind wallops our tin roof, what say we stick to riddles regarding nature?

Namsikia saa zote lakini simwoni. *(I hear him all the time, but I don't see him.)*
Upepo *(Wind)*

Huwafanya watu wote walie. *(It makes all the people cry.)*
Moshi *(Smoke)*

Couched in the call-and-response mode, the Tega gang try to decipher the statement. If the *kitendawili* is old hat, like those first two, then the answer might be recited before the riddle can be fully said. However, if the challenger is worth his salt, asking riddles from a fresher stash, then a peculiar side-trip emerges. Let's play the game for real:

ME: *Pana visu vingi lakini mpini mmoja tu.* (There are many knives but only one handle.)
YOU: *Um . . . er . . . nakupe mji?* (Um . . . er . . . can I give you a city?)
ME: *Ndiyo.* (Yep.)
YOU: Paris.

Day and night [Caribbean]

Zanzibar sidebar

Kitendawili changu cha ajabu kina matone ya dhahabu.
(My wonderful riddle is adorned with spots of gold.)
Qurani Takatifu *(The Holy Koran)*

Uwanja wa mpira mweupe, wachezaji wanyekundu.
(A white soccer field, red soccer players.)
Mchele na maharage *(Rice and beans)*

Mzungu amejishika kiunoni.
(A European whose hand is on his waist.)
Kikombe *(Teacup)*

Nyumba yangu ndogo, wanaishi watu wengi.
(My house is small, many people live there.)
Kibiriti *(Matchbox)*

Mashetani wangu ruahani, akikugusa, huponi.
(My devils, if they touch you, you won't live.)
Ukimwe *(AIDS)*

ME (channelling English all of a sudden): So I went to see the Mona Lisa, who looked sad. Then I tried to climb the Eiffel Tower but the line was too long. Time for coffee instead. But in Paris, if you want a coffee, you have to order food as well. The waiters are super fussy. The cheapest food on the menu was toast—but not French toast—or banana bread or a puffy little cake . . . you know . . . I'm trying to remember—a madeleine.

Feels a million miles from Zanzibar, but this is how things roll in Mangapwani. The guesser can buy some thinking time by naming a city, the springboard for the riddler to spin a story. There's a second purpose, too, if your antennas were attuned. A clue to the riddle's answer can often be smuggled into the follow-up story, just as I've done with you, fabricating my time in Paris. Now can you tell me

What's brown and sounds like a bell?

what has many knives but only one handle? Consult that menu again: it's a bunch of bananas.

The fresher the riddle, the more likely the guesser will be saying Nairobi, or Munich, or Rio de Janeiro, anything to stall defeat. Riddlers in Zanzibar know this. They enter the fray with story ideas to match their new material, a made-up travelogue for every tricky answer. With that inbuilt dynamic, riddles are flourishing in Stone Town, the nickname for Zanzibar City, the topics evolving briskly from wind and smoke (the archaic answers) to the more contemporary kind, as the riddle box shows. Just as well, really. You'd hate to finish a *kitendawili* battle with a wet May still to go.

⌐ 66 ⌐

Why is the mother weak?

If a Masai warrior is waving a clump of grass, he's seeking peace. Kids employ the tactic in games too. Locked in a wrestle, a mock-battle, a child will grab grass as their white flag.

The reason relates to the food chain. Ample grass suggests a generous season. Good supply spells good fodder for the animals that the Masai hunt—the zebra and antelope—as well as the cattle they own. Historically it's cattle that set the Masai apart. Many other tribes in Kenya and Tanzania fall under the Dorobo umbrella, where Dorobo is based on the Masai word *il-tóróbò* (the hunters—or those without cattle).

This livestock love is enshrined in proverbs too. There's a timeworn saying in Masai culture that 'A cow is as good as a man'. Another version claims, 'One cow resembles a man's head.' In plainer English the adage suggests that a man will live well, find a wife and have children, should he care for his animals.

Regardless of the number of animals he owns, a Masai man will know each cow by name, the herd an extension of his family.

Dung

The animals are only killed when ill or when ceremonies dictate. Before a child can be named, say, living as long as three moons before being accepted by the tribe, a bullock must be slaughtered in the child's honour. Nor will any meat or hide be wasted. Every chink of bone will be reborn as jewellery, or weaponry, or decoration within the *kraal* (village). Even the blood is drunk, mixed with milk on occasion, concocting a primal thickshake that goes back to the dawn of time.

Cow's blood is deemed a source of strength. So prized is the elixir that a cow can be tapped like a cask, its neck vein nicked by an arrowhead, the flow controlled by a vine wrapped lasso-like above the shoulder. As soon as several litres are drawn the wound is sealed with clay, and the beast returned to the herd, a tad anaemic but intact.

More recently, owing to drought and general shifts in diet, the custom has waned. Though the tradition survives in riddling if you take the time to look. The Masai have two riddle styles. The first is playful, verging on silly, such as this familiar teaser:

Kidung' ang'ata bkira aare nimiking'amaro.
The two of us cross the wilderness without talking to each other.

The answer is as old as mankind, with shadow-selves thriving in folklore.

When a Masai speaker is asking the frivolous kind of riddle, he will say, *'Oyiote?'* ('Are you ready?'), his listeners obliged to answer, *'Ee-wuo'* ('It has come'). However, when introducing a thornier challenge, a riddle tapping into tribal knowledge, the asker will say, *'Ira ng'en?'* ('Are you clever?'), whereby a simple yes from the audience is a sign to continue. Set up like so, an asker may try:

Why is the mother weak?

Before you glimpsed the Masai *kraal*, you might have floundered to handle such a question. Mothers worldwide could be weary for reasons of irascible kids, lousy sleep, an overload of chores. All of which could apply to Masai mums, yet now you're likely suspicious of a more cultural cause. Go with that hunch. Of course, if you can't imagine the answer,

What do you do with a dead chemist?

Masai was saying

I have many warriors, and one goes out to look after the hut.
Rafters of a hut

What are my warriors like when they stand in a circle, and one cannot
*   see which is the first and which the last?*
The pegs being used to stretch a skin

When your mother leaves her hut, what is seen to be issuing from
*   her garments?*
The leg of her child (in a sling across her back)

What escapes the fire?
A bare spot on which no grass grows

I have two skins—one to lie on, and the other to cover myself with.
*   What are they?*
The bare ground and the sky

then go outside and grab a fistful of grass. Or maybe you're prepared
to take a punt:

> *Because she did not catch the blood in her gourd*

Reasons for this deficit in the mum's diet can range from simple (she
was too engulfed in her children to attend the ritual) to complex (the
village's hierarchy of blood-drinking). Widowhood is another maybe,
with the single mother dependent on the tribe's generosity when it
comes to blood rations. Naturally we'd need the riddle's context for
the answer to be fully fleshed out, in every gory detail, but for now
let's put mum's weakness down to a general shortage of glycoproteins
and plasma enzymes.

⏏ 67 ⏗

Which do you prefer: the death of the moon, or the death of a banana tree?

One day a courtier came to a hut to collect a debt. A boy in tattered clothes answered the door. 'Where is your father?' asked the man.

'He's out looking for money,' said the boy. 'If he sees a butterfly, he'll go to your house. If he doesn't see one, he won't. Success goes to the swift.'

'Where is your mother?' the courtier tried.

'My mother is looking for a thousand captives.'

'Your eldest brother?'

'He's doing a job that never ends.'

'So where is your other brother?'

'He's collecting grass that's been thrown away.'

'So then, what are *you* doing?'

'I'm standing up; I'm making something; I'm amusing myself; and what I've made doesn't suit me anymore.'

By this stage the courtier was ropable. Sick of this peasant talking in circles, he marched the brat to see King Andriambohoemanana, accusing the boy and his family of dishonour.

To reach a considered verdict, Andriambohoemanana asked the young man to explain his answers, the better to determine whether they were insults.

The boy was only too happy to recount the conversation. 'I said my father was looking for money, which can be hard to catch, just like the butterfly.'

The king and courtier exchanged glances.

The boy continued, 'Meanwhile my mother was looking for a thousand captives, which we know are the many grains of rice she gathers, or the roots of the manioc.

What's heavy, yet not backwards?

'As for my older brother, doing a job that never ends, this is the minding of cattle, since our grandparents did this, and our parents, and our children will do the same when their turn comes.'

The boy had Andriambohoemanana's full attention. The child had wisdom beyond his years, plus the eloquence to match.

'My other brother was collecting straw for burning—the grass you lose the moment the fuel catches alight. As for me, I was modelling with clay when the courtier called, amusing myself, shaping the clay into figures that soon lost my interest when they were done.'

Rather than punish the boy, the king paid the father's debt, and retained the young man in his entourage, for riddle-speech was highly prized in Madagascar. So it was, in one swoop, that the *indevo* (peasant or slave) became *ondevohova* (the servant of nobles). And if that sounds like a modest promotion, then consider the mercurial climb to follow, a story to break the cycle of endless cattle-minding. As master of metaphor, the boy soon presided over the entourage, earning the king's trust as *mpikabary*—or speechwriter.

The legend hails from the Betsileo, a highland people of Madagascar, or Malagasy as the nation was once known. Shaped like a guitar, off eastern Africa, the island is a living blend of Bantu and Asian heritage, a proud hybrid race distinct from mainland Africa. You see that defiance borne out in the Betsileo people. Translated, the tribe's name means 'the many invincible ones', an allusion to the people's resilience in the face of numerous raids by rival clans and Europeans alike. The peasant boy's tale underpins the sentiment, a parable celebrating grass-roots wisdom, all the more when such savvy can be packaged into fractured poetry, or riddle-speak, known as *ankamantatra*.

Even the highland's first king was nicknamed Mpatino, or Word-Cutter. If you could wrangle language, then your powers didn't end there. As described in Lee Haring's stellar 1985 essay on the island's folklore, appearing in *The Journal of American Folklore*, many children's games revolved around clever speech in the native Malagasy tongue. One enacts a funeral, a cicada shell the deceased. With great fanfare, the shell is buried, the cue for each child to deliver a eulogy of *hainteny* (metaphor-language) and *ankamantatra*, the winner being the finest orator.

To pigeonhole the Madagascan riddles into neat categories is to attempt to hug my grandmother's bellowing ox—the land's metaphor for a waterfall. Water, meanwhile, can be cut without wound, the paradox a common feature of the local mind-games. The eye, for instance, is God's little lake, although you can't swim in it. And getting ghoulish for a moment, a Madagascan bedstead is the dead that carries the living, where the felled timber upholds a felled sleeper.

Death, in fact, pervades another suite of riddles, the genre known as *safidy*, or choice riddles. Also called dilemma tales, the style is popular across mainland Africa too, but trust the Madagascans to be succinct:

Which do you prefer: an elegant cane or a muddy cudgel?

Temptation may steer you to choose the cane, yet the wiser response is the cudgel, as the instruments are metaphors invoking two animals: the notched tail of a rat, and the spattered oxtail. Now that you know the booby-trap:

Which do you prefer, little eyes in the rocks or big eyes in the grass?

Again, the pitfall is A. Those little eyes belong to the island's wildcat, perhaps the *falanouc*, or small-toothed civet, while the ox is your friend in B.

Winding back the folklore clock, reverting to a time before the first king, there was a *safidy* central to man's existence. Or more specifically, about how death came to be part of life. In a parallel Eden, so goes the Madagascan myth, the world's first man and woman were faced with a cosmic riddle, when God invited the couple to make a choice:

Which do you prefer: the death of the moon, or the death of a banana tree?

Choose wisely, as the fate of humanity rests on your decision. The riddle is a watershed moment in the course of creation, a neck riddle with a twist. The humans, being humans, failed to grasp the celestial metaphor, pleading with God to illuminate the options. God was gracious enough to oblige. Yet before he does, pick a death, either death . . .

Have you made your decision? Are you locked in? Here's the divine footnote from the tale's almighty himself: the moon dies every

It barks in the mountains and is silent at home.

Madagascan medley

Buried but not rotten.
Hair

God's stick has water in its stomach.
Sugar cane

Old man leaning on the wall.
Boiled rice that sticks to a pot's sides

When the little one comes, the great one removes its hat.
Water pot (when a cup scoops from the household water pot, the
    lid must be removed)

Its mother says, 'Let us spread out our hands,' but the children say,
    'Let us curl up our fists.'
The fern (where the mature plant has outspread fronds, while the
    young shoots are furled)

month, yet still continues its existence, returning to life after a few
days. By contrast, a lopped banana tree stays dead, as the bedstead
riddle teaches us, though the tree perpetuates its species via the seeds
the harvester keeps.

The couple considered their choice, and still preferred the tree
metaphor, taken by the lure of furthering their kind. Thus we live and
die—both here and in faraway Madagascar. Wise or otherwise, the
choice underlines the importance of children as much as riddles, the joy
of family the worthy price of mortality.

Axe [Argentina]

⊏⅃ 68 ⅃⊐

You cannot walk without me, yet you grease your body and forget me ...

Marahgoo is a devil who lives near the Pilliga waterhole. He wears swan feathers in his hair and carries a pouch of drink he wants you to try. Whatever you do, don't.

Gwaibooyanbooyan, on the other hand, is the hairless one who lives in the scrub. Given half a chance, he'll jump from the shadows and tear your flesh to ribbons.

The legends hail from the Euahlayi people of northern New South Wales. Their language is Gamilaraay—the source of galah and bindi-eye. Their traditions were first recorded for posterity by a grazier called Katie Langloh Parker in the early 1900s.

Parker moved to the district in 1879. She and her husband took up ownership of Bangate station on the Narran River, near Walgett, the heart of Euahlayi country. The newlywed wife soon grew fascinated by the local Aboriginal people. The affinity was forged when she was a child, growing up on the Darling River, back when she was saved from drowning by a young indigenous girl. The incident was a spur that steered the course of Katie's life, the impetus to learn Gamilaraay and slowly win the trust of the Euahlayi.

Like no other white woman before, Parker was immersed in tribal life. She joined hunting trips, eavesdropped on songs, dug for mussels with her toes. She watched the *wirreenun* (or medicine man) press firesticks on snake bites. She learnt about the *muggil*, a stone knife, and the *bubberah*, or boomerang, cut from the swamp oak. Such details were captured in *The Euahlayi Tribe*, Parker's 1905 bestseller, along with a snatch of children's verse:

> *Gheerlayi ghilayer*
> *Wahl munnoomerhdayer,*
> *Wahl mooroobahgoo,*

What do liars do after death?

Yelgyayerdayer deermuldayer,
Gheerlayi ghilayer.

Kind be,
Do not steal;
Do not touch what to another belongs,
Leave all such alone.
Kind be.

Gamilaraay was a musical language. (It still is, though sadly its speakers
have dwindled to dozens in recent years.) Parker heard the music in
the bird names—from the *baaldharraharra* (spur-winged plover) to the
wululuu (whistling duck)—as well as in the dynamic skipping games, or
brambahl, the old men loved: 'They had a long rope, a man at each end
to swing it. When it is in full swing, in goes the skipper. After skipping
in an ordinary way for a few rounds, he begins the variations, which
consist, among other things, of his taking thorns out of his feet, digging
as if for larvae of ants, digging yams, grinding grass seed, jumping like a
frog . . . striking an attitude as if looking for something in the distance,
running out, snatching up a child, and skipping with it in his arms . . .'

Rhythm and play were touchstones of Euahlayi life. Some songs
taught morals, others parried evil spirits. A third category was a trap,
a piece of Gamilaraay wordplay designed to snare the lazy thinker.
This singsong game was known as *ghiribul*, or riddle.

'Most of these *ghiribul* are not translatable,' Parker wrote, 'being
little songs describing the things to be guessed, whose peculiarities
the singer acts as he sings—a sort of one-man show, pantomime in
miniature, with a riddle running through it.' Minus music and actions,
here's a sample:

> *You cannot walk without me, yet you grease your body and forget me,*
>   *and let me crack. Even though you could neither walk nor run*
>   *without me. Who says that?*

Feet, you may suspect, and rightly so—it's impossible to walk without
them after all. Yet why the grease? Where does it come from, and why
the body rub in the first place? That was my reaction on first reading.
Indeed, the foot is the right area of anatomy, but can you guess the

They lie still

reason for the grease? I was lost, until I read Chapter XIV of Parker's memoir, describing how the Euahlayi loved to swim in summer, their bodies brushed as infants with the feather of the *goomble-guddon* (or bustard) for spiritual protection in the water. The Narran River was the local pool, the clay of its banks a surrogate soap the swimmers rubbed on their skin. Come winter, however, the billabong was too cold for a dip. Instead of bathing, they cooked fish and smeared the flesh's grease all over their bodies. Well, almost all over. The grease lent the body a healthy lustre, yet rubbing the soles must have seemed futile, the extra coating only helping to attract muck underfoot. Besides, the very act of walking would only undo your work, and waste a prized commodity. A sensible decision in the end, not one Parker verifies, but the truth of the age-old matter lies in a singsong *ghiribul*.

Ghiribul glimpses (from *The Euahlayi Tribe*, 1905)

What is it that says to the floodwaters, 'I am too strong for you; you cannot push me back'?
The cod

What is it that says, 'You cannot help yourself; you will have to go and let me take your place; you cannot stay when I come'?
The grey hairs in a man's beard to the black ones

I am not water, yet all who are thirsty, seeing me, come toward me to drink, though I am no liquid.
A mirage

What is it that goes along the creek, across the creek, underneath it, and along it again, and yet has left neither side?
The yellow-flowering creeping water-weed

'Here I am, just in front of you. I can't move; but if you kick me, I will knock you down, though I will not move to do it.' Who says this?
A stump that anyone falls over

My cow in Manila. You can hear her moo.

⊐ 69 ⊏

Fin hrazef vitishera sorfoon?

What horse grows out of the ground?

Khal was the first seed to be planted, a word meaning chieftain or king. Next came *khalasar*, a horde loyal to the *khal*, each warrior prepared to give their life in battle. A few paragraphs later was *arakh*, a crescent-shaped sword similar to a scimitar, followed by the race's word for queen: *khaleesi*.

Alias Emilia Clarke, the blonde sylph known to every adolescent boy who watches *Game of Thrones*, and a horde of middle-aged men, come to that. New American parents have likewise been smitten by the queen, Khaleesi outstripping Imogen and Susannah in the baby-naming stakes, according to social security data released in 2014.

Such is the impact of the HBO series, first aired in 2011. The show is based on *A Song of Ice and Fire* by George R.R. Martin, the American Tolkien, as dubbed by *Time* magazine. A fitting mantle, given the author's gift for imaginary kingdoms, on top of his knack for inventing a language. Where Tolkien engineered Elvish (among others) for his Middle Earth sagas, Martin created Dothraki.

A smidgeon, mind you. The Dothraki people, a fierce race of horse-loving nomads, are just one piece in the rich Martin jigsaw comprising the Seven Kingdoms of Westeros. Thankfully, most realms speak English, compared to the guttural exotica of *rakh* (boy), *maegi* (sorceress) and *hrakkar* (white lion) that Martin sprinkles across Essos, by the Dothraki Sea.

All up, Martin's prose established some 30 new words, the raw material for David J. Peterson to evolve. From a babble of linguists, HBO selected this young Berkeley grad with a gift for phonemes. To extend the Dothraki language, Peterson had to honour the words and grammar already devised by Martin, as well as fashion a dialect that actors could pronounce.

Those rules in mind, Peterson set to work. He strove for a head-initial language, as it's called, where subject-verb-object was the default grammar

Thunder [Philippines]

pattern. He considered Turkish and Estonian, tested out Russian and Swahili; he dabbled in Inuktitut—the native tongue of Arctic Canada. Ultimately he wove together all five, creating a language that sounds like Arabic (to non-Arabic speakers), and has no word for please.

Because that was the challenge's other rule—Dothraki-speak needed to reflect Dothraki-think. You don't want to mess with Khal Drogo or his *khalasar*, his *arakhs* kept sharp for a reason. When push comes to shove, the Dothraki aren't big on manners. Flaunting that deficit, the race can brag three words for push, three for pull, and none for follow. What about polite? Nothing. Neat? Uh-uh. Horse? Try ten, give or take, from *qahlan* (palomino) to *manin* (colt).

Look all you like, you won't find a riddle among the 2000 words Peterson has produced since his commission began. Hardly encouraging then, for a riddle-seeker like your author sifting the last two seasons of scripts in the slim hope of finding an example. The lone spurs to keep my search alive were *astilat*, to joke, and *jasat*, to laugh. For all their machismo, it seemed these nomads could appreciate humour.

A riddle therefore seemed possible. Double meanings were on offer. *Rakh*, say, wasn't only boy, but also lamb. Just as *koala* means medicine, suggesting that the syrups of Essos are laced with eucalyptus oil.

Resorting to another formula, a riddle might behead a word like *arakh*, so making *rakh*, and the Dothraki surely had a talent for removing the *nhare* (head) of their enemy. Palindromes existed, too, where *halah* was flower, and *eve* a tail. The same native lexicon also had its share of joke-worthy anagrams, including *loy* (puddle) and *yol* (born). So why couldn't a Dothraki riddle exist? All the tools were in reach, if only the small-screen's favourite warriors had the inclination to apply them.

Or David J. Peterson had cause to consider the detour. With a verb like *astilat* ringing in my ears, I contacted the *khal* of conlanging (the pastime of language construction) to ask whether the Dothraki had the capacity to riddle. Quicker than an *arakh* flash, Peterson replied, 'Wherever there are homonyms and fathers there are riddles (or puns).'

In a world first, for your cultish delectation, here is the eventual wisecrack as composed especially for *Riddledom*. As David warned in his preliminary email, the quip may fall short of knee-slapping, owing

Where was Solomon's Temple?

to the universal elements of kids and dad jokes, but that doesn't make the exclusive pun any less Dothraki:

> Fin hrazef vitishera sorfoon?
> *What horse grows out of the ground?*

Take a bow. Damn it, take a bow and every *khalasar* arrow if you can answer this double-meaning wincer. As a clue, I've already slipped in the solution's antonym—in both languages—halfway through this chapter. That word was *manin*, or colt. Its flipside is *vado*, the filly, also identifying a certain root vegetable, as everyone in Essos (and the Dothraki fan club) would know. Consult your copy of *Living Language Dothraki*, and you'll see *vado* is also the word for turnip.

Why the silence? Quick, before it's too late: tell the *khal* his riddle was *athdavrazar* (excellent) or you'll end up losing your *nhare*.

◲ 70 ◳

lu/gu/sEn/soi/an bE/si/tu/nEn

A hardwood bridge falls like iron

Despite what you may suspect, my Caps Lock key is working fine. You can blame this toggle case on the Dusun people of northern Borneo, not Bill Gates.

The Dusun-Kadazan language depends on the familiar characters of English, streamlined into an alphabet of 22. For some reason, they ditched *c, f, q* and *x*, making a quick fix next to impossible in Sensuron, a small Dusun village within the Malaysian lobe of Sabah.

It's a tiny place, less than 1000 people back in 1960. That's when Ohio-born anthropologist Thomas Rhys Williams spent his time there, observing Dusun riddles and rituals. His findings were recorded in two essays for *The Journal of American Folklore*. The key revelation, setting the Dusun apart from many other first-nation people, was how tightly ritual and riddle were entwined.

On the side of Solomon's head

As we've seen, religion can be fond of riddles. Novelist Henry Miller wrote, 'All true wisdom comes in the form of riddle.' It's not so rare to find the two elements—ritual and riddle—in cahoots. Yet in the jungles of Sabah, the marriage takes an extraordinary form.

In his first essay, Williams drafts a catalogue of Dusun riddles. They can be vivid, such as the depiction of a squalling nursling:

The panther crying as it looks up at the leaking coconut.

They can be playful, too:

A virgin on the far bank of the river, laughing but with her smile barely visible.

The answer is a particular tree called the *pa/ku/di/ta*, which has a leathery green leaf with a white underside. When a breeze blows, these paler facets can ripple, as if the tree was flirting with a smile.

Many of the riddles require that kind of footnoting, as the cultural gap is significant, doubtless even wider in 1960. Another such example:

The ragged edge of the cloth is tangled badly and nobody knows how to join it except the headman, who spends a day unravelling and repairing it.

Dictionaries of the first world prefer fancier terms, things like mediation or arbitration. Not the Dusun. In the lush backwater of Sensuron, breaches in the social fabric called for unravelling and repairing. The answer to the last riddle is brief: one who settles cases at law. Yet the footnote from Williams lends a greater insight: 'When murder happens, the hearts of the people are tangled with emotion at the deed, for it tears apart the good relationships between people. The headman must spend one day putting the bad feelings right again.'

Of all things, riddles come to the rescue. Village life was not always idyllic. In Dusun culture, the simplest territory quarrel could spark a knife fight. Vendettas ran long, as Williams observed, with the demolition of a rival's hut being par for the course. Rice wine was another problem, freely allowed among young teens. Blend the

What pizza did the Buddhist want?

booze with testosterone and young men were prone to *ko,/m/Eus*—a destructive state similar to amok, that other violent word the island gave us.

Perhaps life has changed in 50 years—I can't say. For the record, the one phone-cum-inbox I managed to locate in Sensuron—belonging to a rafflesia plantation—has been out of service for six months. Consequently I'm not too sure how Dusun life has evolved. What I can report, however, is that when civil disputes threatened a village's harmony back in 1960, the headman invoked the power of riddles.

A sitdown court would be arranged, once the dust had settled. The disputants would meet with the chief, along with any other relevant parties. The gathering had the guise of a tribunal, but instead of he-said-versus-she-said, as most marriage quarrels become, the reconciliation was based on wit. No matter the beef—debts or adultery, assault or battery—the gist was riddling:

lu/gu/sEn/soi/an bE/si/tu/nEn.
A hardwood bridge falls like iron.

That's the metaphor, but what's the subject? Time was critical. If the defendant couldn't solve the image in a few moments, he'd be ribbed by the elders. Not just during the assembly, but for days and weeks afterwards, the derision its own kind of punishment.

Williams saw the upside of the ceremony. The riddle-court served as a circuit-breaker, switching the miscreant's focus from recent wrongs to traditional lore. The hardwood bridge that falls like iron, for instance, is a blowpipe's dart. The logic is elegant, as the ideal wood used for bridges is also the stuff of the hunter's projectiles, the darts capable of felling prey in seconds.

More than a diversion, such a riddle emphasised the Dusun tradition, the hunt-and-gather routine of Sabah life. For that was the court's other purpose: to underscore the values and ideals of the community. In some cultures, that might amount to memorising scripture, or collecting litter on the freeway, but in Sensuron the conduit was riddling. Perhaps it still remains that way. I'm optimistic, though less convinced that rafflesia farmer will ever get his phone fixed in time to ask.

One with everything

◲ 71 ◳

Two calves and an ape, they
made their escape ...

People get confused between stationary (standing still) and stationery (pads and pens), and a little book of 1794 is one big reason why. A flimsy thing, *A Whetstone for Dull Wits* holds a special place on the riddle shelf. Its author is the ubiquitous Anon. Likewise the artist who carved the fifteen woodcuts, one for each rhyming riddle.

The cover's woodcut depicts a gentleman in tricorn, reading a book and looking rather bored. Naturally the book can't be the riddle volume, or so the flyleaf reckons:

> Of Merry Books this is the Chief,
> 'Tis as a Purging PILL,
> To carry off all heavy Grief,
> And make you laugh your Fill.

Who said hype was a modern scourge? Though the inscription deserving greater focus is a few inches lower on the flyleaf: 'Printed at Derby, for the Benefit of the Travelling Stationers'.

That statement tells a story. In mediaeval Latin, a *stationarius* was a trader who kept an established stall. 'Station' shares the root: a fixed point along a route for disembarking or swapping horses. Meanwhile a permanent storekeeper was called a stationer, whether he sold pens or cabbages. Most often, however, the term defined a bookseller, someone licensed by a nearby university to flog paper and academic tomes. As a rule, these wares were too heavy to hoof around. It's why the modern swag of A4 reams and inkjet cartridges gets labelled stationery, thanks to some mediaeval retailer who lacked an oxcart big enough to mobilise his merch.

That brief fell to the flying stationer, as he was known, the kind who scurried laneways hawking broadsheets of newish news. Compare this with a travelling stationer who worked the shire in rounds, porting anything from writing paper to hair oil.

An animal eats on a living table.

Trinkets were critical—the pins and candles that cost a pittance but ensured a steady turnover. Whether a stationer was standing still or roaming the streets, he depended on a flow of clientele. One candle could roll into a ladle sale, or Gutenberg's Bible. This need for exchange paved the way for a riddle collection, a pennyworth of witticisms that set a trend in chapbooks.

I should make clear that chap in this context relates to cheap, not the male of the species. Such volumes were often small and simply produced, keeping their cost in check. As such, a chapman did his rounds of the valley, peddling discount bric-a-brac, be that Spanish combs or riddles about animals:

> *Two Calves and an Ape,*
> *They made their Escape,*
> *From one that was worse than a Spright;*
> *They travelled together*
> *In all sorts of Weather,*
> *But often were put in a Plight.*

At least the riddle seems to refer to animals: two calves and an ape. But don't be too presumptuous. Say the trio aloud and you may hear a shift from zoo to you: two calves and an ape. Can you hear the trap? A minor tweak of Gothic typography and the menagerie mutates into two calves and a nape—both body parts. Here the muscles work in harmony, travelling together in all sorts of weather, much in the vein of chapmen and flying stationers.

Yet what caused this particular body to flee? Who was worse than a Spright, compelling the legs and neck to hit the road? Put it this way: far too many chapbook quips traded on sexism, painting women as irrational nags. In this regard, *A Whetstone for Dull Wits* is no exception. For a mere penny you could read the most unlikely saga that served as the riddle's solution, an answer that somehow also sketched a chapman's nomadic lot:

> *'Tis a man flying from his Scolding Wife; the two Calves and an Ape*
> *signify the Calves of the Legs, and the Nape of his Neck, which*
> *by travelling were expos'd to the weather.*

Child suckling [Lithuania]

⌐ 72 ⌐

Two an' two is four, an' four an' five is nine . . .

When do you tell jokes? Presuming you have a few up the sleeve—wordy ones, dirty ones, riddles for kids—when do they appear? Each style will dictate its audience, of course, but when is a suitable moment?

Jokes can be icebreakers. For better or worse, they help betray the teller's bias in politics and attitudes. Riddles fall under the same umbrella. Often humour is aligned with our worldview—the pessimistic, the karmic, the perverse. We keep the jokes that carry a grain of truth, a punchline that resonates with our own ideology. You know yourself, your favourite comedians are those whose spiel 'clicks' with your own mindset. Memory retains the patter until the right circumstances, but the big question is when will you deliver the goods?

That's the puzzle folklore collectors must solve, working in the field: when are the wisecracks shared within a community? With the subsidiary question: how can the riddles be captured without being corrupted?

Kenneth S. Goldstein faced both challenges in Aberdeen, back in 1959. His hope was to harvest the riddles peculiar to eastern Scotland, particularly in the rural sprawl of the Buchan District.

Goldstein soon discovered there were two popular modes—the casual and the competitive. The first was the hardest to nab. Quips might be traded between farmhands while herding, or among children loitering in the street. The clock and the day seemed secondary to the social exchange, where any waking moment might spark a random outbreak of playful language. Sometimes Scottish riddles were in verse form, sung across the plough like a secular hymn, with no anthropologist in a bull's roar.

Riddle contests, on the other hand, were more bankable occasions of comical recitals. Back in the late 1950s, before TV had gained its footing, the custom among Aberdonians was to gather for a test of wits. I daresay drinking, singing and chatting were part of the same

Water stands.

bill, but Goldstein's grail was the riddle. As he wrote in *The Journal of American Folklore*, in a field report from his stay: 'The collector can then slip into the background and observe, make notes on, and record both the riddling contexts and the riddles.'

Espionage with consent, if you like. Journalists know the compact well. Your job is to watch the subjects in the hope they'll forget they're being watched, allowing the evening to unfold as if you were absent. The year Goldstein spent in Scotland would form the basis of his hallmark work, *A Guide for Fieldworkers in Folklore*, published four years on. The Pennsylvanian academic would later apply his 'invisible' skills to field studies around the world, gathering ghost stories, sea shanties, cowboy songs—and riddles.

In Aberdeen, he collected the casual and the competitive. He soon learnt that the more itinerant workers had the deepest repertoires. He labelled such people the landed tinkers, 'the descendants of travelling metal smiths, horn craftsmen and horse traders who nowadays support themselves by hawking goods about the countryside'. Adds up, really. Just like the modern sales rep, roaming a city, just like the chapman we met a chapter ago, there's acumen in icebreakers, as well as every chance you'll get new patter in reply.

Goldstein's other discovery was conjugal. From pub to party, he stumbled on a joke genre unique to northeast Scotland. While every culture seems to enshrine marriage in its folklore, the Scots took a less reverent stance. For a taste, try this kitchen-sink drama, as recorded by a colleague of Goldstein's, the late Jean Stewart, back in 1960:

> *An auld man an' his wife wis arguin' ae nicht atween themsel' aboot*
> *fa should dae the dishes after tea. The man, he widna dae them,*
> *and the wifie wisna wantin' tae, either. So they mak's a paction,*
> *the smartest een—the een fa kens the bonniest song—needn't dae*
> *the dishes the nicht. The aul' mannie, he sings,*

>> *'Two an' two is four,*
>> *An' four an' five is nine;*
>> *I'll tak' a haud o' yer thing,*
>> *An' ye'll tak' a haud o' mine.'*

Bamboo [Sierra Leone]

The wifie says tae hersel', 'Noo that's a gude song, but I've a better
een than that.' An' she sings,

> *'Two an' two is four,*
> *An' four an' five is nine;*
> *I ken the length o' yer thing,*
> *But ye dinna ken the depth o' mine.'*

The humour is corporeal. The 'auld man' thought his thing would win
the argument, as his appendage was graspable, compared to his other
half's biology, which ye nae can git ya hand aboot. Yet the man dinna
grasp the cunning of his wifie, who switched dimensions from length
to depth, and so escaped dish duties.

During his time in situ, Goldstein heard the mythical spouses locked
in all manner of scenarios, spouting sexual conundrums to settle other
mundane squabbles, hurling riddles that couldn't be answered. Which
suggests the ditties aren't true riddles, unless we can accept that Mr
and Mrs Aberdeen are destined to bicker forever, their impasse immune
from resolution. Either way, the format says much about the Scottish
character—some 50 years back at least. I hazard to say that modern
joking along the North Sea has changed a wee bit.

73

What government measure is like nitro-muriatic acid?

Last year I met Molly Oldfield, a founding researcher on the BBC
TV show *QI*, though 'elf' is the term the show prefers. She told me
the team uses an imaginary nine-year-old as their yardstick. If the
writers ever hesitate over a question's inclusion, they consider whether
an intelligent nine-year-old would find the topic interesting. If the
answer's yes, then the tube-nosed bat, or Aztec popcorn, are keepers.

Which hairstyle has its own comb?

Riddles aren't so different. As a rule, nine-year-olds love them, and they teach you things by stealth. Aged nine, worshipping *1001 Riddles*, I learnt that mistletoe has no feet, a whetstone is dry and Balaam owned an ass. Puns can make you wince and wise in one blow. As for historians, should they suss out that same 1001, they'd glean that people in 1949 (the year of publication) played things called records, smoked pipes and drove garbage wagons.

Yet winding the clock back further, almost a century, we'll discover even more historic gossip among the era's riddles. That's the beauty of the 1800s—editors seemed less worried about sharing their inner thoughts. Politics, culture, religion—the canvas felt wider back then. Not every riddle was seemly. Some were downright sexist. Racism was rampant too:

A negro changed will bring to view a common fruit of brilliant hue.

The anagram is ORANGE, a word you'll also find hiding in arrogance. The brainteaser would be unthinkable in our times, but such bigotry was the currency back then.

In their better moments, the riddles of 1860 made the most of their unmuzzled nature. For proof, let's flip through *Charades, Enigmas & Riddles* (1860), a slim Cambridge anthology that could double as a *QI* script. The jokes might be weaker but the tidbits are delectable. To illustrate the point, let's put the episode to air, treating the posers as a closing round of General Ignorance:

Q: *When Burford's Panorama was burned, why did that make him an orphan?*
A: *He had then no Pa nor a Ma.*

Autocue: According to Mogg's guide to London, Burford's Panorama was a modern wonder of 1844. The gallery stood on Leicester Square, holding extensive paintings of battlefields, the ruins of Pompeii, the tropical sweep of Rio. Despite what the riddle claims, the venue never did burn down. If Mr Mogg is our guide, the venue's greatest risk was overcrowding. That's why he urges an off-season trip, as 'There will be less danger . . . of having one's corns crushed by a duke, of being hustled by an earl, or elbowed about and squeezed by peeresses and maids-of-honour, the bulk of a bishop being, in the meanwhile, interposed between one's eye and the canvas.'

Q: If your house was on fire, what three authors would you invoke?
A: Dickens, Howitt, Burns!

Autocue: The Rowling, Meyer, Picoult of their day.

Q: What government measure is like nitro-muriatic acid?
A: The Divorce Bill; because it will dissolve a wedding ring.

Autocue: Before 1857, if you wanted out of wedlock, you needed the church's blessing. Marriage was deemed a holy union, not just a contractual agreement. Parliament changed all that. The passing of the *Matrimonial Causes Act* (alias the Divorce Bill) shook London's foundations. In one pen stroke, the rules had changed. Divorcees still needed a chunk of change, of course, for the courts this time, instead of the church's coffers, but reversing vows felt far more possible. Plausible, even: as simple as dropping your lifelong bling into a bucket of acid.

Why did the Mafia put a hit on Einstein?

He knew too much

Famous & Forgettable

You know you've made it when you win star billing in a riddle. Yet for every idol, there's also the idler. Here's a section to celebrate both extremes.

74

How does Good King Wenceslas like his pizza?

Tom Smith went to Paris in 1840, on the prowl for new ideas. Pralines and fondants were hardly selling like hot cakes, his East London bakery needing a novelty to sell. The answer to his prayers was the bonbon, balls of bite-sized chocolate wrapped in tissue paper. Salvation (and salivation) was at hand.

Smith took the recipe back to Clerkenwell and baked up a storm. The bonbons were a hit for a short while, the trade cooling over January. To counter the slump, Smith started lining the wrapping with short romantic quotes. Before too long the novelty-within-a-novelty proved a bonanza. Not that Smith rested easy. He wanted a bonus gimmick, something to perpetuate his new success, which is how the pyrotechnics entered his thoughts, a sound to mimic the crackle of a winter's fire. Was it possible? Eventually, yes, after seven years of burnt fingers, and lashings of silver fulminate, the Cosaque was born.

The name saluted the whip-cracking soldiers of the Franco-Prussian War, but Londoners had a better idea. 'Cracker' made more sense as a name, along with the ditching of the interior chocolate. Candy was dandy for quick satisfaction, but quotes and knick-knacks were more immune to detonation. Out went the calories, in came the novelties, and the cracker went off big-time.

Soon the quotes succumbed to riddles. Not everyone could appreciate John Keats opining on sweet sin, though more than a few could tolerate:

What part of your body keeps the best rhythm?
Your eardrums

How does the snail keep his shell shiny?
With snail polish

What do you call a masked banker?

Sorry, blame the crackers they came in. Whenever silly season nears, newspapers start padding their pages with quizzes and fluff pieces. For my own sins, in 2005 I had to interview the cracker-makers of Australia and the UK. The elephant in the room was undoubtedly the question of woeful riddles.

Dr Tim Sharp, a clinical psychologist at Sydney's Happiness Institute, nursed his own theory. 'The typical response to a cracker riddle is a laugh combined with a sigh as well.' That sigh being vital, apparently. 'When a joke is less than good, it creates a communion of fellow suffering in the room.'

The most expensive crackers, I discovered, cost £1000 for a six-pack, sold by Fortnum & Mason in London's Piccadilly Circus, some 5 kilometres from Tom Smith's old bakery. Tucked inside were gewgaws ranging from sterling-silver jewellery to MP3 players. And riddles? Of course. No cracker is complete without its wisecrack.

But just because you spend a grand on frippery doesn't guarantee your riddles will improve. To quote Dr Andrea Tanner, Fortnum & Mason's archivist and cracker copywriter: 'We do not allocate the best jokes to the most expensive crackers—all are equally bad, as should be the case with cracker jokes.'

Let your groans be the judge with this batch. With one small warning: think December. Think family lunches. Think lower standards. Think 'communion of fellow suffering'. That way, Yule laugh.

What's Tarzan's favourite Christmas carol?
Jungle Bells

What do you sing at a snowman's birthday?
Freeze a Jolly Good Fellow

Why didn't Rudolph go to school?
He was elf-taught

What does Miley Cyrus eat for Christmas?
Twerky

How does Good King Wenceslas like his pizza?
Deep-pan, crisp and even

The Loan Arranger

⌐ 75 ⌐

Tarda, gradu lento, specioso praedita dorso . . .

My gait is slow, though splendidly I'm dressed . . .

As an Australian I'm proud of our national anagram: SATURNALIA. (Better than the Croatians, who are stuck with raincoats, or a Swede with weeds.) For those unsure what Saturnalia means, picture a Christmas feast across three days, adding a spot of gambling, an eisteddfod, dwarf wrestling, exotic dancing and a platter of honey-glazed peacock.

The party's excuse was Saturn, of course, the Roman god of harvest. December coincided with the winter solstice, when the god needed appeasing to ensure boom crops in the new year. Or that was old Rome's excuse; the prime motive was pleasure. Some scholars have argued that the festival was the Christmas precursor, since both rituals were marked by cards and gift-giving. There was also a tradition of a silly hat called the *pilleus* to signify a freed man, much like the crepe crown furled inside a Christmas cracker. Indeed, the *pilleus* was worn by both masters and slaves alike, forging an equality for the orgy's duration, just as generations now will unify through the cracker's trinkets.

Seating plans were just as fiddly, too. Check this out:

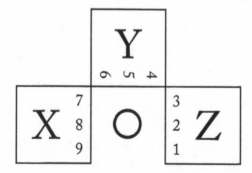

The circle was the dining table; the surrounding squares, the couches. The banquet was arrayed by a servant called a *structor* who oversaw a stream of oysters and pheasant, roast boar and wild mushrooms. The

What do you get crossing a poodle with a dinosaur?

overload was sluiced down by Tuscan plonk blended with water to aid the stamina. After the gorging, the guests would recline on their respective couches. Mine host and honoured others held prime spot at the table's head (numbers 4–6 on Couch Y), trickling down to the poor relations on Couch X.

Glutted, boozed, recumbent—what to do? Answer: indulge in the ageless custom of loll and LOL. Games were played, in tandem with lyres. Stories were told and riddles swapped.

In this regard, Caelius Firmianus Symphosius was the master. (In some accounts he's remembered as Symposius.) Little is known of the poet, and even his dates are tricky to nail down. The first mention of his *Aenigmata* collection appears in the fourth century AD, despite the fact that his 100 three-line ditties (or tercets) echo an earlier style in metre. One thing is clear, however—the work was written with Saturnalia in mind.

Not only did the preface insist as much, but each tercet was headed by its answer. Eccentric, I know, declaring the solution before delivering the riddle, but the tactic gave reciters the luxury of choosing their subject matter, as well as the option of revealing the punchline early, or not at all. Here in translation (by Elizabeth du Bois) is 'The Mirror':

No shape is strange to me, yet none I know,
My glories with an inner radiance glow,
Which, till they're seen before, can nothing show.

If you like that, there are 98 more in the same book. And before you doubt my maths, Riddle XCVI is missing from the manuscript—a puzzle in its own right. The topics are a medley, from flour to sleep, the phoenix to the fox. For history buffs, Symphosius confirms the Roman use of keys (*Great deeds with little strength I do*) and anchors (*I search the waters and I bite the ground*). He shows us glass windows (*Look deep within, I hinder not the light*) and ivory (*A mighty tooth am I, 'neath Eastern skies*). He also tells us how to build a lyre:

My gait is slow, though splendidly I'm dressed,
And learned, though by envious fate oppressed,
Alive, I nothing say, though dead, my voice is blessed.

Yabba-dabba-doodle

A lyre? I lied. Please, as if I'd mirror Symphosius and give the answer upfront! Instead you're chasing the raw material used by lyre-makers. Can you guess the ingredient?

As a boy, according to legend, Hermes fluked the lyre's invention by stretching four strings across the riddle's solution. Or at least the solution's shell, for the answer is the tortoise, a creature prized for the rich acoustics of its shell. Artisans inlaid the base with goat's horn to amplify the 'blessed voice'. Riddle XX whispers these ancient mechanics. Three poetic lines and the banquet's music is newly woken. One riddle and you sense a distant era when late December was a time of alcohol and gluttony. Oh, wait . . .

⌐┛ 76 ┗⌐

Why is the latest *Cole's Funny Picture Book* like the earliest *Cole's Funny Picture Book*?

Focus on the circle below for 20 seconds. If the light's right, and Edward William Cole is telling the truth, you'll notice how the circle starts to revolve.

Not that it worked for me. The room was stuffy and I kept seeing HOT rather than a rolling wheel. Still, E.W. Cole made me try. The man had that kind of clout in the marvel department.

The OT illusion appeared in *Cole's Funny Picture Book*, a mega-seller across Australia in 1879. On top of optical tricks, the omnibus teemed with doggerels and shadowgraphs, stories and puzzles. And riddles, of course, some I still remember from my grandmother's house in Sydney.

What's black on top and red inside?

Grandma Jessie had a shelf devoted to Mr Cole. To settle her grandkids she'd pick out a volume and read about Wotto and Spotto in Fairyland, or the Pongalong Penguin Pouncer. You get the drift. The humour was zany and of its day. Naff, in a word, but the sort of naff that spelt *ker-ching* 140 years ago.

Emerging from a gold rush, cashed-up and confident, the Victorian public was hungry for frolic and diversion. With a zeal for quirk, E.W. Cole was there to offer both. His four-storey bookstore in Melbourne's heart was an imaginarium to rival Willy Wonka's factory. Instead of a Fudge Room, there was a Smiling Gallery of funfair mirrors. Rather than a Bubble Room, you paid a penny to see a mechanical hen lay a golden egg.

To find the man's picture book, a browser would need to brave a corridor of illusions, caged monkeys and talking birds, a fernery and orchestra, a Chinese tea salon. Amid the wonders, Cole claimed his emporium held two million titles, which was doubtless OTT: a commercial illusion, if you like. But still, after the toy alcove, and the photographic studio, there was room enough for thousands of books, tens of thousands, most spines illuminated by a ceiling of domed glass.

Rudyard Kipling and Mark Twain both made detours on their Australian trips to see the palace first-hand. Cole was likely there to meet them, the expat Englishman dressed in scarlet to match his staff's uniforms, a childish grin offset by a prophet's beard. Oddly, bookselling was not his first choice of trade. He'd previously sold lemonade on the goldfields, then pies in the city. Revenue from both ventures funded his grandiose vision, which flyers called 'the prettiest sight in Melbourne', and with good reason.

As a girl, my grandmother felt transformed when she walked under the rainbow that arched over the Collins Street entrance. She recalled the gooseflesh as she tripped past the kooky mirrors, the brass and glass. Reaching the counter, Jessie had pestered her parents for a *Cole's Funny Picture Book*—one of several by then. That was the secret, as E.W. knew all too well. Create an urban fantasia, and families will come. Fashion a book of illusions and riddles and children will harass until they're happy.

What is the best throw of the dice?

Galoshes, of course [Finland]

By way of a clue, Cole was a William Blake-like radical, a blend of moralist and dreamer. Between lemonade and books, he'd tried selling his own manuscript about the Bible—describing Jesus as a visionary rather than a miracle-worker—but the heresy fell on deaf ears. Hence the pies, then the riddle ploy to sow his propaganda. The best throw of the dice, therefore, was to throw them away.

The first book was split into sections such as Naughtiness Land and Travelling Land, where Cole asserted that every religion was fundamentally one. Fanatical or not, the formula clicked, with Pussy Land and Moo-Moo Land converting into cash cow. And Play Land, too, where the riddles were stowed:

What is higher when it's upside down?

The answer was my age when absorbing the puns at Jessie's house. Correct, I was 6, which was also the tally of omnibuses the Cole family produced, give or take. The tally's imprecision owes to E.W.'s

Cole's lore

What goes further the slower it goes?
Money

What did the baby echidna say to the cactus?
'Is that you, Mum?'

Who killed one-fourth of the people in the world?
Cain, when he killed Abel

What age do most girls wish to attain?
Marri-age

What would you do if a dinosaur sat in front of you at a concert?
Miss most of the show

Why is Cole's Book Arcade like a learned man?
Because it is well stocked with literature

Why are riddles like surgeons?

grandson—Cole Turnley—reviving the series in 1951. Sticking to a good thing, Turnley cannibalised the earlier run, keeping the O of OT turning until the mid 1970s.

Is a book a new book if it's a pastiche of older books? That's a riddle for philosophers, a bit like the vintage car that's had every piece replaced. In the meantime, Turnley couldn't resist a waggish self-reference:

> *Why is the latest* Cole's Funny Picture Book *like the earliest* Cole's Funny Picture Book?
> *Because every* Cole's Funny Picture Book *is a* Cole's Funny Picture Book!

Wotto and Spotto—and the late Jessie Mitchell—could only concur.

⌐ 77 ¬

When is Henderson Africanus like Sir Graham Berry's bandy leg?

The book was published in Melbourne back in 1887, its title almost longer than the actual volume: *Christmas Crackers: A book of glorious games, rattling riddles, perplexing puzzles, spirited sports, pleasant pastimes, fantastic fun & jolly jokes.* Not to mention an alliteration addiction.

Ninety pages in total, split into light verse, magic tricks and everything else the title promised. As for those Rattling Riddles, quite a few had a Melbourne flavour. Clearly the editors were locavores, upgrading many wordplay recipes with fresh ingredients. Dunlop, for instance, the latest Melbourne Cup winner, featured front and centre in this pun:

> *Why is the racehorse Dunlop like a hotel waiter?*
> *Because he runs for cups, plates and steaks*

You'll find more Australian overtones in the riddle box, most of the examples losing their crispness over the journey. I must admit,

They keep you in stitches

Christmas wisecracks

What Australian city is a stale egg?
Addle-laid

Why would Sydney naturally be expected to possess a sculler
of the first rank?
Because it has a Manly Beach

What is worse than raining cats and dogs?
Hailing trams

Why is The Age *like the Militia?*
Because it has a leader, columns and reviews

Why do Messrs Munro and Nimmo [two state politicians] *run*
so slight a risk of drowning?
Because they're accustomed to keeping their noses above water

When does the House of Assembly present the most ludicrous spectacle?
During a division, when its ayes are on one side, and its noes on
the other

rummaging through *Christmas Crackers* for a chapter focus, my initial choice was a Melbourne reference I could grasp immediately:

Why is Collins Street like the River Murray?

As a hint, think about a feature that rivers and main streets share. Not beds, not mouths—but keep brainstorming. In 1887, the horse tram was losing ground to the cable kind, with a major route operating along Collins Street. No doubt several daytrippers were aboard to visit the big banks, as Collins had the Bank of Victoria on one side and the Bank of New South Wales on the other.

Or it did, back in 1887. The interim has savaged the quip. Neither bank exists by that name now. The Bank of Victoria was swallowed by

Why was the hearse horse hoarse?

the Commonwealth Bank almost a century after the wordplay, while the Bank of New South Wales has been rebadged into Westpac.

Keen to conduct my own legwork, I caught an electric tram to the riddle's coordinates to see if the punchline could be rescued. Alas, the riddle now fizzles, unless the River Murray rolls between Westpac and Sires Tuxedo Hire.

That was Plan A—a home-baked pun, a city landmark, a testament to time's passing. The chapter was all but written when Henderson Africanus appeared on the horizon. If riddles are parcels of mystery, then surely the best pick from any book is the riddle you can't understand even when the answer is served on a platter.

When is Henderson Africanus like Sir Graham Berry's bandy leg?

To introduce both men, let me paint a quick picture of the political landscape. Back in the late 1800s, Victoria was stuck in a legal rut. Not once but thrice the state had sputtered to a halt, owing to the stalemates between the two Houses of Legislature—the Council and the Assembly. At one point in 1878, the Council blocked funding, forcing the governor to sack a small army of public servants, including several judges and magistrates.

Black Wednesday, as the day was known, was the darkest for Graham Berry, the governor under siege. Just a year into his second term, this Twickenham draper was living on a knife's edge, honed extra sharp by the local press. *The Age, The Argus*—every masthead in the city condemned the impasse, a fact observed by Daniel Henderson, the tall Jamaican who sold papers down on Collins Street.

You couldn't miss the bloke. With plum-dark skin and white top hat, Henderson was one of few Afro-Americans living in Victoria, a bona fide character of the colony. On most days he'd holler headlines from the kerbs, including news about Berry's predicament. As a sideline, under the counter, Henderson also sold his own political pamphlets, using the ironic byline of Snowball to push his diatribes. Meanwhile on Sundays he favoured a different alias, mounting the soapboxes along the Yarra and preaching his politics under the guise of Henderson Africanus. To eavesdrop on the man in full swing, let's sample one of his pamphlets: 'The coloured people of Australia or America are not like the Chinese, for centuries of slavery and its traditional history has [*sic*] taught them a valuable lesson from their so-called masters, and they know well how to better the instruction.'

Come Black Wednesday in 1878, with Victoria teetering on the brink of collapse. Governor Berry was desperate for a solution. The newspapers knew it; the Opposition knew it; the cartoonists knew it. Deep into the turmoil, Berry threatened to travel to England in the hope of dumping the Council from constitutional law in order to wheedle greater autonomy. Of course, such a trip was portrayed as lunacy by most in the wings. Crueller critics went so far as to suggest the governor take Henderson Africanus on the voyage, the Jamaican eccentric likely to make more sense when addressing the House of Commons.

The mockery was cruel, and gives you sufficient background to the riddle in focus. Let's see the barb again, this time in tandem with its xenophobic answer:

> *When is Henderson Africanus like Sir Graham Berry's bandy leg?*
> *When the knee-grows out*

⌐ 78 ⌐

What's black, white and read all over?

Damn, I gave the answer away, committing the riddle to paper. Bloody hell—did I just say paper? This is getting out of hand. Let's start again. Please unread what you've just read and imagine red instead. That's how the trap is meant to be sprung. This time round you hear a different teaser:

> *What's black, white and red all over?*

See? I mean, hear? Much trickier. The red/read homophone is the inbuilt gotcha of this careworn riddle, making the listener imagine anything from sunburnt nuns to gory skunks, rather than the newspaper we all know the solution to be.

What part of London is in France?

The newspaper, in fact, is old news. After a century of rotation, the gag is looking baggy around the eyes. Folklore expert Mac Barrick, writing for *The Journal of American Folklore*, nominated the newspaper routine as 'perhaps the most common example of a folk riddle collected in the United States in the twentieth century', a few steps ahead of the road-crossing chicken. By Barrick's tally, the joke appeared in fifteen collections published between 1917 and 1939, a newspaper dutifully delivered as the punchline on each occasion.

Pushing the calendar further back, I'd hazard to say the pun is even more elderly, mainly due to the homophone trap. The minute you jot the question down, the jig is up. What does that tell you? The wordplay had oral beginnings. Folklore being folklore, it's impossible to isolate the starting point, but safe to say this riddle was circulating long before its print debut.

Repetition can kill a riddle, of course, turning the cleverness stale. Or then again, in some cases the echolalia has benefits, elevating the joke into meme. You knew the newspaper answer long before you started the chapter. Common knowledge like that can either doom a riddle or be its lifeblood. Barrick counts a dozen variants on the newspaper classic. We've already met two alternatives, with additional suspects like embarrassed Dalmatians and embarrassed penguins extending the line-up. The joke, in other words, becomes a springboard, a launching pad for departures.

Crude ones, too, since the combination of colours unlocks a psychosexual impulse. What began as a newspaper has since rolled into aberrations that include a stabbed priest, a harpooned orca, Santa trapped in a chimney or integrated lovers rolling downhill during the girlfriend's period.

By the same token, the riddle's redness has granted licence to throw political grenades, the colour a code for communism in English and other languages. You won't be shocked to learn that the French and Italian newspapers mentioned below have a distinct Leninist lean:

Quel journal est tout rouge et noir et blanc?
L'Humanité

Quale giornale è rosso, bianco e nero?
L'Unità

Back in America, during the 1960s, the riddle was hijacked to demonise the civil rights movement. Lunch counters across the country still practised segregation, inspiring sit-in protests by black and white students alike. Clashes erupted. Arrests soared. Critics of the movement accused the protests of being Soviet-engineered, a bid by Khrushchev to destabilise democracy. Hence the bigot's view of the integration lobby was black, white and Red all over.

Clever or not, you can see how a spoken pun has evolved into a shape-shifting tool. The quaint homophone of red/read has been stranded, much like many quaint newspapers. That was the gist of Jimmy Kimmel's riddle in 2012. The chat-show host was addressing the Correspondents' Dinner at the White House, daring to bait a roomful of journalists about the demise of newspapers by asking:

What's black, white and read all over?
Nothing anymore

◱ 79 ◲

What do you call a nun with a washing machine on her head?

Elvis Costello and The Imposters were rehearsing on set. I can't remember the song, but I do recall the urge I felt to join them. Not that I can play a musical instrument, unless you count a constipated tuba. Or a mean 'Frère Jacques' on glockenspiel. But hey, with a name like Imposters, I felt well qualified.

After all, my job that night was to impersonate a television star. The star was Rove McManus, a big fish a few years back. Not that Rove has vanished from the media radar, but back in 2002 the comedian's smile dazzled on every magazine. As host of his eponymous chat show, he was poised to win three consecutive gold Logies for most popular personality, pulling studio crowds like a Filipino faith healer.

Why didn't the goldfish newlyweds kiss?

Excepting one night, a cold night in June, when Rove wasn't Rove but a bespectacled crossword-maker with a satchel of lame jokes.

The fraud was enacted in the name of journalism. Shelley Gare, my editor at *Sunday Life*, had suggested I fill the shoes of a warm-up guy, one of those network jesters who prime a crowd before a show, get them laughing and feeling good about life. Blindly I accepted the challenge. The people at *Rove* were just as game, allowing us to substitute their own gagster—Kynan Barker—with a gonzo try-hard. My brief was clear: get out there and be funny.

Simple on paper, since paper was my natural habitat, but a different ball of wax when you add the lights and shiny floor, a camera crew and audience. For five minutes just before the show went to air, I had to mimic the idol the crowd had come to see. Not his voice or mannerisms, but a dummy run of comic patter like the schtick the real Rove would do once the tape started rolling—only his would be funny. As the fake McManus I had to make the studio thrum. Soften up the audience. Whet their appetite for the McCoy.

I think the technical term is bombing. Or dying. Or something just as grievous. My best material related to the fact that nobody knew who I was, a possible goldmine if you know how to use it. I didn't. Instead I joked about bogus guests coming up, about wax museums and nicotine patches. Nothing dynamite. Out of respect for Rove, you understand. I waved my hands to orchestrate applause levels and threw lollies like confetti to boost the blood sugar. In the longest five minutes of my life I did everything but tell riddles.

That initiative had been seized the night before. As spadework for my fake job, I'd watched a professional wrangler fine-tune a game-show audience. With a pie-seller's voice, and a dancer's lightness, the man gambolled about the bleachers, belting out a litany of riddles. Bang, bang—one after the other, relentless, merciless, maybe 20 in a row, barely giving the audience time to think, let alone reply.

What do you call a man with a car on his head?
Jack

What do you call a man with sesame seeds on his head?
Big Mac

Two koi

What do you call a man with a paper bag on his head?
Russell

Notice the pattern? None of the puns was sophisticated, but when the sequence was delivered at pace, the effect was delirium. So slick was the expert, so systematic, we were only getting Warren (the guy with the rabbits) before a clumsy Rex was upon us. Women were recruited, too, from the one-legged Eileen to the two-legged Noelene, and I dare say the Chinese Irene was lurching in between. There was even a nun with a washing machine on her head. Quick! Too slow. I've already said the answer a few lines above: Sister Matic. The crowd went nuts.

Writing the story, I went to see several TV jesters in action, from the pie-seller to Sarah Kinsella of kids' TV, whose main job was avoiding wee or vomit situations. I saw the Pontiff of Warm-Ups, Michael Pope, make a crowd guffaw or titter on cue. I went to Circus Oz to see how clowns did it. My research, however, only went to underline my fraudulence. I lacked the razzle-dazzle, the command, and I certainly lacked the riddles. Suffice to say, as a stand-in stand-up, I'm a fine glockenspieler.

⎤ 80 ⎣

Why are some persons who do not like London milk like York thieves?

Professor Buck is a hard man to pin down, damn near Google-proof. The only shred I have on the chap is a lone snippet from the *Colonial Times* of Hobart, 29 June 1852.

Fitting, I guess. To look twice and realise that a 'necromantic performer' has vanished in a puff of smoke. Or that's how it seems. Somehow the conjuror managed to fill York's Theatre Royal on 28 June 1852, and then melt into the floorboards.

Suddenly my new conundrum in this mad riddle quest became Professor Buck himself. I swept the web and dived down rabbit holes

What do you call a time-travelling pedant?

in a bid to trace this man of mystery. My pulse climbed on learning of Arnold Buck, an American magician, who died while attempting the dangerous bullet-catch in a crowded theatre. This new lead sounded plausible until I saw that the tragedy occurred in 1840, a dozen years before the good professor dazzled the good people of York.

Blocked again. Unless . . . unless the necromancer had learnt to chat with the dead from either side of the grave. See how desperate I was getting? Ghosts, after all, tend to have a flimsy presence, and this Buck bloke verged on transparent.

Namesakes abounded. My hunt unearthed an Iowan horticulturist, a Texan engineer and a chicken elocutionist on *Sesame Street* called Professor Buck Awe. Yet no date or bio jibed with the Tasmanian snippet. The article in question was sourced from *The York Herald*, an English organ that's long since atrophied. The trail went cold. Until my research led me to Herr Döbler (1836–1904), the stage name of Aberdeen magician George William S. Buck, who turned out to be Professor Buck's son.

This was exciting. Here was a sniff. Charles Dickens was a fan of Döbler (with or without the umlaut, as the theatrical posters varied). The 'apparatus conjuror' was feted in London circles, a showman using bottomless wine bottles and automatic candles to enchant the gentry. More notably, Lewis Carroll and his friend Alice Liddell went to see a Döbler show, the onstage pageantry echoing the magic of Carroll's Wonderland, created during the same period.

Curiouser and curiouser, but still I drew a blank on Professor Buck. This Hobart scrap loomed as my only substantial clue to the man, though at least the story teemed with riddles. Twenty in total, most oozing showbiz.

According to the article, a silver cup worth five guineas was a prize for the evening's best riddle. I can't speak for Buck as a necromancer, or as a palpable human being for that matter, but he certainly knew the tricks of marketing. By word of mouth, perhaps, or possibly pamphlets, Buck had invited the citizens of York to conjure a riddle, the best creation to win the cup. No surprises, the booty had a catch, with patrons needing to attend the show in order to claim their reward. As the *Herald* reported, the York contest drew 400 entries, however 'the majority of them were either so trashy a character, or so well-known already, that they were consigned to the flames'. This left some 100 redeemable riddles, which naturally inspired their creators to buy a ticket.

The plan was ingenious. Not only did the competition fill the house, but 100-plus riddles also helped to punctuate the evening. Buck selected a jury of theatregoers to perform the teasers in a call-and-response fashion on stage. He then invited the same team to adjourn to the wings to pick the funniest pair.

See what he did there? The reason he sought the top two riddles, rather than a single victor, was to involve the entire audience. Clearly the Buckmeister had missed his calling. Who needs to summon the dead when you can channel a marketing guerrilla a century ahead of the curve? The two best riddles were presented to the audience. In theatre slang the game is known as the clap-o-meter, where an MC invites the crowd to applaud for their preference as each nominee is recited. For your chance to take part, imagine you're sitting in the Theatre Royal in 1852, and these are your choices:

> *Why is learning to play the fiddle one of the worst things a man can do?*
> *Because it leads him into so many scrapes*

Hmm, is that a general *meh* I'm hearing from the gods? A yawn from the stalls? Time to announce Riddle number 2:

> *Why are some persons who do not like London milk like York thieves?*
> *Because they do not like Chalk*

I can hear your *huh?* from here. Perfectly understandable, since the riddle relies on local knowledge. It was only a desperate Twitter plea that alerted me to Chalk being a reference to Superintendent Robert Chalk, the city's principal police officer during that period. This is why riddles intrigue me, along with fugitive sorcerers and research chases: their minor details speak volumes, on several fronts.

In one remote riddle-off we have learnt that Yorkies knew not just the chalkiness of London milk, but also the name of their town's chief enforcer. Furthermore, the same crowd deemed the double meaning to be gold, earning Mr E. Hart of 5 Tower Place a silver cup.

Why did the invisible man go crazy?

Buck the trend

Other riddles on the magician's list included:

Why are ladies and gentlemen in the boxes very sad?
Because they are all in tiers

Why are mammas like beggars of the past days?
Because they are matchmakers

Why is York Minster like the residence of [stripper] Lola Montez?
Because it contains one of the finest bells

Why will the winner of the prize be likely to become a drunkard?
Because he will be fond of his cup

Why is the letter E like Professor Buck?
Because E is the centre of amusement

⌐ 81 ⌐

Why is Blondin like a prizefighter?

Walking on stilts is tricky. Doing a somersault while wearing stilts is more difficult. Attempting to somersault with stilts while balancing on a tightrope is downright certifiable. But that's what Charles Blondin did, 20 metres off the ground, giving the hordes at Crystal Palace one almighty crick. Women swooned as newsmen scribbled. Crimean War veterans held their breath, waiting for the Frenchman to plummet. As for the pubescent boys in the crowd, well, they invented riddles.

Maybe not top-shelf riddles, but their output suffuses *Every Boy's Magazine*, a brother publication of *The Boy's Own Magazine*. Flick through the issues from 1862, a year in Blondin's wake, and you'll register the impact the acrobat had on young lives. For want of pop stars to stir boyish cockles, Blondin was the Blondie of his day.

Out of sight, out of mind

Is it any shock? Back then, Jenny Lind was the toast of the music scene, the so-called Swedish nightingale hitting the high notes in Covent Garden. While the soprano could enthral, she'd never have the power to capture a lad's vitals, let alone inspire a suite of riddles. Instead, she inspired just one:

Why would Jenny Lind make good soup?
Because she's neither Grisi nor Alboni

If not for those last two performers falling off fame's tightrope, that wisecrack might still be admired in bohemian circles. Opera buffs could well be au fait with Giuditta Grisi and Madame Alboni, but I'll admit to looking them up. (While Lind I only know as she's a regular of US crosswords, thanks to those handy letters.) Blondin, on the other hand, seems more deeply etched in Western memory, his name synonymous with derring-do. Which seems only fair, presuming you can cook an omelette while suspended over Niagara Falls, or push a wheelbarrow some 50 metres above terra firma. The man was Evel Knievel in a life before gasoline.

Blondin's circus feats inspired a range of tributes, surfacing in unlikely places. In 1860, just after that Niagara stunt, a cartoonist named Jacob Dallas depicted an aspiring president in circus mode. Dressed in socks and pantaloons, Abraham Lincoln tiptoes on a rope, carrying a balance pole marked 'Constitution', and shouldering an African slave, just as Blondin had piggy-backed his manager the year before.

There have been stage plays and songs about the French funambulist, street names, and a Welsh device dubbed a Blondin that carries rocks along a cable. And let's not forget a serenade of boyish riddles:

Why is Blondin like a prizefighter?
Because he can't make his living without some assaults

Why has Blondin the most wonderful digestion?
Because he lives on a rope and thrives

What is Blondin's profession?
The public line

Why is Blondin a great favourite with the public?
Because his performance is always on cord

What's the liveliest city in the world?

⌐ 82 ⌐

Enfant de l'Art, Enfant de la Nature . . .
Child of Art, Child of Nature . . .

The elevator was straight out of Hitchcock: the sliding grille, the wood panels, the groaning cables. Even down to the dapper attendant with his pince-nez glasses, the pencil moustache, a postcard of every Greek island pasted on the wall behind him. 'What storey?'

Well, that takes telling, the whole escapade, starting from the email I received six weeks before the elevator. The sender was Jarrod Rawlins, an art dealer writing on behalf of a Melbourne painter.

'I haven't seen you before,' said the liftman.

'I'm here to see Amanda.'

'The Marburg,' he corrected.

Amanda Marburg—painter, photographer, sculptor, crossword addict. Her chief fix was the Friday puzzle that appeared in *The Age*, tearing out her hair until she filled in the final word. I was pusher to her junkie, the riddler behind the weekly clues. That's how I fell into the frame, so to speak, with Amanda casting around for her next victim. 'Are you interested?' Mr Rawlins had asked.

Before deciding, I ran a search of my own. Part of me was flattered, of course, but I wanted to investigate the Marburg technique. Call me shallow, but style mattered. As a crossword-maker I was hoping for cubism. Failing that, I hoped for an artistic bent to mirror my own, a twisted way of seeing the world.

I didn't need to worry. The Marburg deserved the notoriety. Surfing the web I found gargoyles and demons, molten lobsters and haunted cats. Rather than panic I felt at home. Here was a painter who understood enigmas, every image its own little mystery. Weirder still, the figures were shaped in clay and then transferred into oil—further reason to meet the oddity who'd created them.

The elevator jolted. The attendant yanked open the grille. 'Fifth door on your left, walking clockwise.'

Berlin—it's always on the Spree

The building was a labyrinth of lino and peeling walls. I looked for numbers on the doors but most were blank, or decorated with symbols, random stickers, stray bits of cloth: the totems of the inmates.

Once upon a time the Nicholas Building was a giant haberdashery, a ten-storey pile in the middle of Melbourne with garment and fabric emporia the principal tenants. That dream fizzled after World War II, the address evolving into a nest of studios. I tapped on what seemed the right door. Music drifted from the other side, guitars and oboe, a tune I vaguely knew but couldn't recall the name. The door inched open. A woman with black curly hair was standing there, mid-thirties, spattered clothes, shy grin: The Marburg.

The kettle took some finding, then the cups. Most in sight had been colonised by brushes, while the sink was choked with turpentine rags. Yet the chaos felt familiar, the sort of bedlam I call home. The music came from the windowsill, a mini-stereo more paint than plastic. By the chorus I'd worked out the song: 'Bye Bye Pride', a sleeper hit for The Go-Betweens. Perhaps the track was deliberate, a caveat from the artist before we signed the contract.

Over black tea we fell into conversation. We touched on anagrams and red herrings, charade clues and hidden messages, a quasi-courtship to assure each other we'd found the right match. As a portrait virgin I figured the dance was important. Having your face reduced to a replica entailed a leap of trust.

No matter the state of your ego, it's hard enough to trust one painter, let alone seven, as was the case with Jean-Jacques Rousseau, the man behind our latest riddle. Maybe the philosopher was a serial sitter due to the first effort, by Maurice Quentin de la Tour in 1753, falling short of expectations. Somehow I doubt it. Rousseau's face is open and handsome, a bookish Roger Federer, if you're trying to imagine him. If The Marburg could make me half as debonair I'd be in her debt.

That's the thing—portraits hang on walls as much as they hang around full stop. You grow old the minute the oil dries. Leave the studio and your art-self is left behind as a permanent back-marker of your advancing decrepitude.

Dramatic, I know, but that was Rousseau's take. Of anyone, he should have known. When he wasn't writing treatises on the nature

What do you call a clean optimist?

of man—our potential goodness in a corrupt society—the Genevan philosopher was posing in a chair, entrusting the next man in the series to capture his essence more truly.

The Marburg, thank God, had a speedy approach. As soon as we agreed to go ahead, she spent half an hour converting my head and torso into plasticine. The method arose from a claymation passion, the paint phase a more recent development after some low-life stole her camera when she was at art school. All she needed from me was stillness, a fair ask at the best of times, but the words of Rousseau were a handy motivation: 'Patience is bitter—but the fruit is sweet.'

Thirty minutes—a jiffy compared to tradition. Perhaps the hours that Rousseau had to observe, the hours multiplied by seven, lent him the time to compose his elegant riddle:

> Enfant de l'Art, Enfant de la Nature,
> Sans prolonger les jours j'empêche de mourir:
> Plus je suis vrai, plus je fais d'imposture,
> Et je deviens trop jeune à force de vieillir.

Unless you've read *Le Contrat Social* in the original, Rousseau's keystone work of 1762, you may need the verse translated:

> *Child of Art, Child of Nature,*
> *Without prolonging life, I prevent death:*
> *The truer I am, the more false I appear,*
> *And I become too young as age creeps on.*

Sooner or later, time makes clay of us all. As a failed watchmaker back in Geneva, Rousseau knew the truth better than anyone. So many aspects of his riddle were obvious—the subject's younger self held captive in the frame, the onward march of the minutes, the false immortality that art can confer. For mine, however, the problem lay in the third line: *The truer I am, the more false I appear.* It made no sense—until the Archibald hit town.

The contest is held every year, a competition run by the Art Gallery of New South Wales to find the finest portrait in the land. Submissions tally in the hundreds. A jury whittles that number down to 40 or so, the pick of the crop hanging in shows across the eastern capitals.

DA, the Marburg portrait, made the cut. At the time, I felt mild shock. Not because Amanda botched her task, but because I looked like a voodoo Medusa. A ballpoint poked out of my pocket, my shirt a boomerang paisley going in ten directions. My eyes resembled polyps, two needle pricks as pupils. Meanwhile my hair had a life of its own, a viper nest infesting my scalp. The so-called replica was a falsehood, or that's what I presumed, until the judges spoke. The portrait came second that year, praised from all quarters as a feat of authenticity. Even Tracy, my wife, surveyed her plasticine spouse and confirmed, 'The Marburg nailed you.'

Rousseau, do me a favour with your Child of Art analogy, and shut up.

◿ 83 ◣

Because I am by nature blind, I wisely choose to walk behind …

The last stop on Gulliver's travels was the Country of the Houyhnhnms. Midway between Madagascar and Australia, the land was ruled by a noble breed of horse-like animals that spoke in neighs and lived in harmony. The Houyhnhnms engaged in art and philosophy, science and reason, plus a two-foal policy: one colt, one filly. Should genders in the family repeat, the offspring would be swapped with that of another broodmare to keep the legal balance. Simple as that. No need for quarrelling. Logic and order lay at the core of Houyhnhnm society.

By contrast, the Yahoos were hell-bent on destroying each other. Naked and hairy, the brutes lived in trees and spent their days grovelling in mud, dragging sledges, or gouging each other with claw-like nails 'for want of such convenient instruments of death as we had invented'.

No sooner had Gulliver arrived on the scene than the Yahoos attacked him. Gulliver saved his skin with a few swipes of his sword,

What bus crossed the ocean?

sending the posse up a tree. But the battle wasn't done. With deadly precision the Yahoos angled their bowels and shat with deadeye aim from the branches. The stench was stifling. Poor old Gulliver couldn't resume his travels quick enough.

Yahoo the word, of course, has come to mean the basest kind of human. (Unless it bears an exclamation mark, in which case it's a search engine.) Lager louts have been equated to yahoos—as have vandals and litterbugs, hooligans and philistines. In short, everything that Jonathan Swift wasn't. As proof, the author of *Gulliver's Travels* reserved his battles for satire on the page, or riddles via correspondence.

His prime opponent was Thomas Sheridan, a fellow Irishman and cleric some 20 years his junior. A lot of *Gulliver's Travels* was actually written at Sheridan's country house in around 1724. Indeed, if the gossip held good, Swift was secretly wed to Sheridan's sister Esther, but this was never proven by biographers, including Sheridan himself, who wrote the first one.

Superstar and satellite—that was the relationship in many ways. Literary lion and dilettante. Yet when it came to the War of Riddles, the two men took up quills as equals.

We can't say for sure who fired the first quip, though we do know the stoush began around 1724. That's right, the same year Swift was writing about make-believe lands in Sheridan's getaway, perhaps when the flirting with Esther did or did not occur. In a subsequent volume of riddles, an editor's foreword suggests, 'Some ingenious gentlemen, friends of [Swift's], used to entertain themselves with writing riddles, and send them to him and their other acquaintance . . .'

Others in the riddle clique included a Dublin professor in medicine, Dr Richard Helsham, as well as some chap named Mr F_____r. (The gap was a deliberate tease.) By and large the gags were good, at least those that qualified for the anthology. The verses were the sophisticated missiles that the yahoos lacked in their own culture. Here's one from Dr Swift:

We are little airy Creatures,
All of diff'rent Voice and Features,
One of us in Glass is set,

One of us you'll find in Jet,
T'other you may see in Tin,
And the fourth a Box within,
If the fifth you shou'd pursue
It can never fly from you.

The answer is beautiful, making Swift's rhyme one of my favourites in *this* collection. Can you guess the answer? With their superior logic, a Houyhnhnm might. The angle is alphabetical, as those airy creatures you seek are the vowels. Look again and you'll see the pattern, how A is set in GLASS, and E found in JET, and so on. I'm not sure whether Dr Helsham or Mr F_____r cracked the puzzle. Perhaps a few hints in the evening mail were needed. Once the solution was reached, Sheridan felt obliged to compose a riposte.

But what could be a riddle-worthy topic? How best to outwit the mansion's lodger? In a fanciful moment, I imagine Sheridan peeking at the manuscript that lay on Swift's desk, fishing the pages for inspiration. That might explain why Sheridan went from vowels to bowels, the erudite circle reduced to the art of fart, as though Ireland had turned to Houyhnhnmland and the hairy tree-shitters had somehow learnt to formulate verse. I shall leave you with an aromatic sample, 'The Fart' by Reverend Thomas Sheridan:

Because I am by nature blind,
I wisely choose to walk behind;
However, to avoid disgrace,
I let no creature see my face.
My words are few, but spoke with sense;
And yet my speaking gives offence:
Or, if to whisper I presume,
The company will fly the room.

How many seconds in one year?

Twelve—January 2nd, February 2nd . . .

Body & Soul

Time to tap the spiritual side of life, where we pay passing worship to the sacred and celestial. (Yet somehow include a Roman candle, a Burmese umbrella and a Celtic beehive.)

⌐ 84 ⌐

趙州和尚、因みに僧問う

Does a dog have a Buddha nature?

Listen. Can you hear it? That's the sound of one hand clapping.

Assuming you're surrounded by silence, or perhaps a jackhammer's clamour, since the one-handed clap is the soundless sound, which doesn't make sense, but only to those standing on the outside looking in.

Let's take this chapter slowly, as Zen Buddhism delights in such paradoxes. Yet the contradictions only exist in a rational mind. A *roshi*, or Zen master, can embrace the psychic tension, the pure consciousness that transcends intellect. To couple the contrary forces of sound and silence, say, or finitude and endlessness, is to reach *satori*: the state of enlightenment.

Getting there may take a lifetime. It's not easy to shed your logic, let alone your earthbound sense of meaning. The ready measure of a disciple's progress is the *koan*, a spiritual conundrum that stems from the Japanese *ko* (public) plus *an* (matter for thought). Tracking the source back, we drift southwest to China, the cradle of Zen that gave us *gong'an*—a public case. A proving ground, if you like, making the *koan* a transcendental yardstick.

American novelist Tom Robbins defines the concept as an unsolvable riddle, which is true and not true, in classic *koan* fashion. He writes further, 'But the contemplation of that riddle—even though it cannot be solved—is in itself transformative. And if the contemplation is of high enough quality, you can merge with the divine.'

The divine is the nub, the Great Unknowing as some schools prefer, means to flee the cognitive and find the sublime. Or, to quote the Chinese monk Engo: 'There is no crack in the *gong'an* to insert one's intellectual teeth.'

What did the whole world hear?

In that sense, the *koan* is also a solvable riddle, yet not in the Western way of Q-meets-A, where every chicken has a road to cross, and every imperfect jigsaw awaits its missing piece. Rather the solution is the inner seeing, a Moebius striptease of the meditative kind. Let's look at our chosen *koan* in a bid to unsee the riddle stereotype:

Does a dog have a Buddha nature?

After so many chapters of knee-jerk responses, you must be tempted to rummage for the funny. I know I am. Nor can we be blamed—riddle immersion encourages the brain to probe for any question's trickery, to find its inbuilt weakness. But the *koan* hails from the opposite school. These quasi-riddles are seeking the wise, not the wise-arse. The outstripping of wit, if you like. A third state between rational and irrational which Zen commentators label the non-rational.

The dog in question is called Joshu's dog, a notable animal in the Zen menagerie. Joshu is the Japanese name for the Chinese master Zhàozhōu Cōngshěn, a prominent monk of the Tang dynasty, dating back to the late eighth century. His many *koan* creations appear in a volume with the ultimate Zen title: *The Gateless Gate*. Indeed, this poser was the gateway to centuries of debate, wrestling with the concept of divinity within animals, as well as insentient objects. But let's leave sober analysis to one side and dive deeper below the challenge. Or beyond.

無

Voilà—there's your answer to an unsolvable riddle, despite what Tom Robbins and yours truly just said. One answer. The start of an answer. If we translate the pictogram we end up with *mu*, which sounds more bovine than canine. But let's peel back what *mu* might mean.

Predictably, *mu* means two things, as the *koan* celebrates duality as much as non-duality. The pairing of hands, and the single hand, is but one example. The gate existing and not existing, heaviness and lightness: the *koan* marries the binary. Here, *mu* can translate into 'nothing'—the concept of nothing. In the same breath, the response also denotes emptiness, which is distinct from nothing. A cup, say, can be empty, just as it's capable of not existing. In a sense, the answer is

The horse farting on Noah's Ark [1300s monk]

an un-answer, the response both recognising and negating the notion of an enlightened mutt in one syllable. No dog has a Buddhist nature; a dog can be capable of having a Buddhist nature, just as any cup can be filled. Joshu's dog, in fact, is a contradiction on four legs, but only if you're standing outside the temple, looking in.

What may follow this inspired stab is *jakugo*, or the capping phrase. Here that rejoinder may relate to karmic delusion, a sure sign his protégé is approaching enlightenment. Deeper into the exchange, a *roshi* will apply a battery of non-riddle riddles, gauging the depth of the disciple's *satori*—that giddy shock of breaching the rational barrier. We may never know such answers, though at least you'll now know why a *koan* is both a riddle and not. As well as the trend among so many Zen followers to favour a certain name, should they own a dog.

Mu? True.

⌐⌐ 85 ⌐⌐

It comes out after fanfare; it opens its white umbrella because it is proud of its royal birth

Surf any Burmese travel site and you're bound to find a vibrant umbrella among the galleries. The colours are important. First there's the matter of fashion, where someone such as Aung San Suu Kyi, the nation's restored opposition leader, is seen brandishing an avocado parasol to match her lime silk blouse. And second, there's tradition to heed. It's a rare Buddhist monk to be seen in Yangon without a red *Pathein hti* shading his crimson robe.

Pathein here is a reference to the city that makes the parasols, while *hti* is the Burmese word for umbrella. Keep scrolling through the site and you're likely to come across a pagoda as well. If the shot's clear, you might make out a small triangular moulding atop the central spire. Typically painted gold, this too is called a *hti*, just like the sun-shields

Five stalls, one gate.

of bamboo and taffeta, an umbrella symbol to thwart the devil as much as the *Pathein* brolly parries the elements.

Golden umbrellas are also an emblem of royalty, in league with pure white. A commoner would be unwise to shade her head with either colour for fear of adopting false airs. Or worse, the colour choice could be viewed by those in authority as tacit treachery—a case of treason via parasol. This colour-coded hierarchy is captured in the Burmese proverb '*Thay yin myay-gyi, shin yin shwe hti*'.

You'll recognise the last word at least. The whole thing translates as: 'Death means going to ground; living means being under a golden umbrella.' Decoding the maxim further, the humour is sardonic. Burmese people believe that the vanquished lie buried in the earth, whereas their conquerors flourish in the aftermath, blessed by the perks of power.

Nowadays, since the fall of Mandalay in 1885, Burma can't brag a royal family in residence, though the majestic colour schemes persist in the national memory. That's seen in the proverb above, and the riddle below:

> *It comes out after fanfare; it opens its white umbrella because it is proud of its royal birth.*

Fittingly, weather plays a part in this teaser. You'd be right to think it was rain, given that *hti* translates as umbrella and not parasol here. So what might the fanfare be? Can you name the noisy chorus that accompanies rain?

Ignore the trumpet and drum. This is nature's fanfare, the symphony of lightning and thunder. The sky-music usually marks the onset of monsoon season, ten times louder than the gongs and drums that might precede a potentate. In response to nature's pomp, the earth bursts forth with mushrooms. Not one or two but thousands, sprouting in the fading light like masses of umbrellas.

Hence the mushroom is your answer, shaped like *Pathein hti*, and no ordinary *hti*, now that you know Burma's umbrella lore. Every May, when the big rains come, the heat and moisture debunk the ancient proverb, as common folk find signs of royalty lie beneath their feet.

A glove [Lithuania]

⊏ 86 ⊏

రౖండు కౖరములు అజ ౖనముకు మూల కౖరణములు

These two spices are the root causes of ignorance

Telugu may look like barbed wire on paper, but India's third most spoken language is capable of immense softness. Take this translation— a riddle encoding the moon:

The one who triggers movements in the womb of an ocean as well as that of mother.

The sky is likewise given joyous treatment:

We can neither fold nor unfold this mat.

And while we're gazing upward, then consider this Telugu stumper:

It flies in the sky but is not a bird; it carries humans but not the wind.

Sounds like the Superman catchphrase? You're getting warm. The answer is an aeroplane, proof that the 21st century has landed in Andhra Pradesh, the southeastern hip of mother India, and the spiritual home of the Telugu people. P.V. Rao—India's prime minister during the 1990s—was a Telugu speaker. Mind you, the same man spoke thirteen other languages, but Telugu was his cradle tongue. Many of the curlicues you see on the page, along with thousands of Telugu words, derive from Sanskrit, one of the world's oldest languages.

Antiquity, in fact, pervades the culture's riddles. That recent aeroplane lies beyond the traditional topics of nature and the spirit, with man's inner world the foremost focus. Indeed, the 'Supermantra' of our aeroplane riddle is typically eclipsed by the *Suprabhātam* of Hindu faith.

Translated, *Suprabhātam* means 'auspicious dawn'. The term hails from a volume of Hindu hymns widely worshipped by the Telugu people. Meander the streets of Hyderabad and Visakhapatnam and you will hear the verses sung from radios and temples, the meditative means

A thing you can find and God cannot.

of welcoming the day, helping the collective mind attune to Vishnu. This ascetic lifestyle is embodied in the riddle for the *Suprabhātam*:

> *It is not for the idol but only for restraining.*

Bhagavad Gita, the other great Hindu work, a wodge of 700 verses lifted from the epic *Mahabharata*, is also embodied in Telugu riddling:

> *This line can change human life.*

To attain enlightenment, however, there are two hurdles the Hindu must clear, two human traits the worshipper must quit worshipping in order to rise above his imperfection. Both obstacles will answer our principal riddle:

> ఈ రెండు కొరములు అజ్ఞానముకు మూల కొరణములు
> *These two spices are the root causes of ignorance.*

Surrender to the *Bhagavad Gita*. Let the *Suprabhātam*'s light wash through your mind and you may well isolate those ignorant spices. In Hinduism, the terms are *Ahamkaram* and *Mamakaram*. In the wood shavings of Telugu script the duo is అహంకొరము and మమకొరము.

Telugu teasers

It makes mind motion less.
Meditation

A weapon to make a human being into a real human being.
Knowledge

Untidy clothes but kids are like gems.
Corncob

If we cut horizontally it is a wheel; if we cut vertically, it is a shell.
Onion

In a wooden house is a snake.
The tongue

A master [Ireland]

In English, we'd approximate the spices as egoism and self-importance, the deep-set roots of spiritual blindness, such a difficult challenge summarised in a simple riddle.

⊏⌁ 87 ⌁⊐

Primum, mi Lovatelle, cum bibissem . . .

I drank the first, my friend . . .

X marks the author of this Latin charade—a mystery behind a mystery. The anonymous verses ran in *Vox Urbis*, a Roman newspaper written entirely in Latin, from headlines to weather to enigmatic contributions. Perhaps not surprisingly, the paper only lasted fifteen years, from 1898 until the Great War, a time when Rome was faced by more urgent matters of state.

Before the war, however, Mr X continued to produce his brain-benders, a poetry book (in Latin) offered to the winner. But wait, there's more. By God's grace the flyleaf would be signed by a bigwig in the Catholic Church, maybe even the Pope himself. Indeed, the Pope was at short odds, thanks to the spadework of *Figaro* journalist Felix Ziegler. Working on a whisper, Ziegler landed a scoop in 1899, declaring that X was none other than XIII, the current Leo in the Vatican.

In many ways, Leo XIII—or Vincenzo Gioacchino Raffaele Luigi Pecci as he was christened—was quite the record-breaker. Not only was His Holiness unmasked as a riddlesmith and a poet, but he also achieved numerous firsts after taking office in 1878. He was the first pope to appear on film, make a sound recording, and convene the Vatican Council, and he also appeared in a print ad for the beefy tea called Bovril. Further to that, Leo was the oldest pope to relinquish his mitre, reaching a respectable 93 on retirement.

The same man was a science buff, too, establishing the Vatican Observatory. And when not pondering the heavens, Leo loved hunting game as well as growing his own grapes. Comically, these two loves

Why do we all go to bed?

combined one day when cardinals heard gunfire issuing from the Vatican's gardens. Fearing an assassination, the brethren rushed outside to find His Holy Father scaring off sparrows with his rifle, hell-bent on protecting the vines.

Biographers claim that the private vineyard was in fact where the Pontiff did most of his X-work, crafting a riddle like this one:

Primum, mi Lovatelle, cum bibissem
Phthisi convalui ocius fugata.
Cymbam, quae liquidis natabat undis,
Alterum maris in profunda mersit.

I drank the first, my friend,
And phthisis had an end.
But with the next, my boat
Must cease, at last, to float.

The quatrain captures the answer's two parts—a drink to ward off phthisis (a wasting disease linked to tuberculosis), plus a boating peril. How good is your Latin? Perhaps what will help is considering the answer in toto:

The whole your eyes have known
Your pallid cheeks have shown;
For oh, the swelling tide
No bravest heart could hide,
When your dear mother died.

The solution you want is the saline kind, for *lac* (milk) plus *rima* (crack) can link to make *lacrima*, or tears: our source of lachrymose. Had you guessed as much, an autographed copy of canonical sestets would be in the mail. Then again, if your Latin is rubbish, or you'd never heard of Pope Leo XIII, you've just met a man more enrapt in the human experience than pontificating, as glimpsed through the handiwork of the marvellous Mr X.

Because the bed won't come to us

⊐ 88 ⊏

There was a she-mule in my house;
I opened the door and she became a heifer

Abraham ibn Ezra was a man of many hats, and several shoes too. Tramping in exile for 30 years, this writer/philosopher/astronomer/ doctor/grammarian must have worn a dozen soles to ribbons.

Not by choice, it should be said. The man was born around 1092—it's hard to be more precise. His hometown was Tudela, a Jewish pocket in northern Spain, but things didn't stay Jewish for long, not after the Almohad Muslims arrived from Morocco in 1140, forcing our hero into vagrancy to avoid persecution.

Like a proto-backpacker, ibn Ezra drifted through France and Italy. He called in on Egypt and Israel, picking up insights into Arabic star-gazing and the astrolabe, a precursor to the sextant. As for income, he banked on his wits, turning out poems or punctuation guides wherever he went, his literary output a self-generated currency. He decoded the books of Moses, Hebrew grammar, Indian mathematics and the Pleiades, all the while rambling from poorhouse to synagogue, his exile as much a lifestyle as anything by 1150.

Unlike a backpacker, ibn Ezra was dubbed the Wise, the Great, as well as the Admirable Doctor. The English poet Robert Browning devoted a poem to the intellect, based on ibn Ezra's own words: 'Grow old along with me! The best is yet to be . . .'

Sadly, time has been less careful with the Doctor's own poems, a bare minimum surviving the millennium since his time on earth. The same is true of his riddles, the kind that possibly earned him a roof over his head or bread on the table. The riddle you've just read as the chapter heading, say, might have been conjured in London or Lucca, Babylon or Rome, a neat piece of wordplay to cadge a mattress. His audience, I hope, were as Jewish and as erudite as he, otherwise ibn Ezra might well have met his maker a little sooner, going by this material:

There is a place where the lasso sits.

> *There was a she-mule in my house; I opened the door and she became*
> *a heifer.*

In its defence, the enigma loses everything in translation. Indeed, keeping to English we have no chance, so let's read the riddle in the original Hebrew:

תא יתחתפ ; ילש תיבב דרפ - איההיה
הרפל הכפה איהו תלדה

Now can you guess? Something tells me that if you were a taverner in Verona, or a coach driver in Provence, you may have demanded cash from the Great One. The pun is Hebrew to its bootstraps, a piece of letter-play so technical it almost qualifies as a private joke; nor does a millennium of meantime do the gag any favours (even chestnuts can stale with shelf-life). I must admit, after consulting two rabbis in Melbourne, one mediaeval historian in Canberra, plus the evergreen dilettante Rahel Meltzer, I'm still at sea. Not drowning exactly, but flapping for a solid lifeline.

The crux is shape-shifting, where many Hebrew words can flex into others by exchanging vowels amid a fixed array of consonants. Relevant to ibn Ezra's riddle, for example, the word for door (or *delet*) can also double as the label for the Jewish *d* (or *dalet*), the vowels bed-hopping among the consonants. Presuming that's not too loopy to grasp, then see how you fare with Rabbi Fred Morgan's insights: 'The Hebrew for she-mule is *pirdah*, while heifer is *parah*. As you can see, the only difference between the two words (ignore the vowels—it's the consonants that matter) is the *d*, which is the door (*delet/dalet*) that I opened—or removed.'

Odd to consider, but in a Hebrew universe, a word like prune could also be construed as apron, or Peroni, or paranoia, given the necessary vowel transfusions. Some 900 years ago, a matching sleight was being performed by a footloose scholar in southern Europe, turning she-mules into heifers by yanking an ambiguous door off its hinges.

For all that, my favourite paradox embedded in Abraham's riddle is not the transformation of livestock, but the very mention of a house. From exile until his death in 1167, Abraham ibn Ezra had little but

A rattlesnake [Mexico]

the open road as corridor, the sky his ceiling, his only house the four walls offered by kind strangers. Maybe this closeness to the heavens gave the nomad his feel for the stars, just as his literary subsistence lent him an affinity for grammar.

Mind you, the wanderer is homeless no more. That vague dimple you detect next time you gaze at the moon could be the Abenezra Crater, the hollow named in the riddle-maker's honour. A humble man by nature, Abraham would might well delight to learn his restless spirit has left a lasting impact.

⌐┘ 89 └⌐

When God by flood was punishing vile sin ...

Sermons can be a snore-fest. Genesis, the Gospels—regardless of the topic, if a preacher can't infuse his message with gusto, his flock will stray. Aldhelm knew the danger first-hand. Up there with greed and hypocrisy was the cardinal sin of a turgid homily. For all his classical learning, the monk had a winsome touch.

True, the abbot of Malmesbury could bang on about celibacy or grammar. As a wonder of erudition, to quote the Venerable Bede, Aldhelm could rhapsodise on the saints, or go to great lengths adjusting the Easter calendar to heed the wishes of Rome. But then again, the same sermoniser was a champion of riddle-writing.

There's something of Chaucer in this Anglo-Saxon forerunner. While there's no doubting his piety—the man invited to Rome in the late seventh century to meet with Pope Sergius I—Aldhelm was also an avid gamester. Read between the lines of this Malmesbury abbot's writing and you'll experience a most nimble mind. He lapped up Hebrew and astrology. He loved to travel. He knew his share of tavern songs, too, in addition to arranging his own poetry to music. Back when 50 was the old 70, the abbot went to retire, but the monks wouldn't have

What's bought by the yard and worn by the foot?

a bar of it. For more than anything, the brethren cherished Aldhelm's sermons, peppered with the wisdom and wit that still distinguish his *Enigmata* today:

When God by flood was punishing vile sin,
And those waters cleansing evil's stain,
I first fulfilled the patriarch's command,
As by a fruitful bough I signified
Salvation to the earth was come. Thenceforth
My heart is ever gentle, and in me,
A happy bird, no black bile ever flows.

A cat is a roving huntress in the Aldhelm universe. A candle drips a rain of teardrops from its brow. 'Greedy gulps of red blood,' the monk writes, are the leech's fare. Less funny than refreshing, the riddles' imagery testifies to a sharp eye: the hooked claws of beavers, the surface-skitter of the water spider. You get a sense of life from 1400 years ago (when 'no star of heaven outshines' fire) as much as a sense of Aldhelm the man—gentle, curious, passionate.

While most riddles focus on secular animals—that is, fauna untouched by biblical allusion—there are some creatures that overlap, appearing in the Bible and the world of Malmesbury. One is the serpent—'I cast off my worn-out skin, and find my body staunch'—and the other is the 'happy bird' in our opening riddle. Have you isolated the chapter and verse? Let me suggest Genesis 8:11, where 'the dove came back to Noah in the evening, and behold, in her mouth was a freshly plucked olive leaf. So Noah knew that the waters had subsided from the earth.'

This passage is how the dove came to be the symbol of peace, the sign for Noah and his bestial shipmates to make a fresh start in a world rinsed of vice. By the same token, the dove riddle is how one Anglo-Saxon monk helped to humanise the church, blending scholarship with wit, discipline and entertainment. Aldhelm was a man of humour, the benign kind, as coursed through his happy bird, the abbot's *enigmata* helping his teachings to soar.

Carpet

⌐⌐ 90 ⌐⌐

I see at a distance through the moor . . .

'Clane, please.'

'Where?'

'Clane.'

'Where?'

'Clane.'

Every time I caught the bus, that was our routine. Maybe if I'd lived in Cork or somewhere else pronounceable I might have redeemed two minutes of my life, five times a week. But that wasn't to be. Clane was my hidey-hole, a stone cottage in Kilkenny. I commuted to Dublin for classes, or groceries, or a bid for sanity. Still, no matter how often I used Bus Éirann, my Australian accent always converted Clane into Clone, or Callan, or Clarinet, bemusing the drivers.

The classes were devoted to James Joyce, the same reason I was trapped in the cottage. By trapped I mean cohabiting with a 78-year-old Chinese poet who spoke flimsy English, and ground his teeth in his sleep. Like Zhang Jing, I'd won a scholarship to spend the winter in Ireland, the better to write some virtuoso fiction and plumb the S-bends of *Ulysses*.

This was 2001, a gloomy winter if you check the almanacs. Riding that bus to Clane—once the driver had unravelled my voice—waited for the hulk of Clongowes College to loom in the fog. That was my landmark. James Joyce went there as a wunderkind in the 1890s. The school was shut for the Christmas holidays, the building a promontory without a lighthouse, yet its shape and substance gave me a peculiar comfort. The rugby posts nearby resembled the masts of lost ships, though at least they signified I was almost home. Or in Clane, I should say.

I didn't write much. I started a novel on a supermarket pad but spent more time trying to name the work without really knowing what the work was about. Zhang was more industrious. He wrote poems in the next room, though I later discovered that his opus in fact was a

What sport is clear to see?

continuum of letters to those he missed, fuelled by green tea and long gazes out the window.

The view was fog. And when that lifted, we saw a row of wizened trees that edged the road to Clongowes. The fog returned by late afternoon. Not that I minded the weather. The fog, in fact, was a third character in our narrative, a constant companion engulfing our cottage. When I wasn't dreaming up book titles, or trying to catch a bus, I'd read slabs of Joyce, or Yeats, or the turf poems of Seamus Heaney, immersing myself in Ireland, when all the while the fog was doing the immersion for me.

> *It is at the bottom, it is on the top;*
> *It is in the middle of the locked chest;*
> *It is from here to the Land of Youth,*
> *And it comes back hither again.*

That's a riddle, in case you didn't guess. An Irish riddle—but can you guess the answer? Yes, it's fog, the Celtic spirits manifested. Seems the obscurity seldom lifts, no matter the time of life. If this riddle doesn't say so, then let's look deeper into the folklore. There we'll see that the Irish have their own way of doing things, with haze and middle distance two key elements of their riddle heritage.

> *I see at a distance through the moor a little red man and a kink in his*
> *fundament; he has a wooden tooth between the two ribs.*

Distilling the wealth of a nation's riddling into one paragon is a fool's mission. Be that as it may, I spent a week drowning in Celtic allusions to thimbles and earthworms, church bells and liquorice, looking for the ultimate Eire riddle, the one that seems to underpin the lot, or illustrates what no other culture attempts. In the end I fell for the flicker of the riddle-maker's fire, that little red man on the moor, as it goes to illuminate the genre's Irishness.

First up, it hints at a story, complete with narrator and sense of place. The Irish don't plump for riddle-me-ree, or can-you-tell-me. Same applies to any of that old reward bullshit if you happen to guess the answer. Perhaps that parlour play is too English, or storytelling is so Irish that even their enigmas mutate into anecdotes.

Irish literature

A hag in the corner, a spike in her eye, and she's doing light work.
Spinning wheel

A bridge over a lake without stick, without stone.
Rainbow

Three sieves full of young fiddlers.
Beehive

Two small well-dressed white girls. They caught fever and died.
Two candles

See up there, my daddy wearing a white cap.
Smoke

The riddle's other essence lies in the little red man, the phrase. Fed on poetry and myth, the Celts animated all the props around them, from castle rubble to wizened trees. A small fat man with a big belly is the kettle. An iron pot of bubbling gruel is the hag in the corner with 200 eyes. Even death is embodied, as the man without a coat, or the man of the slender hard leg, where riddle may entail another jaunt across the moor to meet him—fog optional.

What has ten legs and needs burping?

Quintuplets

Enigma Variations

We finish on innovators—the boundary-pushers, the ground-breakers, the outliers.

Question being, are you ready to tussle with the wordless and the peerless, from blind myth-makers to Inuit warriors?

Kolmasti päivässä päälleen pukee . . .

Three times daily, standing above clothes . . .

Scratch Hymylä off your itinerary. The place may sound mystical but only exiles live there, the gullible and disgraced. Even in translation, the Land of Smiles is out to woo you, selling the promise of bliss to anyone who arrives, but the message is bunkum.

Imagine a place where mice play horses, and cats are the carriage drivers. According to Hymylä survivors, the land has axes for spoons, and ladles for axes. Other visitors have mentioned cows baking reindeer bread. To borrow an iGen phrase, Hymylä is totes cray-cray.

Not that iGen has heard of Hymylä. The land is overlooked by modern atlases, spurned by FIFA, ignored by backpackers. Even in Finland, where the Land of Smiles was created, there's seldom any mention of the place nowadays. Sad in a way, seeing an empire vanish, despite that empire being so humiliating.

For that was the essence of Hymylä, the dreaded Land of Smiles. Riddle lovers in olden Finland hardly planned the trip. Rather it chose you, the moment you took a false turn, or guessed the wrong answer. Them were the rules. One bungle and you were ejected from the riddle circle and into the cold of Hymylä.

Though only momentarily—maybe 20 minutes, depending on the mercy of the other players. The custom was to gather as a village, sharing the warmth of a single cabin and passing the evening with stories and riddles. At its peak, before radio interrupted the conversation, the social nights were mainstays. In the Folklore Archive of the Finnish Literature Society, more than 30,000 *arvoituksia* (riddles) survive from that period, many of them booby-trapped to make the most of Hymylä.

Aside from the umpteen umlauts, the typical Finnish riddle resembles many other folklore snippets from Europe. The topics are agrarian—the

Why couldn't the strings ever win?

ox and candle. The metaphors are evasive, and the telling terse. There's a soft spot for paradox, too, plus a passion for tampering with logic, where clouds don't need legs to run, and sleep can bloom devoid of roots.

Business as usual, until Hymylä enters the picture. Nobody likes to bungle a riddle. Then again, in most cultures, there's no real punishment for a wrong answer. You may lose face, or cop a mild joshing, but the sky doesn't fall. The riddles reload. That's the spirit of the genre. You try to identify that soldier with a thousand swords—a porcupine? A plough? Wrong, a fir tree. Too bad. No hassles—next riddle.

Except in Finland. Maybe iGen should be grateful those long wintry nights have petered out since the 1960s, for the Land of Smiles was no happy place. Solve our chapter's main riddle if you dare:

Kolmasti päivässä päälleen pukee,
Enimmät ajat alasti seisoo.

Three times daily, standing above clothes,
Most times standing naked.

Who could the nudist be? The number is your best clue. What occurs thrice a day? Ask your stomach, I suggest. The answer is a table, as that's where you sit for meals. Well done if you nailed the solution, but imagine you went a different way. Say you guessed a child, or a roof, or the sun—I don't know, anything but a table. You tried but failed. Once upon a time in Finland, the other riddle players would chorus: 'Hyys, hyys, Hymylään! Kun et sitäkään tiedä!' Or in our ears: 'Off, off, to Hymylä! You don't know anything!'

That was it. The jury had spoken. You'd leave your chair and brave the elements, or the woodroom or kitchen, some designated space beyond the cosy hub of the game, and you'd sit there until the group deigned to let you back. Welcome to Hymylä in all its un-fun.

Mind you, exile was a minor humiliation compared to some variations. In the research of folklorist Annikki Kaivola-Bregenho, depending on the era or the region, the Land of Smiles might also entail cross-dressing or performing menial chores. You could be tickled en masse or birched on the knuckles. In one cruel spin-off, an exile had to smear his face with tar, then wipe off the gunk using chaff.

They could only tie [Popsicle]

Your reprieve wasn't merely a matter of time, or the mercy shown by your 'friends', but also depended on the calibre of your imagination. Let's say you picked a hedgehog over a fir tree. Banished, you'd sit in the snow for 20 minutes, or chop wood, whatever the rules decreed, waiting for a delegate to fetch you. Eventually, when that chance came, your sorry bones invited back into the circle, you could only return on one condition. That is, on leaving Hymylä you then had to impress your mates by describing the absurd world you'd witnessed while away.

Release the cray-cray, the reindeer bread and all the other zaniness. This phase of the game is where Hymylä gets its dippy reputation—the horse-mice and axe-spoon. The cats driving carts and the antler marmalade. Paint a funny picture and you were welcome back at the naked table. Fall short, however, and you were out in the cold again—literally and figuratively. Which makes your task clear, should ever you have the chance to go riddling in Espoo. Either you memorise the 30,000 riddles in the national archives, or you say you have a dental appointment.

Finnish lines

Who is that fellow that flies about and praises his own name?
Curlew

Smaller than God, greater than a king.
Death

A stallion in the stable, its tail on the roof.
Kitchen stove

Take away, it increases; put back, it decreases.
Cloth covering a sauna's smoke-hole

Hangs in the daytime, put in a hole for the night.
A door hook (What—you had another answer? To Hymylä
    with you!)

Who sings soulful conundrums?

⌐⌐ 92 ⌐⌐

Madam, I take the liberty of sending the servant whom I mentioned the other day . . .

Mitta Mitta is four hours northeast of Melbourne. I lived there for most of 1990, writing a novel about Old Tallangatta, the town that moved down the road to make room for a dam. When I wasn't writing, or researching, or playing frisbee golf around the paddocks, I taught imagination at the tiny schools in the area.

Classes of ragtag kids somehow created really exciting writing. That was my aim—to spark fresh words and ideas. I drove to Tangambalanga to reinvent onomatopoeia with nine-year-olds. I pulled into Upper Sandy Creek to compose clerihews, or anagram-aliases, or paste up stories using newspaper confetti. I called by Thurgoona to avoid the letter O in our radio dramas. In Granya, a single-room school, I spent the morning making cubby houses, and then after lunch we wrote fairytales from different points of view: Snow White according to Grumpy, Goldilocks from a bear's perspective, etc.

This last game had the strongest life at uni level, where I'd later teach creative writing for a few years. The exercise is handy for empathy too, getting students to understand their characters a little more. Helps if you're trying to compose a script, or a screenplay, or write a riddle in the guise of a letter, perhaps.

When I first came across this document, dated 1805, I was nonplussed. I couldn't understand why a letter of reference was stuck in a book called *London Enigmas*. The document was headed, 'In A Letter To Lady', and I presumed the editors had goofed.

Convinced, I turned to the answers section, expecting an erratum of sorts. Instead I found a nine-letter word, the letter's solution, for the madam's correspondence was a covert riddle like nothing I'd seen before. The letter revives fond memories of those games I played back in Eskdale and Kergunyah, getting the writer to imagine what life might be like for

Mother Hubbard, or a wolf, or a household object as the case may be. See if you can identify the so-called servant described in this unique reference:

Madam,

I take the liberty of sending the servant whom I mentioned the other day, and think, before you retain him, you should know something of his family and qualities. His birth was certainly low, and he was brought up among poor people; a little polishing was bestowed upon him, which to his credit he took well: he is sharp, has bright parts, and I have reason to believe his temper is good. He has undergone some severe trials previous to his entering my service, which has been an advantage to him. He has some skill in drawing, and if you should employ him in that way, he may prove an hour's amusement to you and your friends. He will be useful at your side-board; yet I must confess, if you cannot contrive to keep liquor from him, his head will be frequently turned; though upon such an occasion I must do him the justice to say, I never knew him to give offence, or in any single instance betray his trust. You may rely on him never repeating anything that passes in your family out of doors. I must not further anticipate your opinion of him; but will only add, I should not have parted with him myself, but for the pleasure of recommending him to you.

I am, Madam, &c. &c.

So, would you retain this servant? If you're even slightly convivial, then I can recommend the household helper. As for the solution, let's play the game I taught in Upper Sandy. Read the initials of the sentence that opens this chapter's second paragraph, and pop, you'll extract the answer.

⌐ 93 ⌐

'Tis a true Picture of the Man . . .

The poster belongs to the Ephemera Collection (Portfolio 143, Folder 12), filed in the vaults of America's Library of Congress. Historians know such documents as squibs, a word stemming from the sound

What do you get when you cross a riddle with a rhetorical question?

of a small explosion, as the posters are often loaded with lampoon. Squibs are also small-scale fireworks—a tame Roman candle, say, or a controlled detonation used in mining to loosen a rock face. We mainly hear the term in 'damp squib', describing a flop, as moist gunpowder reneges on the bang.

But let's get back to the ephemera, the political squib under lock and key. We know little of the satire's background, or the satirist for that matter. By 'we' I refer to the dozen experts in American history I consulted for this chapter, from Professor Eric Foner of Columbia University to the Philadelphia Historical Society. Every reply had a similar ring. Ephemera is ephemera by definition, material destined to last a day, and that day was way back in 1770.

That's right, as Captain James Cook was planting a Union Jack in Botany Bay, a mystery hand was pasting a squib on a Philadelphian fence, sending up a political candidate. The author used the byline of 'A White-Oak', while the riddle's target is only identified by a snide description. That's the game, and the reason the poster is emblazoned *A Riddle*. Instead of naming names and possibly courting libel, A White-Oak opts to outline his nemesis with a shadowy portrait, allowing passers-by to guess:

> There has appeared in the City, a tall Man, well made, of a fair Complexion, Buckram Gait, majestic Look, but of an unaccountable disdainful Countenance, and of a haughty imperious Disposition . . .

Enjoy the politesse while it lasts. After the opening, the portrait plunges into vitriol. In one swoop the tall man is accused of Vanity, Arrogance, venal Complaisance, and marrying above his pay grade. The bile concludes on the sarky assertion:

> He would be glad of a Seat in the ASSEMBLY, which would make him a great Statesman indeed!

Lastly, returning to his theme, A White-Oak turns his hand to poetry:

> 'Tis a true Picture of the Man,
> Pray solve this Riddle if you can.

[No answer]

Modern-day academics have drawn a blank, along with archivists and passionate amateurs. I knocked on every likely door, seeking to identify the 'tall Man' mentioned in the poster. Professor Eric Foner, an authority on the American civil war and slavery, said, 'I find the document intriguing, but I can't solve the riddle.'

Which neatly goes to reinforce (the anagram of Eric Foner) the benefits and risks of resorting to riddles as your means of attack. While libel lawyers can't touch you, the attack may end up missing its intended target. Perhaps the strategy won the ephemeral day back in 1770, but 250 years on, *A Riddle* is one damp squib.

⌐ 94 ⌐

前前在后后 后后在前前

Front-front at the back-back, back-back at the front-front

Fracture a fistful of raw spaghetti. Now spread the aftermath on a table to see if you can spell DARKNESS, using the pasta to construct each letter—the D's curve, the A's crossbar. Once you've done that, remove all the excess pasta. Next, gently blow on your handiwork, making the letters disperse into random pieces again. For your final challenge, realign the debris to make out DAYLIGHT with no crumb wasted.

The task may seem impossible, but that's a Western mind speaking. Chinese riddle-solvers perform such mental exercises with nonchalance, treating ideograms as anagrams, tones as stepping stones, moving deftly from one concept to another. I've spent three months seeing a mathematical whizkid called Yi Huang for riddle tutorials and can't believe the convolutions that go by the name of Chinese wordplay.

For starters, consider such categories as 'shrimp whiskers', 'boot removal' and 'brocade screen'. Each label is a different approach to manipulating characters. The nearest we get in the West, perhaps, are cryptic clue recipes, where solvers must identify homophones and hiddens, containers and reversals. Tricky, yet nothing so aerobatic as

What did the blonde call her pet zebra?

the Chinese equivalent. Crossword games are kindergarten compared with the postgrad marvels of Chinese riddling.

A boyish 28 years, Yi is a postgrad too. He juggles his days between tutoring in pure maths at the University of Melbourne and finalising his PhD. 'What's it about?' I ask.

Yi glances at a bluestone wall as if the answer's hiding there. 'See all the shapes on that wall? All the bumps and facets? I'm developing a theory that can distinguish complex shapes like that—things like protein chains, or a piece of Nutri-Grain. It's all about the geometry of moduli spaces.'

A stroll in the park compared with the challenge before us. Somehow Yi and I are hoping to convert a bunch of Chinese riddles into English, all the while maintaining their beauty and sense. A goose chase, really, but we're optimists.

First up, let's walk among the lanterns. The lights hang during New Year's festival, à la fairy bulbs adorning Christmas rooftops. Beyond that, the parallels sputter. Where Western lights blink, the Chinese lanterns balance light with the darkness of riddles. Each lantern carries a challenge, printed on duplicated tassels that dangle from the base. What say we tear one off? That's the custom. Pick a lantern, any lantern, and pit your skills against the riddle, like this one:

前前在后后　后后在前前

Unfortunately, translation doesn't help too much:

Front-front at the back-back, back-back at the front-front.

What if I said we're seeking some green vegetables—would that help? Didn't think so. To untie the knot you'd need to know that the Chinese word for front is 前. Your chances will improve if you know that any Chinese ideogram is made up of various radicals, the ticks and strokes that comprise the whole, just as bits of spaghetti went to make that R in DARKNESS. In the case of 前, the initial radicals that the writer puts on the page are the twin antennae atop the horizontal bar. Treating this configuration as one distinct piece, you now have the front of front.

Step two: we head for back, or 后 as a Chinese scribe would write. Examining the character closely, you'll see that the last radicals are

Spot

the central crosspiece and the lower square: the so-called back of back. Interchange these two segments, as the riddle advises, and you'll solve the lantern challenge: 豆.

Look again at the symbol and you'll spot those same antennae supporting the square inside the new character, the front-of-front upholding back's back, if you still follow the logic.

Together the combo spells 'beans', the vegetables the tassel may have suggested to the passerby. Crack the code on New Year's Eve and you'll be entitled to visit the lantern-owner's house, or take the tassel to the nearest kiosk, and thus claim a prize. Something better than 豆, I hope.

To contrive a parallel in English, I suggest to Yi a word like SINGLET. The moment you take the top of this top to the bottom, and move the top's bottom to the top, you create TINGLES. 'Maybe for you,' laughs Yi.

November, the day is gusty. Pollen falls across our notes, a mess of arrows and squiggles, crossbars and shrimp whiskers. For all our brain strain, we've only scratched the surface of Chinese riddles, though surfaces can be complicated, as Yi knows better than most. Time to push on, we decide. Time to shine our lanterns on another aspect of radical thinking.

救护车

rescue-protect-car

Green beans are easy pickings compared with other Chinese methods. Thought you should know that before we carry on, the beans an entrée for a richer feast. I suggest you find a comfy chair in a room with decent ventilation, as vertigo is liable to strike.

Worse, you may need an ambulance, or 救护车. Character by character, the word translates as 'rescue-protect-car'. But before we summon the paramedics, let's talk about bodies.

What has branches and leaves but no bark?

For most people, riddles are split into question and answer. Oedipus and Samson thought in those terms, Fijians and Lithuanians. The Chinese, however, prefer to rely on anatomy. Ambulance is a case in point. The actual word is 救护车, which is also a riddle's opening statement—no query, no block, no obvious pun. Just the word, pure and simple. Hence a term like 'question' isn't helpful, for there's no explicit question in presenting this vehicle to the audience. So let's be wise and adopt the Chinese way by calling the opener a 'face'.

Still in the mood, let's ditch the label of answer as well, going with the local trope of bottoms. Seems only sensible. If ambulance is the riddle's so-called face, then the opposite of a face is the backside. So then, using our noodles, and grasping the new Chinese formula, we may well make our way to the ambulance's base.

And just as it is for the ambulance, speed is vital to Chinese enigmas. Many riddle categories—dropping the hat, removing a boot—depend on solvers excelling as decoders, showing prompt recall of classical texts and figurative language. According to Mandarin, a riddle isn't so much solved as hit at, shot at, or knocked off. With all that in mind, moving at our own pace, let's now contemplate the ambulance.

To unravel the lantern riddle in the last chapter, we recycled elements of two characters (front and back) to create beans. This ambulance puzzle belongs to the subset known as rolling the blind, where the radicals stay intact, the subterfuge banking more on reversal than rearranging.

Picture an old-fashioned Holland blind, or a retractable awning if you like. As the sun dictates, the operator rolls the cloth into position, or rolls the cloth back to its niche, regulating the day's glare. Furling is the principle in play here—furling and unfurling. Where the riddle asker presents the cloth, the askee usually needs to find a phrase whose pure reversal matches the 'cloth'—or 'head'—of the original.

In a vain bid to mimic the feat in English, let's imagine that the riddle's head was 'brilliant sun'. Abiding by the blind principle, a solver would need to locate a common expression that's capable of being furled back to satisfy the sense of brilliant sun. A possible 'backside'—so to speak—is 'light fantastic', the vaudeville idiom for dancing. Reverse the cloth and you make 'fantastic light', not just a fair reflection of the sun, but a reasonable description of the brain-flash you needed to conjure the answer.

That said, no Chinese riddle can be so easily boxed and labelled. As part of the same furling family, a solver could well offer the synonym as first response, rather than twist the intermediary phrase to reach the synonym. In our English example, say, a solver could be justified in offering 'light fantastic' at the top, the so-called 'cloth' then rewinding to expose the 'brilliant sun' as the head's loose synonym.

Feeling light-headed? I can't blame you. Chinese riddling is an exclusive sport. Let's call an ambulance to see how this particular blind operates:

救护车

In a show of mercy, the riddle's face we see above would be identified as a blind-roller, telling the solver how the bottom can be reached. 救护车 is standard Mandarin, the sort of word you might see on a sign or building in Beijing. But how do you manipulate the right phrase to end up with an ambulance in a good way, and not just as one more riddle casualty?

In this case the Chinese solver needs to think of a phrase that can be reversed to capture an ambulance's essence. (How simple does a PhD in geodetic calculus seem right now?) Three seconds later, however, after meeting the face of an ambulance, a shrewd Chinese solver would kick arse with:

危之人乘

Dismantled, that's 'danger-belonging-person-carry'. Or put more simply, something to carry a person in danger. Bingo, a reasonable phrase to denote an ambulance.

But your job's not done, of course. Not in this two-step mode; the sun has gone and the blind needs lifting. Or night has fallen and we need to roll it down. Either way, your cloth needs refurling. And here that means rewinding your synonym to nail the tail:

乘人之危

See the flip? We've rolled the blind. But what have we created?

What font do skywriters use?

As they stand, the pieces above spell 'carry-person-belonging-danger', but that's like saying that thin-gummy-jig means a skinny toothless dance, when really it means thingummyjig. In Mandarin, carry-person-belonging-danger is an established compound, or *chengyu*, in the same way as rescue-protect-car is a familiar cluster for ambulance. So what do you think carry-person-belonging-danger actually means? What's the idiom in play? We don't really have this notion in English, so maybe I should spill the 豆 to ease your misery. Indeed, the nearest Yi and I could manage was something like 'to take advantage of someone who's in trouble'. The closest English cousin would be 'to exploit', or 'extort', but that's only half the Chinese story.

By now you realise the folly of trying to fumble for English counterparts when it comes to illustrating Chinese artistry. Some literary fragments are destined to defy translation, from Rilke sonnets to the Chinese blind highlighting how blind the West can be to Chinese.

Still, we've dabbled in Chinese beans and a rescue-protect-car, snapping and rebuilding, furling and rewinding from arse to apex, looking at two recipes inside out and back to front. If your brain is still reeling, I wouldn't panic. Instead, just remind yourself that CHINESE PROBLEM is only truly COMPREHENSIBLE as an Anglo-Saxon anagram.

This chapter is PECUL_AR, code-speak for ODD ONE OUT. That quirky thinking lies at the heart of the rebus, a conundrum built of symbols, pictures and manipulated letters.

Aerial

Rebus itself is pure Latin, meaning 'by things', for that's how this school of riddling communicates. Can you solve our puzzle on the facing page, for example? Tag each drawing first, then say the three labels aloud. If you're stuck, reread the opening paragraph, and you'll soon realise you're dealing with a different kind of cone-nun-drum.

Of course, being picky, the 'con' of conundrum doesn't fully sync with 'cone', requiring a measure of puzzler's licence to work, but that leeway is integral to the formula. OPM & BR hardly harmonise with 'opium and beer', as asserted by an 1864 New York riddle collection, *The Santa Claus Book of Games and Puzzles*. Not precisely, anyhow. But say the letters hastily to a friend some 10 metres away in a lashing headwind, and the message will be received loud and clearish.

Santa Claus himself, writing the book's introduction, resorts to pictures to convey his words. CFU can identify this phrase that appears:

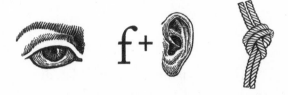

Will these painful puns ever ab8? I fear not. Homophones and hieroglyphs are the rebus tools, the formula calling on artwork as much as the artful use of letters. In the same volume, a plea is written to a mysterious girl:

O MLE B9 & FMN8 B4 U X10U8 NE XS C A YY DET

To decipher the sound-bite, the message reads: 'Oh Emily, benign and effeminate, before you extenuate any excess, see a wise deity.'

A rebus variation from around the same era veils the solution in a cryptic brand of geometry. Try this riddle 4 size:

> *Three-quarters of a cross and a circle complete;*
> *Two semicircles and a perpendicular meet;*
> *A triangle standing on two feet;*
> *Two semicircles and a circle complete.*

What has ears yet cannot hear?

If a circle is O, then we know the answer has O as its second and last letters. Does that get you any warmer? In a roundabout way, warmer is a clue, too—or more the fire you need to ignite your TOBACCO. Of course, if the Santa of 1864 was encapsulating the word, he'd fancy that addictive leaf called 2-back-O.

The rebus genre is a cyclical craze within riddles, just as texting is taking English to new extremes at this TI.ME (point in time). In the 1960s, humour magazines were mad keen on 'doodles', as the genre was labelled. Simple cartoons, like sketches in semaphore, a doodle might purvey something like this:

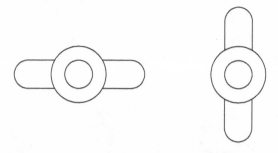

A ship's wheel? A flying doughnut? Seriously, I'm disappointed. Surely you can see the aerial view of a sombreroed Mexican riding a bicycle. In the 1980s, Wacky Wordies took off, with ECNALG meaning 'backward glance', and UJUSTME 'just between you and me'. As proof there's nothing new under the sun, that last rebus-sandwich only goes to mirror a trick pulled by an English anthology back in 1860:

I am
Man making mischief wife

Which translates into the puritan vow, 'I am above making mischief between man and wife.' A relief, really, since your typical

LOVE
LOVE
LOVE
LOVE

usually ends in a HE   ART.

Fire [Guatemala]

⊐ 97 ⊏

é gál-tak –a

An open house . . .

Cuneiform is anything but uniform. Take its name, say. Pedantically, despite what many think, the ancient writing doesn't even rhyme with uniform. (To sound less like Indiana Jones and more like a real archaeologist, try *koo-nay-ee-form* next time, the bonus syllable honouring the Latin source.) The root is *cuneus*, or wedge, a nod to the script's triangular nature, imprinted into clay by a cut reed.

Sumerians, the people of ancient Iraq, developed the language a good while back. Make that a very good while, around 5300BC, where BC may as well mean Before Confucius, or Before Cleopatra was a baby. The city of Ur, clustered on the Euphrates River, is arguably the cradle of Western civilisation, a walled network of brick homes and ziggurats—plus a school or two.

We know this last fact from the tablets left behind. Several shards hold evidence of rote lessons, the clay equivalent of a Victorian copybook. In one case, as discovered by Irving Finkel of the British Museum, a writing tablet wore the indentations of the seven-year-old student biting his homework. Perhaps this same ancient kid was the target audience for the 25 riddles that E.I. Gordon unlocked in 1960, the posers dating back to the eighteenth century BC, making these Ur riddles the true ur-riddles within this collection, the oldest among the elderly.

The godsend is script—tactile proof with a carbon-dated window. With tactile evidence, these riddles can stare down the oral iffiness of Oedipus, which was only later scripted by Sophocles, or the legends plundered by Homer. Examining the relics, scholars can calculate an exact vintage. Well, exactish. It's hard to set your watch by Mesopotamian crockery.

Translation involved just as much estimation. The Sumerian word for riddle, say, has been lost to time, though Gordon deduced *ki-búr-bi* to represent 'solution'. The word ends most of the quatrains, each riddle

What do you always get on your birthday?

resembling a limerick-lite, with steady repetition and a singsong rhythm, according to the syllables. Here's an example:

é gál-tak –a
é sag-gi –a
igi bí-in-du
ù en-na sag ba-an-gi
ki-búr-bi ú-hú[b]

How's your cuneiform? A little rusty, I'd imagine. You already know one word there, opening the last line—*ki-búr-bi*, the solution. As for its neighbour—*ú-hú[b]*—that translates as 'deaf person'. The *[b]*, I should add, constitutes Gordon's educated stab, since particles of the clay had worn or were missing. So, now you know the *ki-búr-bi*, care to intuit what the riddle may be asking?

Early in its evolution, cuneiform was more a picture-language, giving outsiders a fighting chance to enter the dialogue. 'Orchard', say, was originally depicted by three parallel trees, yet over centuries this grove morphed into stems and triangles. For the riddle we now confront, the dominant symbol is 'house', starting its life as a cocoon-like blob and metamorphosing into a four-barred gate, at least in appearance. As a whole the translated riddle reads:

An open house,
A locked-up house,
He sees it,
But even then it remains closed.

Beware—humour can date. The best lines of Bob Hope or Benny Hill may fail to get a titter in the modern comedy lounge. You wouldn't expect a petrified fig to make great jam, but this riddle from four millennia back still has an ounce of juice.

Treating house as a metaphor for head—the early pictographs shared a resemblance—the conundrum takes on more meaning. When talking, your 'house' is open, your mouth a door, the words spilling out. When silent, your door is shut. Either way, a deaf person is oblivious. To them, an open door is as good as closed.

One year older

Dipping into nuance, the riddle has a deeper subtext. Sumerians had three words for deaf, despite the epoch's absence of jet engines and thrash metal. As such, *ú-húb*, *ú-ug* and *geštú-lá* doubled as metaphors for stubborn, or difficult to teach, since a resistant learner is one who is deaf to instruction. Examining the riddle a second time, you'll detect how the open-and-shut business could well imply the reluctant student, a creature who hears but doesn't listen, whose eyes are open but who fails to see. In both senses, this is the deaf receiver—a person denied by handicap, or by stupidity. In either case, the best remedy is to take two tablets—for writing, not biting.

⌐⌐ 98 ⌐⌐

##ERE DO #OU F##D SOU# GRAP#S?

I make riddles for a living. That's how I bankroll the groceries, meet the mortgage, keep the kids in symmetrical teeth.

The riddles are part of a rolling roster of puzzles appearing in a daily box called Wordwit, published by the Fairfax newspapers in Sydney and Melbourne. Across any given week, solvers may face a vocab quiz, scrambled painters, mystery acronyms, palindromes and more. I've been crafting the brainteasers since uni days, which means I'm approaching my thirtieth year in the riddle racket.

How do I invent a riddle exactly? This page alone could yield the right prompt. Whenever I read, or write for that matter, my brain is scouting for puzzle potential. POTENTIAL alone is a twin bathroom, since it combines TOILET and PAN. While a simple word like 'stun' has me thinking about other reversible words, or a longer synonym like 'astound' cradling stun inside its own letters. The white noise never quits. The moment I see the right morsel—the pun-ripeness of Kuala Lumpur, say—I tweak the target into a riddle's solution:

What computer can sing?

What Asian place is okay with marsupials?
Koala Lumper

Trouble being, riddles don't really sell. Not cold like that. You can always share the puns on Twitter, or bounce the quips across a dinner table, but to monetise a riddle you need to groom the pun into puzzle, which is where my riddle-mongering differs from Anon.

If the wording of that KL riddle felt a little strange, there's a good reason. Once I find the punchline, I next need to customise the question in order for its letters to smuggle the answer. Renovated, the Malaysian moaner would now read this way:

WH#T ASI#N ##AC# IS ##AY WITH #A#S#PIA#S?

Tailored like so, I can then introduce the puzzle with these simple instructions:

Can you mix the 11 letters missing from today's riddle in order to spell its punny two-word answer?

This added twist makes the riddle saleable, since the game transcends a guessing contest and becomes a twofold challenge. First, you need to restore the missing letters. Then, assuming you've guessed correctly, you need to jumble the absentees to create a pun that satisfies the question. Do it right, and you'll get a laugh. Or moan.

Now that you know the jig, see if you can swirl the seven letters missing from this next example. You're seeking a word that evokes the riddling vault where our whole odyssey began:

##ERE DO #OU F##D SOU# GRAP#S?

That seven-letter word, I should add, is a comical fabrication, *à la* Koala Lumper in the opener. Feel free to grab a pen and paper and rearrange the likely letters. While you're doing that, let me tell you how some puns almost defy this puzzle treatment.

Take a pastry like a Leia cake, the ideal dessert for a Star Wars party. Only trouble being, to implant those same eight letters into the question makes the resultant riddle sound like Yoda was doing the asking:

How can you mark a Star Wars jubilee?

Puzzlified riddles

1. *WHAT #TORIE# C#N #O EITHER W#Y?* (5)

2. *WH#T'S T#E UN##UE FE## #F #NVISI#LE WEA## #S?* (12)

3. *WHA# BO#K DO YO# BUY A ##U#Y GR###A#IAN?* (5,5)

4. *WHAT #PTI#A# D###AD #ETS YOU S## #M#A#T#?* (7-1-5)

Any luck with the other riddle? Restored, the question reads:

Where do you find sour grapes?

Now that you know the right letters, you'll soon arrive at whinery. Neat and succinct, and not unfunny—that's how the formula works. Though longer answers can demand the most elaborate questions, such as:

WHA# #OVI# WOUL# B##N# #I# ##RTO#'S #ON#ER# #N# #ITH TH# FA#R#LLY #ROTH#RS' LEW# O##VR#?

I'll spare you the hernia, since you're chasing a whopping 26 letters removed from the original. Those same 26 can be reshaped into a bogus movie of three words. What movie, you ask. Well, let's now read that riddle with all 26 truants back in place:

What movie would blend Tim Burton's Wonderland *with the Farrelly brothers' lewd oeuvre?*
Tweedledumb and Tweedledumber

A nip here, a tuck there, the surgery upgrades a silly question into a deeper diversion, but there's also something quintessentially riddlesque

ANSWERS—1. What stories can go either way? (Sagas) 2. What's the unique fear of invisible weapons? (Iraqnophobia) 3. What book do you buy a saucy grammarian? (*Comma Sutra*) 4. What optical doodad lets you see impacts? (Collide-o-scope)

about the exercise. Consider the bulk of the 97 riddles we've already encountered. So many questions carry the shadow of their answers anyway. The concept is classical, where the mystery may send you wandering all over the place, just like Oedipus, only to return to the source, finding the solution lying at your feet. Often it's a simple block that prevents you from seeing the obvious. Or here, a block plus hashes.

⌐⌐ 99 ⌐

What do you call a shout that has a pixel?

Andrew Martin was very human for an android. He felt things. He loved and pined. His wiring was alive with curiosity. And he told jokes. His maiden gig was by the pool one morning. There, Andrew (played by the late Robin Williams) delivered coffee and zingers to the Martin family who owned him:

> *How do you make a hanky dance?*
> *Put a little boogie in it*
>
> *What do you call a brunette between two blondes?*
> *Translator*
>
> *Do you know why blind people don't like to skydive?*
> *It scares their dogs*

Bam. Bam. The riddles were relentless, told flat and fast—but were they original? Did Andrew's engineers—or his wit—engineer them? I'm siding with Option B. Not only do the cracks feel familiar, even in 1999 when *Bicentennial Man* was released, but the humour also seems a giant leap too far for robot-kind to make solo. A sensate android isn't the same as one that's intuitively funny.

Comedy is tough to define, let alone create. Plato and Socrates understood power to be an intricate part of humour, the wicked thrill of seeing the mighty undone, the custard-pie comeuppance for the town's hypocrite.

Ten tickles

A millennium later, French philosopher Blaise Pascal linked laughter to inconsistency. Humour often lurks in the mismatch or surprise outcome:

What do you call a phony psychiatrist?
Sigmund Fraud

As for the real Sigmund, he suspected our *haha*s were entwined with our *aaah*s—the punchline a trigger releasing unexpressed desires. Riddles can be dirty or perverse, just as they can denigrate race or gender, such taboos appealing to the uncivilised id:

How do Italian men propose to their girlfriends?
'You gonna hava what?'

Australian writer Clive James sees comedy a different way, defining humour as 'common sense, dancing'. This theory is best borne out in stand-up brackets, where performers leave the riddles to kids and robots, preferring to throw light on the flaws and foibles of society. When English comic Bill Bailey describes most of jazz as a surrealist car alarm, the Albert Hall laughs with a sense of acknowledgement.

More recently, Joel Warner and Peter McGraw, the US authors of *The Humor Code*, have floated the idea of benign violation. Riddles and jokes allow for safe disasters. Risk-free danger. Clowns can taste funny in cannibal pots; four skindivers can circumcise a whale. Or guide dogs can die while parachuting, getting back to Andrew the android. The calamities belong in a remote bubble.

For a robot then, Andrew's riddles weren't too shabby. They worked on the Martin family at least, and no doubt moviegoers of the day. For that you can credit the writer, Nicholas Kazan, or Robin Williams himself, the improv king. Either way, no IT coding was involved. I can say that with confidence, as I've seen the genuine article.

The experiment began in 2003, a few years after *Bicentennial Man*. Software programmers from Dundee, Edinburgh and Aberdeen universities devised a virtual comedian called STANDUP, or System To Augment Non-speakers' Dialogue Using Puns. The project aimed to give kids with speech problems a chance to play with novel language. Too many software tools in the communication area fixate on the

The box opens; out spill the hazelnuts.

fundamentals rather than the fun. Being silly and creative with words is equally important to a growing mind. Riddles don't just buy social cachet, their booby-traps help the brain thrive in reading and thinking, as shown by a Sussex University study in 1998. Immerse a child in double meaning and deception and she will develop a flair for hypothesis, as well as a healthy suspicion of words at face value.

STANDUP made a splash in Scotland, and elsewhere via the internet. Kids delighted in this new toy, a self-generating gag machine in league with its sister program JAPE, the Joke Analysis and Production Engine. On the social score, both tools were big hits, lending a voice and ally to thousands of marginalised young lives. As for the funny haha, I'll let you be the judge.

The challenge was equipping an electronic brain with the knack of pouncing on decent wordplay. Most of the computer's DIY material belonged under the pun banner, with spoonerisms another category. Quoting Dr Graeme Ritchie from Aberdeen University's Department of Computing Science, 'The STANDUP software makes simple puns by looking for suitable patterns in the words and phrases which are available.'

A glossary called WordNet was square one, a database of 150,000 words with concise definitions as tabled by Princeton University. Input these, plus the words' phonetic patterns, and STANDUP was taking shape.

A further challenge for Ritchie and his team was the realm of meronyms. The word derives from Greek, literally meaning 'part-name', applying to those items that belong to something larger; for example, twig and leaf make up elements of a tree, just as tree is part of a forest. So many meronyms are second nature to a human mind. We don't just see a car but the chassis, the wheels, the hubcaps, etc. Our brain can subdivide at will, whereas the computer needs spoon-feeding, enabling the software to zig and zag between things and their components: a staple tool of riddle-making.

The trick is played out in this chapter's riddle, as conjured by the STANDUP brain:

What do you call a shout that has a pixel?

Camel poo [Arabic]

JAPE japes—pick the category

1. *What do you call a marvellous price?*

2. *What's the difference between a swollen machine and a principal citizen?*

3. *What is a tender document?*

4. *What do you call an elastic curve?*

On the surface, the riddle lacks finesse. A pixelated shout is a peculiar brand of nonsense, but let's move on. Riddles aren't meant to be realistic, after all. Guess the answer? The pixel is a meronym of the computer—your first big clue. As for your second, the answer belongs in Category 4 of STANDUP's armoury:

1. What's the difference between . . . ? (Spoonerism answers)
2. Two similar-sounding words used one after the other
3. Swaps a word for one that sounds like it
4. Swaps a word for one that rhymes with it
5. Part of a word that sounds like another.

Did you get it? I can't hear you laughing. But that's not surprising, as the pixelated holler you're after is a computer scream. At this point, you may be wanting the android back on stage, but therein lies the difference between a Hollywood script and programming script. The first is made by a mind that gets meronyms, avoids wheezy puns and arranges sleeker questions, quality-tested on trial audiences and delivered by the stand-up genius who was Robin Williams, albeit in a robot's monotone. While the pixel joke is the fruit of bits and bytes. Not quite a scream, though the whispers of artificial riddles are only strengthening.

ANSWERS—1. A tall toll (Category 2) 2. One is a vain motor, the other is a main voter (Category 1) 3. A sore-ce (Category 5) 4. A rubber bend (Category 3)

Why is the spider an excellent correspondent?

⌐┘ 100 └⌐

In a riddle whose answer is chess, what is the only prohibited word?

Ts'ui Pên had a plan. Two, if we count the manuscript.

Step 1. Write a novel embodying life.
Step 2. Build a labyrinth.

And no flimsy thing either, but a labyrinth to swallow all trespassers, a Minotaur maze on steroids, an endless torment where the only exit was oblivion.

At first glance, he failed on both counts. The manuscript he left behind was a dog's breakfast, thirteen years of wayward drafts and false trails, while the maze was nowhere to be seen. A major relief for elephants, apparently, since Ts'ui Pên had intended to make his labyrinth of ivory.

Maybe the Chinese scholar became so mired in his sentences, he neglected his other pledge. So went one theory considered by Dr Stephen Albert, an English sinologist whose own lifework was to unravel Ts'ui Pên's lifework.

Among the conundrums Albert faced, aside from this missing maze, was the absence of time in the manuscript. Not just the word 'time' but any concept of hours and minutes, days and nights. A madness, really. How can you tell a saga and disregard the sundial, or the tide of history?

Take this chapter you're reading. Its timeframe is 1916, a detail vital to understanding what happens next, as a man named Yu Tsun nears Albert's house in London. See him pause at the gate. Hear the music that floats through the twilit air, Chinese strings playing somewhere in Albert's garden. A shoal of paper lanterns sways in the foliage.

Tsun opens the gate. He walks up the path, heading for the light deeper in the property. In real life, I should add, Tsun is not who he seems. That's why the year is important. The Chinese visitor is actually a Nazi

He drops a line by every post

spy on the verge of being unmasked. His life is in danger and he knows it. All the wiser then to screen his anxiety in front of Dr Albert, instead emphasising the fact that he's a descendant of Ts'ui Pên, which is true, as well as being a former professor of English back in China—another truth. The men shake hands. A spy in jeopardy, Dr Tsun has possibly found a sanctuary. As for Dr Albert, the stymied academic has a dazzling new theory, one he's keen to share with Ts'ui Pên's relative.

The maze was made, he said. It exists! Not in a physical sense, nothing tangible, but lying inside the manuscript—inside and throughout. The novel *was* the labyrinth! The ivory of its walls was the ivory of the writer's tower. All the twists and turns, each tangent and capillary, were none other than the sentences that wound through the narrative, just like this one you're reading now. Albert draws breath. He then asks Tsun a question:

In a riddle whose answer is chess, what is the only prohibited word?

Take a punt. That's what Jorge Luis Borges is asking of you, for he's the creator of the story we're reliving. The music and the lanterns, the garden and the Great War—the Argentine fabulist crafted each detail, composing *The Garden of Forking Paths* in 1941.

Oops, there goes another time marker. Most writers are enslaved to the march of minutes. Our own grammar system has the ticking clock as pulse. Unless you happen to be a writer called Ts'ui Pên, it seems. This is Albert's breakthrough. The timelessness of the manuscript—which we never get to see—is the infinitude of the labyrinth, he tells Tsun, where every outcome is possible, every forking path a mutual experience of at least two realities, potentially a myriad, since the tyranny of time has been suspended. Banished. Erased from the equation.

In riddle terms, if you wished to install time as an answer, then you wouldn't mention time, the word, in your approach. In essence then, Ts'ui Pên's novel was one giant riddle, ejecting time throughout its breadth in order to highlight time as the solution. The verbal maze symbolised life itself, one messy multiplicity that authorised all outcomes, given time.

Keen readers will know Borges to be equally capable of such kinked reality. For a blind librarian the writer clearly saw the untold scope

What do you call a useless elephant?

of literature. His tales often dwell on memory and dream, myth and paradox. His work has been deemed the seed that spread magic realism across the Americas, as well as a key driver of non-linear thinking throughout the sciences. *The Garden of Forking Paths* is a living emblem of his style, a short story melding genres and cultures, fusing sci-fi and espionage, Eastern and Western outlooks. In a mere ten pages, a riddle embalming a riddle, the reader is left with an altered mind, as well as a deeper feel for the essence of enigma.

So then, what is the one word prohibited in a riddle whose answer is chess? A Nazi spy named Yu Tsun knows—do you? The Chinaman sees the solution, not just to Albert's riddle, but to his own dilemma, his secret identity on the brink of exposure. I won't spoil the tale's deeper resolution, though the obvious solution to Albert's riddle is the game of chess itself—the one thing you can't afford to mention in a riddle that implies chess. Now it's your move. Read the Borges story before time gets away from you.

⌐⌐ 101 ⌐⌐

[Smell of burning hair]

The women went out to the forest to gather blueberries. Late in the day, their baskets full, they turned for home. Distracted, the youngest among them stepped in a fresh pile of bear shit, making a mess of her moccasin. She cursed *shih tthoo*—the Gwich'in word for grizzly—and scraped her shoe against a tree, half the berries spilling in the fuss.

Her noise alerted a young man walking nearby. He appeared from nowhere and saw the depleted basket. Never mind, he knew where more berries were growing, juicier than the ones she carried, bigger and sweeter. 'Come,' he said, 'follow me.'

So she did, deeper into the forest, away from her party. The man was handsome, and his promise held good. The berries were delicious. She filled her basket to the brim. She'd never seen this man before.

He spoke perfect Gwich'in and knew the forest like a native. Soon the light was fading, the woman growing anxious to make her way back.

The man had a better idea. He made a bed of leaves. He built a fire—it looked like a fire—and knew how to catch gopher. The meat was superb. They slept the night, lying close to each other to stay warm. Come the morning the man said, 'Don't open your eyes to look at me.'

They shared a breakfast of cold meat, the woman saying she needed to get home, her family would be worried. The man leant over. He slapped his hand atop the woman's head, then ran his finger around her scalp, the way the sun goes around the earth, and the woman never thought of home again. Or not the home she knew, back in the village, for she'd found a new life in the forest, and even though she knew that her husband was a *shih tthoo*, there was no going back.

The legend of the woman who married a bear is just one among many stories belonging to the Gwich'in people of northeast Alaska and the outer reaches of Canada. There's a long oral history of the *shih tthoo* and *shoh* (black bear) charming the pants off local girls, luring them into their lairs and taking them as wives. In the story you've just sampled, the young berry-picker has twins by her bear, a boy and girl, and raises them as cubs. Later, come hunting season, the woman is torn in her loyalties, unsure whether to help her one-time brothers in flesh, or protect her furry babies.

Care to guess her decision? As a hint, let's turn to the rituals of the Gwich'in hunters. The watchword is stealth—the wiliness you need to find a bear's hideout, and then the guile required to recruit the men to help you kill it.

Before rifles came to the Yukon, it took a full-scale posse to kill a bear. If the first blow was a flesh wound, the bear could double in strength, often charging his aggressor, all fangs and muscle. Five or six men made a big difference. The hunters could encircle the lair and fire arrows from multiple angles. Yet in order to assemble those men once the lair was found, a hunter had to be subtle. Returning to the village, he needed to spread the word without actually saying the word. Reason being, he couldn't risk any woman or child getting wind of the hunt. A boy might blab to his mother. A girl might seek the cave herself to warn the *shoh*, or shack up with the animal, never to be seen

What is higher than a hill?

again. The Gwich'in legends are full of these betrayals, making the risk of open dialogue too great. A code among the men was the best strategy, a lost art known as *gwizhii ideeridlii* (wisdom that is told), as well as *gwizhii ideegwidlii* (wisdom that is performed).

Dr Craig Mishler, professor of anthropology at the University of Alaska, strayed upon these modes of communication in the early 1980s, writing his doctorate on the Alaskan people. One day Mishler was browsing a junior dictionary of Dinjii Zhu' Ginjik—the Gwich'in tongue—and lucked on the word for riddle: *gwizhii ideeridlii*. As he wrote in *The Journal of American Folklore* back in 1984, 'Struck by the nearly homophonous but apparently coincidental resemblance between riddle and -*ridlii*, I renewed my attempts to elicit riddles from several Gwich'in speakers . . .'

Sadly, the language is one of the most endangered in North America. Just a handful of elders retain Dinjii Zhu' Ginjik, those numbers dwindling as English continues to dominate the airwaves. This fragile situation made Mishler's discovery all the more valuable, as pockets of the Gwich'in people shared their memories of the hunting riddles.

What's the brown stuff on your cheeks?

So went one *gwizhii ideeridlii*, a question a hunter might put to a friend, returning to the fold with news of the hiding place. Puzzled, the mate might rub his face, or go look in a mirror, only to find his cheeks were clean. What brown stuff? The question was obviously a prank. His friend was having fun, but then the penny would drop. The wisdom of the comment emerged. The brown stuff was an allusion to the grizzly coat, the mirror-looker realising he was going on a bear hunt.

Secrecy was paramount. The lair-finder had to pick his moment to transfer the news without raising any suspicions among others in earshot, the women in particular. Dinner time was one such chance. No matter what meal the household was sharing, the hunter might ask:

Where's the fat and grease that goes with this?

The cook might be insulted. Though the insider would detect the inner meaning, the *gwizhii ideeridlii* a nod to the rich supply of fat a bear-kill offered.

The grass that grows on top

Dr Mishler records several of these Gwich'in techniques in his article 'Telling about Bear'. Some are verbal, while others involve miming or the senses—the *gwizhii ideegwidlii* of the elders' memories. Bears, for example, have a distinctive gait when lumbering, their front claws almost pigeon-toed to widen their haunches. Given the right moment, the hunter could walk in similar style to alert a potential posse, or use a hut's central pole to scratch his back in ursine fashion.

Words were optional. Around women, in fact, the fewer words the better. Veteran hunters would only need a look, a bear-like gesture, and the hunt was on, launched as subtly as it was announced.

One ploy ignored the usual senses of sight and hearing. Even speech was off the agenda, the riddle being conveyed through campfire fumes, a smoke signal of a different kind. The gesture is ancient, a wordless question imbued in the power of scent. Furtively, with no witnesses, the lair-finder would pull a few strands of hair from his scalp and drop them into the flames. The pong fulfilled the role of riddle, a coded question only the initiated would receive: *I have found a bear. Are you ready?*

Written plainly, that's no riddle. But encoded in odour, the query transforms into mystery. To a nose in the know, the reek translated into the sizzling hide of a bear, should the hunt be successful. And should the smeller be wise to the invitation, and care to join the party.

I felt staggered on reading about this ritual, so vividly captured in Mishler's paper. Like a hunter I had ranged the hills and valleys in search of riddles, thinking each specimen would entail words—strange words, extinct words, but words nevertheless. Or pictures at the very least, the likes of rebus and hieroglyph, yet still comprising the building blocks of language. Then I happened on the Gwich'in lair, astonished to learn that a small population in northeast Alaska had moved the goalposts, ignored the rules, and thus made riddling their own.

But really, why the shock? Here we are at Riddle 101, wiser to the exceptions in so many corners of the world, from the East to the past, from fatal to flippant, from slave song to fairytale. Latitude, in fact, seems the only common ground. From high in the Andes to the deep Finnish night, every culture has been busy testing the bounds of what a riddle can be and do, including the hunters of Gwich'in country, whose curly question is phrased in a plume of pungent smoke, engulfing you.

Black crows on a white bank. They say Caw, Caw!

Postlude

What is a riddle (and why)?

After food, after shelter, after sex,
The brain's fun part interjects,
That longing to mock what we fear
And turn Mother Nature on her ear.
We love the deception, the metaphor,
How riddles unlock a perception door.
We relish how riddles attain
Enjoyment amid the life mundane.
By we I mean those of Lithuania,
Guatemala and Tasmania,
The cracker decoders of Christmas Day,
The long-lost skippers of the Gamilaraay.
Lewis Carroll, Jonathan Swift,
All of us who dream and sift.

Riddles nourish a piece of mind
That other confections fail to find,
Whether the mode is sacred or dirty,
Lamenting war or turning flirty.
There's witchery involved as well,
The askee striving to break the spell,
Desperate to dodge the block, and gain
Wisdom via wholesome pain,
Whether that's sung in coffee groves
Or clues to hidden treasure troves.
Plus humour, let's not forget
(Be it dry, wry or wringing wet)
Underpins the ingredients

To school our brains in disobedience.
We adore the delusion, the diffraction, the joke,
Should riddles be written in pictures or smoke,
Etched on clay, arranged in rhyme,
Boxed in a crossword to signal a crime,
Or treated like a blind unfurled:
Riddles are vital to the human world.

So that's the why, but as for the what,
I can only hope your brain has not
Reverted to that first impression
Of riddling being a kids' obsession.
While that's how our quest was triggered,
Urging us past the pap, prefigured,
We've jemmied wide the vault folkloric
And found the exceptions: the meteoric,
The Twitter-ised and prehistoric,
The Grimm, the deep and the euphoric.
To celebrate how elsewhere thinks,
To risk the homicidal Sphinx,
To meet a riddle-wrangling Pope,
Or Monsieur Blondin on his canyon rope.
We met the subtle, the anti-, the sarky,
The ideographic and Dothraki,
Until now, where the riddling wraps—
No more punchlines, no more traps;
No more puns, Potters, perversions.
Enough Galileo! Goodbye Persians!
Let's leave the secrets of the Telugu soul,
Ambiguous Mrs Hurst, old King Cole,
Since our oddball odyssey is done and dusted.
I trust your mindset's been readjusted
To realise riddles are playful and more,
From poultry in motion to variants galore.
For *Riddledom* has reached its last aha,
So go forth and riddle, wherever you are.

What's an optimist's blood type?

Acknowledgements

How can you thank everyone?
Answer: *You can't.*

Not if you wish to name every name, cite every source, salute every tipster. I don't care how fussy an author's bookwork might be, he'll never repay every debt of kindness he incurs along the way. But still, an author can try.

Which prompts a second riddle:

Where to start?
Answer: *Just start already. Before the orchestra times you out.*

First let's turn to seminal books. Aside from those 1001 riddles that ignited the lifelong romance, there's *The Journal of American Folklore*. When proposing a fragile idea like *Riddledom*, I drew strength from the culture hounds whose curiosity preceded mine.

Diving into the journal's century-old archive, I found six key essays that went to unlock five chapters here. These papers are listed in the bibliography, but let me give three cheers to Ann K. Ferrell, the journal's editor, and her far-flung anthropologists, including Mac E. Barrick (the newspaper gag), Kenneth S. Goldstein (Scotland), Lee Haring (Malagasy), Craig Mishler (the Gwich'in of Alaska), Charles T. Scott (the Amuzgo of Mexico) and Thomas Rhys Williams (the Dusun of Borneo).

Another work to lend me nerve was *Untying the Knot*, an essay collection edited by Galit Hasan-Rokem and David Shulman. From Sophocles to Chinese, this book revels in the enigmatic mode, a human trait that endures across the ages. Details of the work likewise appear in the bibliography.

So too does the third folkloric godsend—*Riddles Ancient and Modern* by Mark Bryant. In tandem, these pioneering works gave *Riddledom* its early momentum, boosted by the warmth of Jeremiah Farrell, editor of the erudite mayhem that is *Wordways*.

Bookwise I could go on. The mess that is my desk testifies to the support library I needed to advance *Riddledom*. When you reach the bibliography, presume my gratitude to each and every author listed as read.

Across 101 chapters, I tapped a babel of languages. To make that happen I recruited a battalion of bilingual angels. I'd like to thank the mathematical genius who is Yi Huang. We met amid a Melbourne Uni treasure hunt back in 2014, though the real trove lay in Yi's immeasurable mind.

Then there's the clan of benign spirits who met the question: *Is there a riddling tradition among indigenous Australians?*

I presented that stumper to Jenny Gibson of the Koorie Heritage Trust. Her simpatico response would open the doors of Dr Christina Eira (a linguist with the Victorian Aboriginal Corporation for Languages), Dr Harold Koch (a senior lecturer at ANU in Aboriginal languages) and his Sydney counterpart, Dr Michael Walsh. Ultimately the answer lay in the work of Dr Murray Garde, an associate researcher at ANU, whose 2008 paper said it all: 'The pragmatics of rude jokes with Grandad: Joking relationships in Aboriginal Australia'. My thanks to you all.

Others to clarify opaque words were rabbis Fred Morgan and Jonathan Keren-Black (Hebrew), as well as the quick-acting Gillian Polack and Rahel Meltzer. I'm likewise grateful to Hannah Burrows (Old Norse), Danute Levickis (Lithuanian), Roy Morris (Japanese—both in Zen and slapstick mode) and Professor Eric Foner (one quaint American poster).

Still on translation, I'm beholden to David J. Peterson, the conlanger to conjure his own Dothraki wisecrack for this book. (I'd thank David in his own TV tongue but Dothraki warriors have no use for etiquette.)

A winemaker named Dan Buckle illuminated Domain Chandon's cellars, explaining the topsy-turvy logic of riddling in a booze sense. His generosity fuelled the book's opening analogy, plus one classy hangover. And here a nod to *The Australian*'s Max Allen for playing matchmaker.

How do a sailor and a landlubber differ?

Margaret Ruwoldt, the communications maven at the University of Melbourne, was kind enough to time-travel back to Pompeii, alerting me to the excellent filth she found on that city's walls. Not that such scribble would embarrass Brose Avard—the big-hearted warm-up guy who helped enliven Riddle 79.

Early in the quest I threw down the gauntlet to readers of my Wordplay column in *The Sydney Morning Herald*, asking for relevant folklore. Rising to the challenge were Gillian Kendrigan (who outed Professor Buck), Sam Spiers (the unmasker of mediaeval monks), and Philip Du Rhone, who shared a funny story about umbrellas going down (but not up) chimneys.

Thanks to the SchadenFreezer duo of Jason Kreher and Matt Moore for their bittersweet anti-riddles. (Watch their dark riddles melt at http://schadenfreezers.tumblr.com.) And while online, pry into Greg Ross's www.futilitycloset.com for more wonders.

Seven hundred words? Usually that means the orchestra is restless. I need to wrap, and fast. Though I can't quit the rostrum until making mention of the Allen & Unwin team.

First, cheers for my publisher Sue Hines, who heard two riddles over lunch and wanted to read 99 more. Then Ann Lennox, for ever daring to accept the manuscript, and later Angela Handley, her energetic locum. For her paring and caring, Susin Chow was a dream editor, equalled only by Clara Finlay's eagle sight at proofing phase. And of course, I owe too much to Tracy O'Shaughnessy, a former A&U cohort, who's never relinquished her talents for imagining good books.

Lastly, as the flyleaf says, this book is dedicated to Heather May Astle, aka Mum, who somehow turned my rowdiness into wordiness. Mum, I only hope *Riddledom* is some small recompense for all the hours I tormented you with electric gorillas, ticking watchdogs and drizzly bears.

One goes to sea, the other ceases to go

Selected bibliography

Along with every chapbook mentioned through the text, every *Boy's Own Magazine* and *Fashionable Lady* collection, here's the honour board of books and papers that helped propel *Riddledom* into reality. My lasting thanks to every wordplay warrior.

Barrick, Mac E., 'The newspaper riddle joke', *Journal of American Folklore*, vol. 87, no. 345, 1974: 253–7

Benefiel, Rebecca R., 'Dialogues of ancient graffiti in the House of Maius Castricius in Pompeii', *American Journal of Archaeology*, vol. 114, no. 1, 2010: 59–101

Berrington, Benj S. and John S. Berrington, *English Riddles: With explanations and notes in Dutch*, Purmerend, [1905] 2013

Biggs, B.G., 'Fijian riddles', *Journal of the Polynesian Society*, vol. 57, no. 4, 1948: 342–8

Borges, Jorge Luis, *Collected Fictions*, Penguin, 1999

Bryant, Mark, *Riddles Ancient and Modern*, Peter Bedrick Books, 1983

Burrows, Hannah, 'Wit and wisdom: The worldview of the Old Norse-Icelandic riddles and their relationship to Eddic poetry', in Martin Chase (ed.), *Eddic, Skaldic, and Beyond: Poetic variety in medieval Iceland and Norway*, Fordham University Press, 2014

Cousineau, Phil, *Riddle Me This: A world treasury of word puzzles, folk wisdom, and literary conundrums*, Conari Press, 1999

Crossley-Holland, Kevin, *The Exeter Book Riddles*, Enitharmon Press, 1993

Du Bois, Elizabeth Hickman, *The Hundred Riddles of Symphosius*, Elm Tree Press, 1912

Dutton, Kevin, *The Wisdom of Psychopaths: What saints, spies and serial killers can teach us about success*, Farrar, Straus and Giroux, 2013

Eckler, Faith and Ross, and Jeremiah Farrell, *Wordways: The Journal of Recreational Linguistics*, <www.wordways.com>

Freud, Sigmund (translator Joyce Crick), *The Joke and its Relation to the Unconscious*, Penguin Classics, 2003

Goldstein, Kenneth S., 'Riddling traditions in northeastern Scotland', *Journal of American Folklore*, vol. 76, no. 302, 1963: 330–6

The more you take, the more you leave behind.

Haring, Lee, 'Malagasy riddling', *Journal of American Folklore*, vol. 98, no. 388, 1985: 163–90

Hasan-Roken, Galit and David Shulman (eds), *Untying the Knot: On riddles and other enigmatic modes*, OUP, 1996

Hecimovich, Gregg, *Puzzling the Reader: Riddles in nineteenth-century British literature*, Peter Lang, 2008

Hollis, A.C., *Masai Myths, Tales and Riddles*, Dover Publications, 2003

Hull, Vernam and Archer Taylor, *A Collection of Irish Riddles*, University of California Press, 1955

Isbell, Billie Jean and Fredy Amilcar Roncalla Fernandez, 'The ontogenesis of metaphor: Riddle games among Quechua speakers seen as cognitive discovery procedures', *Journal of Latin American Lore*, vol. 3, no. 1, 1977: 19–49

Kwapisz, Jan, David Petrain and Mikolaj Szymanski (eds), *The Muse at Play: Riddles and wordplay in Greek and Latin poetry*, De Gruyter, 2012

Milnor, Kristina, *Graffiti and the Literary Landscape in Roman Pompeii*, OUP, 2014

Mishler, Craig, 'Telling about Bear: A northern Athapaskan men's riddle tradition', *Journal of American Folklore*, vol. 97, no. 383, 1984: 61–8

Nelson, Diane M., *A Finger in the Wound: Body politics in quincentennial Guatemala*, University of California Press, 1999

Parker, K. Langloh, *The Euahlayi Tribe: A study of Aboriginal life in Australia*, Archibald Constable and Company, 1905

Potter, Beatrix, *The Tale of Squirrel Nutkin*, Warne, [1903] 2002

Scott, Charles T., 'Amuzgo riddles', *Journal of American Folklore*, vol. 76, no. 301, 1963: 242–4

Seyed-Gohrab, A.A., *Courtly Riddles: Enigmatic embellishments in early Persian poetry*, Leiden University Press, 2010

Sherzer, Joel, *Speech Play and Verbal Art*, University of Texas Press, 2002

Starr, Frederick, *A Little Book of Filipino Riddles*, World Book Co., 1909

Taylor, Archer, *An Annotated Collection of Mongolian Riddles*, American Philosophical Society, 1954

Williams, Kit, *Masquerade*, Jonathan Cape, 1979

Williams, Thomas Rhys, 'The form and function of Tambunan Dusun riddles', *Journal of American Folklore*, vol. 76, no. 300, 1963: 95–110

Williams, Thomas Rhys, 'Tambunan Dusun riddles', *Journal of American Folklore*, vol. 76, no. 300, 1963: 141–81

Woolf, Jenny, *The Mystery of Lewis Carroll*, St Martin's Press, 2010